Entertaining

Inspirations for Your Table

Minnetonka, Minnesota

Entertaining

Inspirations for Your Table

Printed in 2013.

Tom Carpenter
Creative Director

Jen Weaverling
Managing Editor

Wendy Holdman
Senior Book Designer

Stafford Photography
Commissioned Photography

Special thanks to:
Mike Billstein, Terry Casey, Donna Holzinger, Terri Hudoba, Bea Krinke and Betsy Wray.

5 6 7 8 / 15 14 13
© 2010 Cooking Club of America
ISBN 978-1-58159-478-2

Recipe Development
Bruce Aidells, Melanie Barnard, Bev Bennett, Mary Lorraine Binchet, Georgeanne Brennan, Carole Brown, Liz Clark, Janice Cole, Member Beth Colla, Jesse Cool, Rosalind Creasy, Charla Draper, Mary Evans, Member Heather Gardner, Marcy Goldman, Member Pat Goodwin, Hallie Harron, Kate Heyhoe, Member Kimberly Hill, Raghavan Iyer, Dana Jacobi, Patsy Jamieson, Member Simon Kaplan, Elinor Klivans, Diane Kochilas, Stephen Larson, Member Eva LaTorre, Tim Lauer, Karen Levin, Nancy Maurer, Nancie McDermott, Alice Medrich, Member Betty Nickel, Beatrice Ojakangas, Member Carolyn Olesen, Ray Overton, Loretta Paganini, Lisa Saltzman, Member Kathy Sawyer, Member Marilyn Slater, Candy Schermerhorn, Member Jennife Simpson, Carole Smoler, Jerry Traunfled, Jill Van Cleave and Eberhard Werthman.

Cooking Club of America
12301 Whitewater Drive
Minnetonka, MN 55343
www.cookingclub.com

ON THE COVER:
Roast Pork with Shallots and Chestnuts, page 40.
ON BACK COVER:
Flaky Bisteeya Bites, page 11.
Roasted Asparagus with Lemon-Tarragon Vinaigrette, page 112.
Hazelnut-Cherry Reine de Saba, page 133.
ON PAGE 1:
Crown Roast of Pork with Porcini, Fennel and Apple, page 30.

Contents

Roast Pork with Shallots and Chestnuts, page 40

Introduction

It is at once the most enjoyable yet fretful proposition in one's cooking life: The opportunity to entertain. When people are coming over — be it a small knot of close friends for an intimate dinner party or a larger group for a special celebration of some kind — we want to do the cooking ourselves, and do it right.

It's work, yes. But it's also the reward. As Cooking Club of America members, cooking is an integral part of our lives. Plus, kitchen time is always a good time. That's where folks like to gather. And later on, hearing guests' praises for a job well done — a dish well made, a meal to remember fondly forever — that's more than worth the time and effort it took to create.

Oftentimes, a little inspiration is all you need to start your journey toward those rewards. You want ideas for something new to create, something exciting to serve, something that will make heads turn due to both its beautiful presentation and the special culinary touch you added with your own skill and cooking flair.

Strawberry-Chocolate Meringues, page 120

That's where *Entertaining* comes in. In the upcoming pages, you'll find over 200 *Inspirations for Your Table*. Here are best-of-the-best recipes from the Cooking Club of America, brought directly to you from the archives of your award-winning magazine, *Cooking Pleasures*.

We've divided up the book into five sections, to help you locate exactly the recipes you need to make any and every entertaining event a success. From a small dinner for couples, to a big holiday party for family and friends, here are the recipes you'll want to have waiting in your repertoire:

Roasted Italian Potatoes, page 109

Strawberry, Gorgonzola and Chive Bruschetta, page 20

Tossed Orange-Walnut Salad with Balsamic Dressing, page 93

Appetizers — From *Figs Stuffed with Gorgonzola and Walnuts* to *Pistachio Coated Shrimp, Provençal Stuffed Baguette* and *Mini Herbed Quiches Lorraine*, you'll start any gathering off right with all these ideas.

Main Courses — The variety and creativity here is almost endless — from *Rosemary Roasted Salmon, Peppered Roast Beef with Cranberry-Red Wine Sauce* and *Crown Roast of Pork* for your more formal occasions, to *Spicy Pork Burgers with Asian Slaw, Tomato-Olive Pizza with Fresh Mushrooms* or *Beef and Black Bean Chili*.

Salads — Choose from an exciting array of all-time-great salads, some of which are on the traditional side of the plate while others come from the more adventurous side. You'll love *Mediterranean Rice and Fennel Salad, Walnut-Pear Salad with Cranberry Vinaigrette, Red Potato Salad with Feta and Olives*, and autumny *Roasted Butternut Squash Salad* too.

Side Dishes — Sides make the meal, adding accent and accompaniment to the main dishes you choose to feature. Try *Porcini, Fennel and Apple Stuffing, Braised Tarragon Carrots, Cranberry-Port Relish*,

Black Pepper Biscuits, Rainbow Italian Zucchini and *Roasted Asparagus with Lemon-Tarragon Vinaigrette*.

Dessert — Dive into this enjoyable collection of the Club's very best desserts. Try a *White Chocolate Raspberry Tart, Strawberry-Orange Whipped Cream Cake* or *Coconut-Key Lime Meringue Tarts* for more formal occasions, or *Best Ever Pecan Pie* and *Very Lemon Cake with Lush Lemon Frosting* for your more informal gatherings.

You'll also find a very special value-added section. Look at the back pages of the book, behind the hundreds of wonderful recipes. Here are carefully-planned **Menu Ideas** for a variety of occasions. We've divided the menus by season, so that spring, summer, fall or winter, you'll be able to plan a delightful combination.

Entertaining is a joy. It's a chance for you to show off your cooking skills, treat people that matter to you to something special, and collect all the accolades that come your way. We hope these *Inspirations for Your Table* guide you to grand success in each of these regards.

Appetizers

Aged Cheddar and Ale Fondue

A take-off on beer-cheese soup, this hearty fondue pairs aged cheddar with your favorite microbrewed ale. Serve it with cubed rye bread on toothpicks or with vegetables.

2 tablespoons canola oil	**½** teaspoon celery salt
1 tablespoon finely minced onion	**¼** teaspoon hot pepper sauce
3 tablespoons all-purpose flour	**1½** cups (6 oz.) shredded aged cheddar cheese
1¼ cups milk	**2** cups lightly packed cubed (1 inch) dark rye bread or
1⅓ cup ale or nonalcoholic beer	**3** cups assorted fresh vegetables

1 Heat oil in medium saucepan over medium-low heat until hot. Add onion; cook 3 to 4 minutes or until softened, stirring frequently. Stir in flour; cook 1 minute, stirring frequently. Slowly whisk in milk and ale until smooth. Whisk in celery salt and hot pepper sauce. Increase heat to medium; bring to a boil. Boil 2 minutes or until slightly thickened, stirring constantly.

2 Remove from heat; slowly stir in cheese until melted. (Fondue can be prepared to this point up to 1 day ahead.

Cover and refrigerate. Reheat gently over medium-low heat, stirring constantly.) Place in fondue pot on low heat or heat-proof ceramic pot or bowl over candle warmer.

2 cups

PER 2 TABLESPOONS: 90 calories, 6 g total fat (2.5 g saturated fat), 4 g protein, 5 g carbohydrate, 15 mg cholesterol, 155 mg sodium, .5 g fiber

Aged Cheddar and Ale Fondue

Warm Cheese with Nuts

There are two delicious contrasts in this appetizer: the shift in texture from the cheese's crunchy crust to its soft, gooey center. A variation is to make individually sized medallions and place them, after baking, on a salad of mixed greens tossed with a classic vinaigrette.

½	cup walnuts or hazelnuts
2	tablespoons grated lemon peel
1	tablespoon chopped fresh tarragon
12	oz. soft goat cheese
1	egg, beaten
	Crackers or bread

1 In food processor, combine walnuts, lemon peel and tarragon; pulse until finely ground. Place in shallow bowl.
2 Shape cheese into 3 (½-inch-thick) rounds.
3 Dip each cheese round in egg, then ground nut mixture, coating all sides thoroughly. Place on baking sheet. Refrigerate 30 minutes to 2 hours.

4 When ready to serve, heat oven to 375°F. Bake 10 to 12 minutes or until nuts are lightly toasted and cheese is warm. Let stand 5 to 10 minutes. Serve with crackers or bread.

6 servings

PER SERVING: 215 calories, 18 g total fat (9 g saturated fat), 10 g protein, 4.5 g carbohydrate, 75 mg cholesterol, 205 mg sodium, .5 g fiber

Figs Stuffed with Gorgonzola and Walnuts

Slightly sweet poached dried figs contrast with the rich taste of pungent blue cheese. This recipe serves double duty: You can use these festive nibbles to whet your guests' appetites before dinner or serve them after the main course, accompanied by a glass of port.

1½	cups water
2	black tea bags
¼	cup sugar
24	dried Mission figs (about 9 oz.)

⅓	cup (2 oz.) reduced-fat cream cheese, softened
2	oz. (½ cup) Gorgonzola or Roquefort cheese, crumbled
2	tablespoons chopped walnuts, toasted*

1 Bring water to a boil in medium saucepan. Remove from heat; add tea bags. Cover; let steep 5 minutes.
2 Remove and discard tea bags. Add sugar to tea; bring to a simmer over medium heat, stirring to dissolve sugar. Add figs; partially cover. Reduce heat to low; poach gently 20 to 30 minutes or until figs are tender but still firm.
3 With slotted spoon, place figs on plate; cool completely. (Discard or reserve liquid for poaching other dried fruits.)
4 In small bowl, beat cream cheese at medium speed until smooth and creamy. Add Gorgonzola cheese; beat until blended. Spoon mixture into pastry bag fitted with ½-inch star tip or small plastic food-storage bag with ½-inch hole cut in one corner.
5 Line baking sheet with waxed paper. With paring knife, trim stems from figs. Make slit along 1 side of each fig;

place on baking sheet. (If necessary, trim fig bottoms so that figs rest upright.) Pinch each fig gently to open cavity; pipe rosette of cheese mixture into each cavity.
6 Place walnuts in small bowl. Dip cheese-filled side of each fig into nuts to coat. (Appetizers can be made up to 2 days ahead. Cover and refrigerate.) Serve at room temperature.

TIP

*To toast walnuts, spread on baking sheet; bake at 375°F. for 4 to 6 minutes or until lightly browned. Cool.

24 appetizers

PER APPETIZER: 65 calories, 1.5 g total fat (1 g saturated fat), 1.5 g protein, 13 g carbohydrate, 5 mg cholesterol, 50 mg sodium, 2 g fiber

Bayou Cakes with Rémoulade Sauce

Southern crab cakes are quite similar to the classic Chesapeake Bay ones, except that they usually contain Worcestershire sauce. Here, shrimp is added to the crabmeat for an additional twist. These cakes are served New Orleans-style, with a tangy rémoulade sauce of mayonnaise, gherkins, horseradish, capers and a hint of lime.

CRAB CAKES

- ½ cup chopped green onions
- ¼ cup chopped fresh parsley
- 2 teaspoons Dijon mustard
- 2 teaspoons Worcestershire sauce
- 1 teaspoon seafood seasoning, such as Old Bay
- ¼ teaspoon salt
- ¼ teaspoon freshly ground pepper
- 2 eggs, beaten
- 8 oz. cooked crabmeat, drained
- 8 oz. shelled, deveined cooked medium shrimp, chopped
- 1½ cups fresh bread crumbs*
- ⅓ cup unseasoned dry bread crumbs
- 3 tablespoons vegetable oil, divided
- 8 lime wedges

SAUCE

- 1 cup mayonnaise
- 1 tablespoon finely chopped gherkins or pickles
- 1 tablespoon small capers, drained
- 2 teaspoons prepared horseradish
- 2 teaspoons lime juice

1 In large bowl, stir together green onions, parsley, mustard, Worcestershire sauce, seafood seasoning, salt and pepper. Stir in eggs until well-blended. Gently stir in crabmeat and shrimp. Stir in fresh bread crumbs until well-blended.

2 Gently form mixture into 8 (3-inch) patties. Place dry bread crumbs in shallow dish; dip crab cakes in bread crumbs, shaking off excess. Place on baking sheet; cover and refrigerate at least 1 hour or up to 8 hours.

3 Meanwhile, in small bowl, stir together all sauce ingredients.

4 Heat 2 tablespoons of the oil in large nonstick skillet over medium heat until hot. Add crab cakes in batches; cook 4 to 6 minutes or until golden brown, turning once and adding remaining 1 tablespoon oil as necessary. (Crab cakes can be made up to 4 hours ahead. Cover and refrigerate. To reheat, heat oven to 425°F. Place wire rack on rimmed baking sheet; place crab cakes on rack. Bake 8 to 10 minutes or until hot and crisp.) Serve crab cakes with rémoulade sauce and lime wedges.

TIP

* To make fresh bread crumbs, tear day-old whole-grain or white bread into pieces; place in food processor. Pulse 30 to 60 seconds or until coarse crumbs form. One bread slice yields about ¾ cup crumbs.

8 crab cakes

PER CRAB CAKE: 370 calories, 30 g total fat (4.5 g saturated fat), 15 g protein, 10.5 g carbohydrate, 145 mg cholesterol, 645 mg sodium, 1 g fiber

Spicy Oven-Roasted Feta Cheese Squares

Spiced-up feta is a favorite meze, or appetizer, in northern Greece. In this version, red pepper and cayenne provide some heat, which contrasts nicely with the creamy cheese and tangy lemon and herbs. The cheese softens during baking but stays firm enough to serve and eat easily. Accompany the dish with toasted pita wedges or bread.

- 1 (1-lb.) block Greek feta cheese
- 2 tablespoons extra-virgin olive oil
- 2 teaspoons crushed red pepper
- ¼ teaspoon cayenne pepper
- 1 tablespoon chopped fresh oregano
- 3 tablespoons chopped fresh Italian parsley
- 8 lemon wedges

1 Heat oven to 375°F. Lightly oil 8- or 9-inch shallow square baking dish. Cut feta into 8 equal slices; arrange slices in baking dish. Drizzle cheese with oil; sprinkle with crushed red pepper, cayenne pepper and oregano. Cover with foil.

2 Bake 15 to 20 minutes or until feta just begins to melt. Sprinkle with parsley; serve hot with lemon wedges.

8 servings

PER SERVING: 185 calories, 15.5 g total fat (9 g saturated fat), 8.5 g protein, 3.5 g carbohydrate, 50 mg cholesterol, 635 mg sodium, .5 g fiber

Flaky Bisteeya Bites

This variation on a savory Moroccan phyllo pie provides sweet, savory, crisp and tender sensations in every bite. The recipe is a little involved, but can be prepared well in advance.

Flaky Bisteeya Bites

  1 **cup butter, melted**
  3 **eggs, beaten**
  3 **cups finely diced cooked chicken**
 ¼ **cup raisins**
 ¼ **cup finely chopped walnuts**
  1 **tablespoon sugar**
 ½ **teaspoon ground ginger**
 ½ **teaspoon cinnamon**
 ¼ **teaspoon salt**
 ¼ **teaspoon crushed saffron dissolved in**
    1 tablespoon water
 ⅛ **teaspoon freshly ground pepper**
 18 **sheets frozen phyllo dough, thawed**

TOPPING

  2 **tablespoons sugar**
 ½ **teaspoon cinnamon**

1 Line baking sheet with parchment paper. Place 2 tablespoons of the melted butter in small nonstick skillet. Add eggs; cook over low heat, stirring until cooked but still soft and moist.

2 In large bowl, combine cooked eggs, chicken, raisins, walnuts, 1 tablespoon sugar, ginger, ½ teaspoon cinnamon, salt, saffron with water and pepper; mix well. Set aside.

3 Place 1 sheet of phyllo dough on work surface. Brush lightly with melted butter. Cover with second phyllo sheet; brush lightly with butter. Cut the two phyllo sheets crosswise into 5 strips.

4 Place 1 tablespoon chicken mixture in lower right corner of each strip. Fold corners up and over to enclose filling, forming a triangle. Continue to fold, triangle fashion, brushing dough occasionally with melted butter until strips are folded over chicken. Brush edges with melted butter to seal; place on baking sheet. Repeat with remaining phyllo and chicken mixture. (Appetizers can be covered with plastic wrap and refrigerated 24 hours or frozen up to 3 weeks. Do not thaw frozen phyllo triangles before baking.)

5 Heat oven to 350°F. If appetizers were refrigerated or frozen, brush again with melted butter before proceeding. In small bowl, combine topping ingredients; mix well. Sprinkle over appetizers. Bake 20 to 25 minutes or until golden brown.

45 appetizers

PER APPETIZER: 95 calories, 5 g total fat (3 g saturated fat), 35 mg cholesterol, 80 mg sodium, 0 g fiber

Spicy Oven-Roasted Feta Cheese Squares

Garlic-Lime Chicken Drumettes with Chipotle Mayonnaise

Drumettes, also called party wings, are the meatiest part of chicken wings. They look like miniature drumsticks and are the right size to serve as appetizers. This marinade gives them lots of flavor in a relatively short amount of time.

CHICKEN AND MARINADE

- 6 garlic cloves, minced
- 2 teaspoons grated lime peel
- 2 teaspoons kosher (coarse) salt
- 2 teaspoons dried oregano
- 2 teaspoons cumin seeds, toasted, crushed*
- ½ cup lime juice
- ⅓ cup olive oil
- 24 chicken drumettes or party wings

1 Place garlic, grated lime peel, salt, oregano, crushed cumin seeds, lime juice and oil in nonreactive shallow pan large enough to hold chicken in one layer. Add chicken; turn to coat completely with marinade. Cover and refrigerate at least 2 hours or up to 4 hours.

2 In small bowl, stir together all mayonnaise ingredients. Refrigerate 30 minutes.

3 Heat grill or broiler. Remove chicken from marinade; discard marinade. Place chicken on gas grill over medium heat, on charcoal grill 4 to 6 inches from medium coals or on preheated broiler pan 4 to 6 inches from broiler. Grill or broil 12 to 14 minutes or until browned and juices run clear, turning once. Serve with avocado slices.

MAYONNAISE

- 1 cup mayonnaise
- ½ cup light sour cream
- 1 tablespoon Dijon mustard
- 2 to 3 chipotle chiles in adobo sauce, drained, finely chopped**
- 1 tablespoon adobo sauce

GARNISH

- 2 avocados, sliced

TIPS

*Toast cumin seeds in dry skillet over medium-low heat, stirring frequently, 1 minute or until slightly darkened in color and aroma is toasty. Crush with mortar and pestle or flat side of chef's knife.

**Chipotle chiles are dried, smoked jalapeño chiles. They come dried, pickled or canned in adobo sauce. Look for them in the Latin section of the supermarket.

8 servings

PER SERVING: 475 calories, 43.5 g total fat (8.5 g saturated fat), 17.5 g protein, 6 g carbohydrate, 75 mg cholesterol, 470 mg sodium, 3 g fiber

Garlic-Lime Chicken Drumettes with Chipotle Mayonnaise

Artichoke-Blue Cheese Crostini

Crostini, thin slices of toasted bread topped with savory ingredients, make easy hand-held appetizers. The bread slices can be prepared in advance and stored in an airtight container or bag. If desired, crisp them briefly in a 400°F. oven for a few minutes before serving.

- 1 (8-oz.) baguette, cut diagonally into 24 slices (½ inch)
- 2 tablespoons extra-virgin olive oil
- 1 (14-oz.) can quartered artichoke hearts, well-drained
- 1 garlic clove, minced
- ½ cup (2 oz.) crumbled blue cheese
- ¼ cup chopped Kalamata olives
- ¼ cup sour cream or reduced-fat sour cream
- 2 tablespoons chopped fresh parsley
- 1 teaspoon lemon juice
- ⅛ teaspoon freshly ground pepper
- 1 tablespoon freshly grated Parmesan cheese

1 Heat broiler. Brush both sides of bread slices lightly with oil; place on baking sheet. Broil 4 to 6 inches from heat 4 to 6 minutes or until lightly browned, turning once. Cool. (Bread can be prepared up to 1 day ahead. Store in airtight container.)

2 Lightly brush 1½- to 2-cup gratin or baking dish with oil. Pat artichokes dry with paper towels; remove any tough or prickly bits. Place in food processor; pulse until chopped. Or chop by hand into ½-inch pieces. (You should have about 1 cup.)

3 In medium bowl, stir together artichokes, garlic, blue cheese, olives, sour cream, parsley, lemon juice and pepper. Spread mixture in baking dish; sprinkle with cheese. (Spread can be made to this point up to 1 day ahead. Cover and refrigerate.)

4 Heat oven to 375°F. Bake 20 to 30 minutes or until bubbly and lightly browned. Serve with toasted baguette slices.

24 crostini

PER CROSTINI: 55 calories, 3 g total fat (1 g saturated fat), 2 g protein, 6 g carbohydrate, 5 mg cholesterol, 130 mg sodium, .5 g fiber

Artichoke-Blue Cheese Crostini (left), and Mozzarella-Tomato-Olive Cocktail Skewers (right)

Mozzarella-Tomato-Olive Cocktail Skewers

These colorful skewers will liven up any appetizer buffet. They are especially delicious with very soft, fresh mozzarella cheese. Look for smaller balls labeled boconccini (little mouthfuls) or ciliegini (small cherries).

- 4 oz. fresh mozzarella (small balls, if available)
- 16 grape tomatoes
- 16 pitted Kalamata olives
- 2 tablespoons extra-virgin olive oil
- ½ teaspoon minced garlic
- ¼ teaspoon dried thyme
- ⅛ teaspoon salt
- ⅛ teaspoon freshly ground black pepper
  Dash crushed red pepper
- 32 small fresh basil leaves plus additional for garnish, if desired
- 16 (4- to 6-inch) wooden skewers

1 Cut mozzarella into bite-sized pieces. If using small balls, keep whole. Place in medium bowl; stir in tomatoes, olives, oil, garlic, thyme, salt, black pepper and crushed red pepper. Cover and refrigerate 1 to 3 hours.

2 If basil leaves are large, cut into smaller pieces.

3 Thread marinated cheese, tomatoes and olives onto skewers, placing basil leaves in between. Place skewers on platter; garnish with additional fresh basil.

16 skewers

PER SKEWER: 45 calories, 4 g total fat (1.5 g saturated fat), 1.5 g protein, 1 g carbohydrate, 5 mg cholesterol, 90 mg sodium, .5 g fiber

Spicy Herbed Olive Mélange

This recipe was inspired by olives sold at the Marché Grenelle in Paris. It can be prepared quickly and will keep for a month in the refrigerator.

- 8 oz. jumbo Kalamata olives
- 8 oz. cracked green olives
- 8 oz. niçoise olives
- ½ cup diced red bell pepper
- 4 Italian parsley sprigs
- 2 tablespoons minced fresh Italian parsley
- 2 kumquats, thinly sliced
- 2 teaspoons grated lemon peel
- 2 tablespoons lemon juice
- 2 tablespoons extra-virgin olive oil
- ⅛ teaspoon crushed red pepper

In large bowl, stir together all ingredients. Cover and refrigerate at least 1 day. When ready to serve, discard parsley sprigs. Serve at room temperature.

24 (¼ cup) servings

PER SERVING: 45 calories, 4 g total fat (0.5 saturated fat), 0.5 g protein, 2 g carbohydrate, 0 mg cholesterol, 265 mg sodium, 1 g fiber

Provençale-Style Cracked Olives

In the colorful, open-air markets of the seventh district of Paris, you can find hundreds of varieties of olives from France, Italy, Greece, Turkey and Tunisia. Some are simply cured, but many are infused with spices, herbs and other ingredients. They're perfect as appetizers!

- 1 lb. large cracked green olives
- ½ small red onion, thinly sliced
- ½ cup finely chopped green onions
- 3 garlic cloves, sliced
- 2 bay leaves
- 1 large fresh thyme sprig
- ½ cup dry vermouth
- 2 tablespoons extra-virgin olive oil

In large bowl, stir together all ingredients. Cover and refrigerate at least 1 day. When ready to serve, remove garlic slices, if desired. Serve at room temperature.

16 (¼ cup) servings.

PER SERVING: 45 calories, 4 g total fat (0.5 g saturated fat), 0.5 g protein, 1.5 g carbohydrate. 0 mg cholesterol, 370 mg sodium, 1 g fiber

Spicy Herbed Olive Mélange (top), and Provençale-Style Cracked Olives (bottom)

Salmon Saté with Cucumber-Chile Dipping Sauce

Saté is a popular street food in Thailand. Pork is the most popular meat, followed by chicken, but this salmon version offers a refreshingly light appetizer option.

SATÉ

- ½   cup coconut milk
- 4   teaspoons lime juice
- 2   teaspoons grated lime peel
- 1½   teaspoons Asian fish sauce
- ½   lb. center-cut skinless salmon fillet (1 inch thick), cut into 3/8-inch slices (long pieces halved crosswise)

SAUCE

- ¼   cup coarsely grated seedless cucumber*
- ¼   cup rice vinegar
- 2   tablespoons water
- 1   tablespoon minced shallot
- ½   to 1 small red Thai chile, thinly sliced
- ½   teaspoon grated lime peel
- ¼   teaspoon salt

1 Soak 20 (6- to 10-inch) wooden skewers in water 30 to 60 minutes. Meanwhile, combine all saté ingredients except salmon in medium bowl. Gently stir in salmon; refrigerate at least 1 hour or up to 4 hours.

2 Combine all sauce ingredients in small bowl.

3 Heat broiler. Line 2 baking sheets with foil; spray with cooking spray. Remove salmon from marinade. Thread salmon onto skewers; place on baking sheet, brushing some of the marinade over skewers. Discard remaining marinade. (Skewers can be prepared 8 hours ahead. Cover and refrigerate.)

4 Broil skewers 2 to 5 minutes or until light golden brown and fish just begins to flake (do not turn). Serve with sauce.

TIP

*Seedless cucumbers, also called hothouse or English cucumbers, are thinner and longer than regular cucumbers. They're sold wrapped in plastic.

4 servings

PER SERVING: 115 calories, 6 g total fat (3 g saturated fat), 12.5 g protein, 2.5 g carbohydrate, 35 mg cholesterol, 280 mg sodium, .5 g fiber

Salmon Saté with Cucumber-Chile Dipping Sauce

Pistachio-Coated Shrimp

Kick back and relax with the sun-drenched tastes of the Mediterranean.

- ½   cup hummus
- 3   tablespoons olive oil
- 2   tablespoons dried mint
- 1   teaspoon lemon juice
- ½   teaspoon grated lemon peel
- 16   shelled, deveined uncooked medium shrimp
- ¾   cup chopped pistachios
- 1   red bell pepper

1 In medium bowl, combine hummus, olive oil, mint, lemon juice and grated lemon peel; brush over shrimp.

2 Press shrimp into pistachios to coat.

3 Thread onto 16 (6- to 12-inch) wooden skewers that have been soaked in water 30 minutes; top off each skewer with 1-inch piece red bell pepper. (Shrimp can be made to this point 3 hours ahead. Cover and refrigerate.)

4 Gently brush with olive oil; sprinkle with coarse salt.

5 Grill, covered, over medium heat or coals 2 to 4 minutes or until shrimp turn pink, turning once and brushing with oil before turning.

16 appetizers

PER APPETIZER: 85 calories, 7 g total fat (0.1 g saturated fat), 3 g protein, 4 g carbohydrate, 10 mg cholesterol, 40 mg sodium, 1.5 g fiber

Mexican Black Bean-Orange Dip (top), and Smoky Steak Skewers with White BBQ Dipping Sauce (bottom)

Smoky Steak Skewers with White BBQ Dipping Sauce

Sirloin steak is perfect for this recipe because the short cooking time preserves the steak's inherent tenderness. You also could use an equal amount of chicken tenderloins, halved lengthwise. White barbecue sauce is a traditional Southern condiment that's also good with chicken or pork.

½ cup mayonnaise
1 tablespoon cider vinegar
1 tablespoon lemon juice
   Dash ground ancho chile powder plus
½ teaspoon, divided

1 tablespoon smoked paprika*
1 tablespoon packed brown sugar
1 teaspoon ground cumin
¾ teaspoon garlic salt
1¼ lb. beef sirloin steak (1 inch thick)

1 Soak 24 (6- to 7-inch) wooden skewers in water 30 minutes.
2 Meanwhile, combine mayonnaise, vinegar, lemon juice and dash chile powder (or more if desired) in small bowl. Cover and refrigerate. (Sauce can be made 1 day ahead.)
3 Combine paprika, brown sugar, cumin, garlic salt and remaining ½ teaspoon chile powder in another small bowl. Rub mixture onto steak, pressing to make it stick.
4 Heat grill. Cut steak into ¼-inch-thick strips, cutting longer ones in half crosswise. Thread steak onto wooden skewers. Grill, covered, over medium-high heat or coals 4 to 6 minutes for medium-rare, turning once. Serve skewers with sauce.

TIP

* Smoked paprika comes in mild and hot versions and adds a pleasant smoky taste to foods. It can be found in markets carrying foods from Spain or online at tienda.com. Chipotle powder can be substituted for smoked paprika, but it will add a spicy bite to foods.

24 skewers

PER SKEWER: 65 calories, 4.5 g total fat (1 g saturated fat), 5 g protein, 1 g carbohydrate, 15 mg cholesterol, 65 mg sodium, 0 g fiber

Mexican Black Bean-Orange Dip

The fresh flavor of orange brightens this spicy dip. It's based on pico de gallo, a Mexican relish made with vegetables such as bell peppers, jalapeño chiles and onions. Here the vegetables are grilled to bring out their natural sweetness. Serve the dip with tortilla chips.

5   large plum tomatoes, halved lengthwise, seeded (about 1 lb.)
½   sweet onion, sliced (½ inch)
½   green bell pepper, cut into wedges
4   large garlic cloves
1   jalapeño chile, halved, seeds removed if desired
2   tablespoons olive oil
1   (15-oz.) can black beans, drained (do not rinse), coarsely crushed

¼   cup chopped cilantro
3   tablespoons lemon juice
1   tablespoon chopped fresh oregano
2   teaspoons grated orange peel
1   teaspoon garlic salt
½   teaspoon sugar

1 Heat grill. Brush tomatoes, onion, bell pepper, garlic and chile with oil. Grill, covered, over medium-high heat or coals 4 to 6 minutes or until vegetables begin to char and are crisp-tender, turning frequently. (Use a perforated grill tray or thread small pieces onto skewers.) Cool slightly.
2 Meanwhile, combine all remaining ingredients in large bowl.
3 Remove and discard skin from half of the tomatoes; puree in blender until smooth. Add to bean dip. Finely chop remaining tomatoes and grilled vegetables; stir into bean dip. (Dip can be made 2 hours ahead. Cover and refrigerate.) Drain slightly before serving.

About 3 cups

PER 2 TABLESPOONS: 35 calories, 1 g total fat (0 g saturated fat), 1.5 g protein, 4.5 g carbohydrate, 0 mg cholesterol, 90 mg sodium, 1 g fiber

Traditional Guacamole

For classic guacamole, keep it simple. Creamy avocados paired with the piquant mix of onions, tomatoes, chile and cilantro are all that's necessary. Here, the onion, chile and cilantro are ground into a paste before being combined with the avocado, result-ing in a richer, more flavorful guacamole.

5   tablespoons finely chopped white onion, divided
5   tablespoons chopped cilantro, divided
1   serrano chile, chopped
¼   teaspoon coarse salt
3   avocados
2   small plum tomatoes, chopped

1 Crush 3 tablespoons of the onion, 2 tablespoons of the cilantro, chile and salt in molcajete or with large mortar and pestle, or pulse in food processor, until paste forms.
2 Cut avocados in half; remove pits. With large spoon, scoop out flesh; add to chile mixture. Coarsely crush avocados, keeping mixture chunky, not smooth.
3 Gently stir in tomatoes, remaining 2 tablespoons onion and remaining 3 tablespoons cilantro.

2¼ cups

PER 2 TABLESPOONS: 50 calories, 4.5 g total fat (.5 g saturated fat), .5 g protein, 3 g carbohydrate, 0 mg cholesterol, 25 mg sodium, 2 g fiber

Traditional Guacamole

Pork and Spinach Potstickers

Gathering with family and friends to make and eat dumplings is a tradition throughout China, particularly in the north. Here, to save time, we substituted purchased wrappers for homemade dough. Another timesaver: Use an inexpensive plastic dumpling-maker that can be found at most kitchen stores.

Pork and Spinach Potstickers

1	lb. ground pork
1	(9- to 10-oz.) pkg. frozen chopped spinach, thawed, squeezed dry
¼	cup thinly sliced green onions
1	tablespoon soy sauce
1	tablespoon dark sesame oil
2	teaspoons minced fresh ginger
¾	teaspoon salt
½	teaspoon sugar
36	round gyoza potsticker wrappers or square wonton wrappers*
2 to 3	tablespoons vegetable oil
1½	cups water, divided

1 Combine all ingredients except gyoza wrappers, vegetable oil and water in large bowl. (Filling can be made 1 day ahead. Cover and refrigerate.)

2 Place scant 1 tablespoon filling in center of each gyoza wrapper; lightly moisten outside edge of wrapper with a bit of water. Fold wrapper in half to enclose filling, pinching center and each end to make a tight seal. Holding wonton in hand, seal remaining edges, pinching dough toward center, forming a couple of small pleats. Press sealed edge down lightly to plump up dumpling and make it stand up straight.**

3 Place potstickers in rows on baking sheet so they don't touch. Heat 10-inch nonstick skillet over medium-high heat until hot. Add 1 tablespoon of the oil; heat until hot. Place 12 potstickers in skillet (packing them tightly is fine). Cook without disturbing 1 to 2 minutes or until bottoms are pale golden brown.

4 Add ½ cup of the water around sides of skillet; immediately cover. Cook 8 minutes. Uncover; cook 1 to 2 minutes, shaking skillet gently to prevent sticking. When water has evaporated and potstickers are crispy brown, place, bottom-side up, on platter. Repeat with remaining potstickers, adding additional oil as needed. Serve hot or warm with sauces for dipping.

TIPS

* Cut rounds from wonton wrappers using 3¼-inch round cookie cutter, or round off corners with knife. Any leftover wrappers can be tightly wrapped and frozen 3 months.

** Potstickers can be made to this point and frozen 1 month. Place them on a baking sheet 1 inch apart; freeze 3 hours or until completely frozen. Place in resealable plastic freezer bag. They can be cooked frozen; follow instructions, adding an additional ¼ cup water and an extra 1 to 2 minutes cooking time.

36 appetizers

PER APPETIZER: 55 calories, 3 g total fat (1 g saturated fat), 3 g protein, 3.5 g carbohydrate, 10 mg cholesterol, 85 mg sodium, .5 g fiber

Sauces for Potstickers

GINGER-SOY SAUCE

Vinegar and ginger provide a counter-point to the richness of the dumplings in this traditional accompaniment for potstickers.

- ¼ cup soy sauce
- 3 tablespoons white wine vinegar
- 1 tablespoon minced fresh ginger
- 2 teaspoons sugar
- 2 teaspoons dark sesame oil

Whisk all ingredients in small bowl until sugar is dissolved.

About ½ cup

TANGY PLUM SAUCE

Bottled plum sauce, made from a traditional salt-preserved plum, is available in Asian markets as well as many supermarkets. You could also use duck sauce, a popular sweet-and-sour dipping sauce.

- ½ cup Asian plum sauce
- 1 tablespoon white wine vinegar
- 1 teaspoon packed brown sugar
- ¼ teaspoon salt

Whisk all ingredients in small bowl until sugar and salt are dissolved.

About ½ cup

SPICY PEANUT SAUCE

This dip uses prepared Thai-style peanut sauce, fortified with a splash of heat.

- ½ cup purchased peanut sauce
- 2 tablespoons white wine vinegar
- 1 teaspoon sugar
- 1 teaspoon Asian chili-garlic sauce or any hot sauce
- ¼ teaspoon salt

Whisk all ingredients in small bowl until sugar and salt are dissolved.

About ¾ cup

Provençal Stuffed Baguette

Westphalian ham is smoked slowly over beechwood and juniper branches, which imbue it with a light, smoky flavor.

- 1 red bell pepper, cut into 8 wedges
- 1 onion, cut into 8 wedges
- ¼ teaspoon dried thyme
- 2 tablespoons olive oil
- 1 tablespoon balsamic vinegar
- 1 (8-oz.) sourdough baguette
- 4 oz. shaved Westphalian or Black Forest ham
- 1 cup (4 oz.) grated fontina cheese

Provençal Stuffed Baguette

1 Heat oven to 400°F. In large bowl, combine bell pepper, onion, thyme, oil and vinegar; toss to mix. Place in shallow baking pan. Bake for 30 minutes or until vegetables are tender and lightly browned. Cool to room temperature. (Vegetables can be prepared up to 24 hours ahead; cover and refrigerate.)

2 Slice off top ⅓ of baguette. Hollow out inside of top and bottom halves of baguette. Place, cut side up, on baking sheet; bake at 400°F. for 5 minutes. (This will prevent bread from becoming soggy when vegetables are added.)

3 To assemble, place ham in bottom half of baguette; top with half of cheese. Place roasted vegetables over cheese; top with remaining cheese. Cover with top half of baguette. Wrap in foil.(At this point, baguette can be refrigerated 2 to 3 hours.)

4 Heat oven to 350°F. Bake foil-wrapped baguette 20 minutes or until vegetables are hot and cheese is melted. Slice to serve.

18 slices

PER SLICE: 90 calories, 5 g total fat (2 g saturated fat), 10 mg cholesterol, 175 mg sodium, 1 g fiber

Strawberry, Gorgonzola and Chive Bruschetta

Wild Mushroom Turnovers

The combination of mushrooms lends a rich, almost smoky flavor to these turnovers.

- ¼ cup unsalted butter
- 8 oz. specialty mushrooms (shiitakes, portobellos, chanterelles or crimini), finely chopped
- 4 garlic cloves, minced
- ¼ cup (2 oz.) cream cheese
- 2 tablespoons minced fresh chives
- ½ teaspoon lemon juice
- ¼ teaspoon salt
- ⅛ teaspoon freshly ground pepper
- 1 (17.3-oz.) pkg. frozen puff pastry, thawed
- 1 egg, beaten

1 Line baking sheet with parchment paper. Melt butter in large skillet over medium heat. Add mushrooms and garlic; sauté 8 to 10 minutes or until liquid is absorbed.

2 Remove from heat. Stir in cream cheese, chives, lemon juice, salt and pepper. Cool.

3 On lightly floured surface, roll 1 sheet puff pastry to 12-inch square. Cut into 25 squares, each about 2¼ inches square. Brush lightly with egg. Place 1 teaspoon mushroom mixture in center of each square. Fold in half diagonally to form triangles; press edges to seal. Place on baking sheet. Repeat with remaining puff pastry sheet and mushroom mixture. Cover; refrigerate until ready to bake. (Turnovers can be made up to 2 weeks ahead. Cover and freeze. Bake directly from freezer 20 to 25 minutes.)

4 To bake, heat oven to 400°F. Bake 15 to 20 minutes or until golden brown. Serve warm.

50 turnovers

PER TURNOVER: 75 calories, 6 g total fat (2.5 g saturated fat), 1 g protein, 4 g carbohydrate, 10 mg cholesterol, 40 mg sodium, 0 g fiber

Strawberry, Gorgonzola and Chive Bruschetta

This luscious bruschetta pairs an assertive, chive-spiked blue cheese with ripe strawberries—unbeatable!

- 3 tablespoons olive oil
- 1 tablespoon balsamic vinegar
- 12 slices (⅜ inch) crusty French bread
- ¼ teaspoon salt
- 6 oz. Gorgonzola cheese, softened
- 4 tablespoons chopped chives
- 2 cups thinly sliced strawberries
- ⅛ teaspoon freshly ground pepper

1 Heat broiler. In small bowl, combine oil and vinegar. Lightly brush oil mixture on one side of each slice of bread. Sprinkle lightly with salt. Place on ungreased baking sheet.

2 Broil 4 to 6 inches from heat 1 to 2 minutes or until browned. Set aside.

3 In medium bowl, combine cheese and 2 tablespoons of the chives. Spread toasted bread with cheese mixture. Arrange strawberries on top. Sprinkle with remaining chives and pepper.

12 appetizers

PER APPETIZER: 120 calories, 8 g total fat (3 g saturated fat), 4.5 g protein, 8.5 g carbohydrate, 10 mg cholesterol, 320 mg sodium, 1 g fiber

Shrimp with Bloody Mary Sauce

This snappy cocktail sauce is inspired by the Bloody Mary drink. The recipe is ideal for entertaining because both the shrimp and sauce can be prepared ahead of time. Although hot pepper sauce lends a bit of heat, it's not enough to overpower the other flavors.

SHRIMP

    2½ cups water
     2 tablespoons white wine vinegar
     2 (1-inch-wide) strips lemon peel*
     1 teaspoon salt
     1 lb. shelled, deveined uncooked medium shrimp

SAUCE

     1 (14.5-oz.) can diced tomatoes, well-drained
     1 small garlic clove, minced
     1 tablespoon lemon juice
     2 teaspoons Worcestershire sauce
    ¾   teaspoon paprika
    ¼   teaspoon freshly ground pepper
    ¼   teaspoon hot pepper sauce
    ⅛   teaspoon celery seeds
    ⅛   teaspoon salt
     1 tablespoon vodka, if desired

1 In medium saucepan, combine water, vinegar, lemon peel and salt; bring to a gentle simmer over medium heat. Add shrimp; cook 3 to 6 minutes or until shrimp turn pink. Strain; spread shrimp on plate to cool. Cover and refrigerate until ready to serve.

2 Place all sauce ingredients except vodka in food processor or blender; process until sauce is almost smooth. Stir in vodka. Refrigerate at least 30 minutes. (Shrimp and sauce can be prepared up to 1 day ahead.) Serve shrimp with sauce.

TIP

*Peel lemon with vegetable peeler.

6 servings

PER SERVING: 75 calories, .5 g total fat (0 g saturated fat), 12 g protein, 3.5 g carbohydrate, 110 mg cholesterol, 455 mg sodium, .5 g fiber

Shrimp with Bloody Mary Sauce

Baby Shrimp Crostini

Baby shrimp are perfect for this appetizer. They're just the right size to be served on slices of bread, and because they're sold cooked and peeled, preparation time is minimal. The shrimp mixture is best made a day before serving to allow time for the flavors to blend.

    ¾   cup mayonnaise
     2 tablespoons capers, chopped
    1½ tablespoons chopped fresh dill
    1½ teaspoons fresh lemon juice
    ¾   teaspoon grated lemon peel
    ⅛   teaspoon freshly ground pepper
     1 lb. cooked baby or small salad shrimp
    20 thin slices firm white or pumpernickel bread
     3 tablespoons olive oil

1 In medium bowl, stir together mayonnaise, capers, dill, lemon juice, lemon peel and pepper. Add shrimp; gently stir until shrimp are evenly coated. Place in serving bowl; cover and refrigerate at least 4 hours or overnight.

2 Meanwhile, heat oven to 400°F. With 1¾-inch round cookie cutter, cut bread slices into rounds. Brush both sides with oil; place on baking sheet. Bake 7 to 10 minutes or until toasted; cool. Serve with shrimp.

20 appetizers

PER APPETIZER: 135 calories, 9.5 g total fat (1.5 g saturated fat), 6 g protein, 7 g carbohydrate, 50 mg cholesterol, 190 mg sodium, .5 g fiber

Summer Tomato Tart

Sprinkling Romano cheese between the phyllo layers of this tart adds a rich, pleasant saltiness. You can bake the crust and slice the tomatoes and cheese ahead of time, but don't assemble the tart until just before serving to prevent the crust from getting soggy.

CRUST

10 (18 × 14-inch) sheets frozen phyllo dough (from 16-oz. pkg.), thawed
⅓ cup butter, melted
½ cup (2 oz.) freshly grated Pecorino Romano cheese

TOPPING

8 oz. small fresh mozzarella balls, halved*
5 plum tomatoes, sliced (¼ inch)
⅓ cup thinly sliced fresh basil, divided
2 tablespoons freshly grated Pecorino Romano cheese
½ teaspoon salt
½ teaspoon pepper

1 Heat oven to 375°F. Unfold phyllo dough; cover with clean kitchen towel. Lightly brush 17 × 11-inch rimmed baking sheet with some of the butter. Place 1 sheet phyllo on baking sheet. Brush with butter; sprinkle with some of the Romano cheese. Repeat layers until all phyllo is used, brushing each with butter and sprinkling with cheese.

2 Bake 12 to 14 minutes or until crust is golden brown and crispy. Cool completely. Wrap tightly until ready to use.

3 Arrange mozzarella cheese evenly over crust; top with tomatoes. Sprinkle with half of the basil, 2 tablespoons Romano cheese, salt and pepper.

4 Bake 5 to 7 minutes or until cheese is slightly melted and tomatoes are warm. Cool slightly; sprinkle with remaining basil. Cut into 40 pieces.

TIP

* Fresh mozzarella is made in different sizes. Look for balls about ¾ inch in diameter or the size of a cherry. Cubed mozzarella also can be used.

40 pieces

PER PIECE: 55 calories, 3 g total fat (2 g saturated fat), 2.5 g protein, 4 g carbohydrate, 10 mg cholesterol, 115 mg sodium, 0 g fiber

Summar Tomato Tart

Cambozola and Pear Skewers

Cambozola is a mild blue cheese from Germany. If you can't find it, substitute a fairly firm, not-too-ripe Brie or another mild blue cheese, such as Blue Castello.

- 2 large firm but ripe Bartlett pears, peeled
- 2 tablespoons butter
- 1 tablespoon powdered sugar
- 12 oz. Cambozola cheese

1 Cut each pear into 24 cubes.

2 Melt butter in large skillet over medium-high heat. Add pears; cook and stir 2 minutes or until browned and beginning to caramelize. Sprinkle with powdered sugar; cook 2 minutes or until lightly caramelized. Cool.

3 Meanwhile, cut cheese into 48 cubes. When pears are cool, skewer 1 pear cube and 1 cheese cube with 8-inch wooden skewers or toothpicks. Cover and refrigerate until ready to serve. Serve at room temperature.

48 appetizers

PER APPETIZER: 35 calories, 2.5 g total fat (1.5 g saturated fat), 1.5 g protein, 1.5 g carbohydrate, 10 mg cholesterol, 50 mg sodium, .5 g fiber

Cambozola and Pear Skewers

Creamy Summer Vegetable Dip

Toasted cumin is the secret ingredient that brings this creamy, flavorful spread to life. The spread can be made up to 1 day ahead. Serve it with pita wedges or crackers and fresh vegetables.

- 1 cup sugar snap peas
- 1 cup halved green beans
- ½ cup asparagus tips
- ⅓ cup peas
- 4 oz. cream cheese, chilled, cut up
- ½ cup garlic-herb cheese spread

- 3 tablespoons lemon juice
- 2 garlic cloves, minced
- 2 teaspoons cumin seeds, toasted, ground*
- ½ teaspoon coarse salt
- ½ teaspoon pepper

1 Cook snap peas, green beans, asparagus tips and peas in large pot of boiling water 1 to 2 minutes or until bright-green and crisp-tender. Cool completely in ice water. Drain well; pat dry.

2 Place vegetables and all remaining ingredients in food processor; pulse until almost smooth.

TIP

* Toast cumin seeds in small dry skillet over medium-high heat 1 minute or until seeds turn reddish brown and become fragrant, stirring occasionally. Cool. Grind in spice grinder or with mortar and pestle.

2½ cups

PER 2 TABLESPOONS: 40 calories, 3.5 g total fat (2 g saturated fat), 1 g protein, 1.5 g carbohydrate, 10 mg cholesterol, 70 mg sodium, .5 g fiber

Tapas-Style Shrimp

Tapas-Style Shrimp

These very tasty Spanish-style shrimp get their distinctive flavor from smoked paprika. Chipotle chile powder can be substituted, but it will add a spicy bite.

½ cup tomato sauce	2 teaspoons plus ⅛ teaspoon mild smoked paprika, divided
1 tablespoon tomato paste	5 teaspoons minced garlic
3½ tablespoons sherry vinegar, divided	¼ teaspoon salt
1 tablespoon capers, rinsed, drained, coarsely chopped	1 lb. shelled, deveined uncooked large shrimp (16 to 18 count), tails on
¼ teaspoon crushed red pepper	1 tablespoon olive oil

1 In small bowl, stir together tomato sauce and tomato paste until blended. Stir in 1½ tablespoons of the vinegar, capers, crushed red pepper and ⅛ teaspoon of the paprika. When ready to serve, microwave on high 1 minute or until hot. (Sauce can be prepared up to 1 day ahead. Cover and refrigerate.)

2 In medium bowl, stir together remaining 2 tablespoons vinegar, garlic, remaining 2 teaspoons paprika and salt. Add shrimp; toss to coat.

3 Heat oil in large skillet over medium-high heat until hot. Add shrimp; cook 3 to 4 minutes or until shrimp turn pink, turning frequently. Place on plate. (If liquid remains in bottom of skillet, cook liquid until almost evaporated. Remove skillet from heat. Return shrimp to skillet; toss to coat.) Serve warm with dipping sauce.

About 18 appetizers

PER APPETIZER: 30 calories, 1 g total fat (0 g saturated fat), 4 g protein, 1 g carbohydrate, 35 mg cholesterol, 130 mg sodium, .5 g fiber

Olive-Pastry Spirals with Goat Cheese

Black olives provide the rich filling for these crispy little pastry bites. You can use either olive tapenade or olive paste; both are made from ground imported black olives, but tapenade also usually includes anchovies and additional flavorings. Look for them in the same aisle as the olives.

1 sheet frozen puff pastry (from 17.3-oz. pkg.), thawed

3 tablespoons Kalamata olive tapenade or
olive paste

2 tablespoons thinly sliced green onions

¼ cup (1 oz.) soft goat cheese, room temperature

3 tablespoons thinly sliced fresh basil or 24 small leaves

1 Heat oven to 425°F. Line baking sheet with parchment paper.

2 Place puff pastry on work surface. Spread tapenade over surface of puff pastry, leaving about ½-inch border on two short ends; sprinkle with green onions. Starting at one of the short ends, roll up puff pastry; pinch seam to seal. Freeze 15 minutes. Slice into 24 pieces, turning roll to keep round when slicing. Place on baking sheet.

(Spirals can be prepared to this point up to 1 day ahead. Cover and refrigerate.)

3 Bake 15 to 18 minutes or until golden brown and crisp. Top with goat cheese and basil; serve warm.

24 appetizers

PER APPETIZER: 60 calories, 4.5 g total fat (1.5 g saturated fat), 1.5 g protein, 4 g carbohydrate, 10 mg cholesterol, 45 mg sodium, 0 g fiber

Mini Herbed Quiches Lorraine

Using herbes de Provence and chives in these appetizers gives them a Mediterranean twist. Herbes de Provence, a blend of herbs used in southern France, typically includes basil, fennel seed, lavender, marjoram, rosemary, sage, summer savory and thyme.

CRUST

1⅔ cups all-purpose flour

1 teaspoon herbes de Provence

¼ teaspoon salt

10 tablespoons butter, cubed (½ inch)

¼ cup chopped fresh chives

4 to 5 tablespoons water

FILLING

¼ lb. bacon (5 to 6 slices)

¾ cup grated Gruyère or Emmentaler cheese

2 eggs

½ cup half-and-half

½ teaspoon herbes de Provence

¼ teaspoon salt

⅛ teaspoon ground nutmeg

1 In medium bowl, stir together flour, 1 teaspoon herbes de Provence and ¼ teaspoon salt. With pastry blender or 2 knives, cut in butter until mixture resembles coarse crumbs with some pea-sized pieces. Stir in chives. Stir in 4 tablespoons of the water, mixing until dough begins to form. Add additional water 1 teaspoon at a time, if needed. Divide dough in half; shape into flat rounds. Cover and refrigerate 1 hour.

2 Meanwhile, cook bacon in large skillet over medium heat 5 minutes or until crisp. Drain on paper towels; crumble into small pieces.

3 Heat oven to 375°F. Spray mini muffin pans with non-stick cooking spray. Roll each dough half into 10-inch round. With 3-inch round biscuit cutter, cut each dough half into 12 circles; gently place dough into cups of muf-

fin pans. Sprinkle bacon evenly into muffin cups; top evenly with cheese.

4 In medium bowl, whisk eggs until blended; whisk in half-and-half, ½ teaspoon herbes de Provence, salt and nutmeg. Pour into muffin cups. Bake 25 to 30 minutes or until puffed and browned. Remove from pan with tip of knife; serve warm or at room temperature. (Quiches can be made and frozen up to 1 month ahead. Reheat, without thawing, in shallow baking pan at 350°F. for 15 to 20 minutes or until hot.)

24 mini quiches

PER QUICHE: 105 calories, 7.5 g total fat (4.5 g saturated fat), 3 g protein, 7 g carbohydrate, 35 mg cholesterol, 120 mg sodium, .5 g fiber

Phyllo Triangles with Goat Cheese and Roasted Peppers

Crispy, bite-sized triangles of phyllo encase a distinctive medley of Mediterranean flavors. If you can't find pitted Kalamata olives, you can pit them yourself with a chef's knife. Simply press on the olive with the side of a knife blade to gently crush it and loosen the pit.

- 4 oz. soft goat cheese
- ⅓ cup diced roasted red bell peppers (from 7-oz. jar), well-drained
- ¼ cup coarsely chopped pitted Kalamata olives
- ½ teaspoon dried oregano
- ⅛ teaspoon freshly ground pepper
- 12 sheets frozen phyllo, thawed
- 6 tablespoons melted butter,divided

1 Heat oven to 400°F. Line baking sheet with parchment paper. In medium bowl, stir together goat cheese, bell pepper, olives, oregano and pepper.
2 Unroll phyllo sheets; cover with dry towel. Place 1 phyllo sheet on work surface; cover with second sheet. Brush lightly with some of the melted butter. Cut into 4 (16 × 2½-inch) strips. Place 1 rounded teaspoon of the goat cheese mixture at bottom of each strip; fold like a flag up the length of the strip to form a triangle. Place on baking sheet. Repeat with remaining phyllo sheets.
3 Brush tops of appetizers with remaining butter. (Appetizers can be made to this point up to 1 day ahead. Cover and refrigerate.) Bake 12 to 14 minutes or until golden brown and crisp. Cool on wire rack 5 minutes.

24 appetizers

PER APPETIZER: 70 calories, 4 g total fat (2 g saturated fat), 2 g protein, 7 g carbohydrate, 10 mg cholesterol, 90 mg sodium, .5 g fiber

Roasted Red Pepper Hummus

Because no chopping by hand is required, you can prepare this sweet-and-spicy red pepper dip, as well as homemade seasoned pita crisps to serve alongside, in just 10 minutes.

- 2 medium garlic cloves
- 1 (15-oz.) can garbanzo beans, rinsed, drained
- ½ cup purchased roasted red bell peppers
- ⅓ cup tahini paste*
- ⅓ cup lemon juice
- ½ teaspoon salt
- ¼ teaspoon cayenne pepper
- 1 (12-oz.) pkg. pita bread
- 2 tablespoons olive oil
- 2 teaspoons dried Italian seasoning

1 Heat oven to 350°F. With food processor running, add garlic; process until finely chopped. Add garbanzo beans, roasted peppers, tahini paste, lemon juice, salt and cayenne pepper; process until smooth. (Hummus can be made 2 days ahead. Cover and refrigerate.)
2 Cut pita bread into triangles; brush one side lightly with oil. Arrange in single layer on baking sheet; sprinkle with Italian seasoning. Bake 5 to 8 minutes or until lightly toasted. (Pita crisps can be made 1 day ahead.)

TIP

*Tahini paste is available in the Middle Eastern food section of supermarkets.

16 servings

PER SERVING: 135 calories, 5 g total fat (.5 g saturated fat), 4.5 g protein, 18.5 g carbohydrate, 0 mg cholesterol, 230 mg sodium, 2 g fiber

Main Courses

Baked Cavatelli with Italian Sausage and Eggplant

My favorite eggplants for this dish are the small, slender Japanese or Asian ones, which have fewer seeds. Look for smooth, firm, slender eggplants.

- 1 lb. bulk Italian sausage
- 1 large onion, finely chopped
- 2 garlic cloves, minced
- ½ teaspoon crushed red pepper flakes
- 2 medium eggplants, peeled, cut into ¾-inch cubes
- 2 (8-oz.) cans tomato sauce
- ½ cup water
- ¼ teaspoon freshly ground pepper
- 8 oz. cavatelli (narrow shell pasta)
- 2 tablespoons chopped fresh Italian parsley
- 1 cup (4 oz.) shredded mozzarella cheese

1 Heat oven to 400°F. Grease 2-quart casserole. Heat large skillet over medium-high heat until hot. Add sausage, breaking into pieces; cook, stirring, until browned. Add onion, garlic and red pepper flakes; cook 1 minute.

2 Add eggplant; cook 5 minutes, stirring occasionally. Add tomato sauce, water and pepper; mix well. Cook 10 minutes.

3 Meanwhile, cook cavatelli according to package directions.

4 Drain cavatelli; toss with sauce. Place half of mixture in casserole dish. Top with half each of the parsley and cheese. Cover with remaining cavatelli mixture. Sprinkle with remaining parsley and cheese. Cover with foil. (Casserole can be made up to 4 hours ahead. Cover and refrigerate. Bake at 400°F. for 25 to 35 minutes or until thoroughly heated.)

5 Bake 15 to 20 minutes or until thoroughly heated.

6 servings

PER SERVING: 530 calories, 24 g total fat (9 g saturated fat), 28.5 g protein, 51.5 g carbohydrate, 70 mg cholesterol, 1835 mg sodium, 8 g fiber

Baked Cavatelli with Italian Sausage and Eggplant

Rosemary Roasted Salmon

This recipe is one of the easiest and quickest ways to serve salmon; it cooks in just 10 minutes. During the summer, try one of the great wild salmon species, such as king, coho or sockeye.

- 1½ lb. salmon fillet (1 inch thick)
- 4 medium garlic cloves, minced
- 2 tablespoons olive oil
- 1 tablespoon country-style Dijon mustard
- 1 tablespoon finely chopped fresh rosemary
- ¼ teaspoon salt
- ¼ teaspoon freshly ground pepper

1 Heat oven to 475°F. Line small rimmed baking sheet with foil. Place salmon fillet, skin side down, on baking sheet.

2 In small bowl, stir together garlic, oil, mustard and rosemary. Sprinkle salmon with salt and pepper. Spoon rosemary mixture over salmon. Refrigerate 10 minutes.

3 Bake salmon 8 to 10 minutes or until it just begins to flake.

4 servings

PER SERVING: 310 calories, 16.5 g total fat (3.5 g saturated fat), 36.5 g protein, 1.5 g carbohydrate, 110 mg cholesterol, 340 mg sodium, 0 g fiber

Beef and Balsamic with Arugula

Sweet balsamic vinegar harmonizes perfectly with the richness of the steak and adds a delicious counterpoint to the peppery arugula. Use the best extra-virgin olive oil you can find; just a small amount of a fruity oil delivers robust flavor when gently warmed by the beef.

VINAIGRETTE

- 2 teaspoons minced garlic
- 1 teaspoon salt
- 2 tablespoons balsamic vinegar
- 1 teaspoon Dijon mustard
- ¼ cup extra-virgin olive oil

BEEF

- 1½ lb. beef top sirloin steak (¾ to 1 inch thick)
- ½ teaspoon salt
- ¼ teaspoon freshly ground pepper
- 4 cups packed arugula
- ¼ cup chopped fresh basil

1 With side of knife, mash garlic with 1 teaspoon salt to form paste. Place in small bowl; whisk in vinegar and mustard. Slowly whisk in oil.

2 Heat grill. Sprinkle beef with ½ teaspoon salt and pepper. Place on gas grill over medium heat or on charcoal grill 4 to 6 inches from medium coals; cover grill. Grill 8 to 10 minutes for medium-rare or until of desired doneness, turning once. Place on cutting board; cover loosely with foil. Let stand 5 minutes.

3 Cut steak into 4 pieces or thinly slice; place over arugula. Drizzle vinaigrette over steak; sprinkle with basil.

4 servings

PER SERVING: 345 calories, 19 g total fat (3.5 g saturated fat), 39.5 g protein, 2 g carbohydrate, 95 mg cholesterol, 970 mg sodium, .5 g fiber

Lemon-Garlic Grilled Chicken with Basil Aïoli

Lemon-Garlic Grilled Chicken with Basil Aïoli

Basil aïoli—mayonnaise flavored with garlic and basil— is quick to fix and makes a tasty accompaniment to these garlicky grilled chicken breasts. To turn the chicken into a sandwich, slather it with the aïoli and serve it between slices of a good-quality bread.

- 6 boneless skinless chicken breast halves
- 1 tablespoon olive oil
- 4 large garlic cloves, minced, divided
- ⅓ cup grated lemon peel (from about 3 large lemons)
- 2 tablespoons chopped fresh parsley
- 1½ teaspoons lemon pepper seasoning
- ½ cup mayonnaise
- ½ cup chopped fresh basil

1 Heat grill. Brush chicken breasts with oil. In small bowl, stir together 3 of the minced garlic cloves, lemon peel and parsley; rub onto both sides of chicken breasts. Sprinkle with lemon pepper seasoning.

2 Place chicken on gas grill over medium heat or on charcoal grill 4 to 6 inches from medium coals; cover grill. Grill 8 to 10 minutes or until no longer pink in center, turning once.

3 In another small bowl, stir together mayonnaise, basil and remaining 1 minced garlic clove. Serve aïoli with chicken.

6 servings

PER SERVING: 310 calories, 21 g total fat (3.5 g saturated fat), 27 g protein, 2.5 g carbohydrate, 85 mg cholesterol, 255 mg sodium, 1 g fiber

Beef and Balsamic with Arugula

Crown Roast of Pork with Porcini, Fennel and Apple Stuffing

A crown roast is formed by tying together two pork loins, a task you can ask your butcher to do.

PORK

- 2 medium carrots, coarsely chopped
- 1 medium onion, coarsely chopped
- 1 small fennel bulb, fronds removed and discarded, bulb coarsely chopped
- 1 tart apple, peeled, coarsely chopped
- 1 cup apple cider
- 2 tablespoons olive oil, divided
- 2 teaspoons dried sage
- 1 teaspoon salt
- ½ teaspoon freshly ground pepper
- 1 (12-rib) crown roast of pork (5½ to 6 lb.)
- 3 cups Porcini, Fennel and Apple Stuffing (page 96)

SAUCE

- ½ cup reduced-sodium chicken broth
- ½ cup hard apple cider or apple cider*
- ½ cup white wine or additional apple cider

1 Heat oven to 450°F. In shallow roasting pan, stir together carrots, onion, fennel, apple, 1 cup cider and 1 tablespoon of the oil. Evenly spread vegetables in pan. Place roasting rack over vegetables. In small bowl, stir together sage, salt and pepper. Rub pork with remaining 1 tablespoon oil; rub sage mixture into crevices of pork. Place pork on rack in pan. (To keep rib bones from getting too dark, wrap bones in foil.)

2 Bake 20 minutes. Reduce oven temperature to 325°F. Bake 45 minutes; spoon stuffing into center of roast.** Bake an additional 1 hour or until internal temperature reaches 145°F. to 150°F. Carefully place roast on serving platter; cover loosely with foil. Let stand 15 to 20 minutes.

3 Meanwhile, spoon off any excess fat from pan juices. Place roasting pan with vegetables over medium-high heat; add all sauce ingredients. Simmer 3 to 5 minutes or until slightly thickened, scraping up browned bits from bottom of pan.

4 To serve, cut pork between ribs. Spoon sauce over meat; serve with vegetables and stuffing.

TIPS

* Hard apple cider is cider that has been fermented. It has a light, crisp taste that can be slightly effervescent. Its alcohol level can vary. Regular sweet apple cider or apple juice can be substituted.

** Remaining stuffing (recipe on page 96) can be baked along with roast. Put stuffing in oven 45 minutes before roast is done baking.

12 servings

PER 1/12 OF RECIPE (EXCLUDING STUFFING): 270 calories, 12 g total fat (4 g saturated fat), 29 g protein, 9 g carbohydrate, 80 mg cholesterol, 280 mg sodium, 1 g fiber

Crown Roast of Pork with Porcini, Fennel and Apple Stuffing

Peppered Beef Roast with Cranberry-Red Wine Sauce

A boneless beef sirloin tip roast is a tender and affordable cut. This elegant recipe acquires a savory crust during baking thanks to the rub and herb mixture spread over the outside. It's paired with a sweet-tart sauce that provides a nice counterpoint to the rich meat.

BEEF

- 1 (3-lb.) boneless beef sirloin tip roast
- 2 teaspoons Dijon mustard
- 2 teaspoons tomato paste
- 2 teaspoons minced garlic
- 1 teaspoon canola oil
- 1 tablespoon coarsely ground pepper
- 1 teaspoon dried thyme
- ¾ teaspoon dried rosemary
- ¾ teaspoon salt
- ¼ teaspoon ground coriander

SAUCE

- 1 tablespoon butter
- ¼ cup minced shallots
- 1 teaspoon sugar
- 1 cup red wine or cranberry juice
- 1 cup fresh or frozen cranberries
- ½ cup reduced-sodium beef broth

Peppered Beef Roast with Cranberry-Red Wine Sauce

1 Heat oven to 350°F. Pat roast dry; place in heavy shallow roasting pan. In small bowl, stir together mustard, tomato paste, garlic and oil; rub over entire surface of roast. In another small bowl, stir together pepper, thyme, rosemary, salt and coriander; sprinkle over surface of roast. Bake 1 hour 25 minutes to 1 hour 35 minutes or until internal temperature reaches 140°F. for medium-rare or until of desired doneness.

2 Meanwhile, melt butter in medium saucepan over medium-low heat. Add shallots; cook 3 to 5 minutes or until shallots begin to brown. Sprinkle with sugar; cook 1 minute. Add wine, cranberries and broth. Increase heat to medium. Bring to a boil; gently boil 5 minutes. Strain into medium bowl, pressing on cranberries to extract pulp and scraping accumulated pulp on bottom of strainer into wine mixture, repeating pressing and scraping several times. (Sauce can be made up to 1 day ahead. Cover and refrigerate.)

3 Place roast on platter; cover loosely with foil. Let stand 10 to 20 minutes.

4 Meanwhile, add sauce to roasting pan. Bring to a boil over medium heat, scraping up any browned bits from bottom of pan; boil 1 to 2 minutes to combine flavors. Serve sauce with roast.

8 servings

PER SERVING: 235 calories, 7.5 g total fat (2.5 g saturated fat), 34.5 g protein, 4.5 g carbohydrate, 95 mg cholesterol, 355 mg sodium, 1 g fiber

Garlicky Lamb Kebabs

Garlicky Lamb Kebabs

A savory mélange of spices and herbs punctuates this super-flavorful marinade. For the most juicy, tender kebabs, cook the lamb to medium-rare. Try the marinade on lamb chops, lamb leg steaks or venison too.

½	cup chopped shallots
4	garlic cloves, minced
¼	cup red wine vinegar or cider vinegar
2	tablespoons lime juice
2	tablespoons lemon juice
1	tablespoon ground coriander
1	large bay leaf, broken into small pieces
1	teaspoon salt
1	teaspoon pepper
½	teaspoon ground allspice
½	teaspoon dried oregano
½	teaspoon dried thyme
2	lb. boneless leg of lamb, cut into 1½-inch pieces
2	tablespoons olive oil

1 Combine all ingredients except lamb and oil in large bowl. Add lamb; stir. Cover and refrigerate 2 to 8 hours, stirring occasionally.

2 Heat grill. Remove lamb from marinade; discard marinade. Thread lamb onto 4 (10- to 12-inch) metal skewers. Brush lamb with oil. Grill, covered, over medium-high heat or coals 8 to 10 minutes for medium-rare to medium, turning to brown all sides.

6 servings

PER SERVING: 285 calories, 15 g total fat (4.5 g saturated fat), 32.5 g protein, 3 g carbohydrate, 105 mg cholesterol, 350 mg sodium, .5 g fiber

Balsamic-Tossed Pasta with Fresh Tomato, Arugula and Mozzarella

Fresh garden produce and mozzarella combine with a sauce that is simply dressed with olive oil and a splash of good-quality balsamic vinegar. There is no need to cook the sauce; the heat from the pasta helps melt the cheese and warm the sauce.

2	cups chopped seeded tomatoes (2 large)
2	cups coarsely chopped arugula
2	large garlic cloves, chopped
8	oz. fresh mozzarella cheese, cut into small cubes
1	teaspoon sea salt
½	teaspoon freshly ground pepper
¼	cup extra-virgin olive oil
12	oz. strozzapreti (thin, twisted pasta) or penne
2	tablespoons balsamic vinegar

1 In large bowl, stir together tomatoes, arugula, garlic, mozzarella, salt, pepper and oil. Refrigerate 30 minutes.

2 Cook strozzapreti in large pot of boiling salted water according to package directions; drain. Toss with sauce. Add vinegar; toss.

4 servings

PER SERVING: 635 calories, 29 g total fat (10 g saturated fat), 24 g protein, 72 g carbohydrate, 0 mg cholesterol, 1015 mg sodium, 4 g fiber

Balsamic-Tossed Pasta with Fresh Tomato, Arugula and Mozzarella

Butterflied Chicken with Garlic

Butterflying the chicken makes it cook evenly and quickly. After straining the garlic from the pan juices, spread it on bread as a condiment.

- 20 garlic cloves*
- 1 (4-lb.) whole chicken, butterflied, or cut-up pieces**
- ¾ cup white wine or additional chicken broth
- ¾ cup lower-sodium chicken broth
- 2 teaspoons flavored sea salt
- 1 tablespoon chopped fresh rosemary
- 1 tablespoon chopped fresh thyme
- ½ teaspoon pepper

1 Heat oven to 400°F. Scatter garlic in bottom of roasting pan; top with chicken. Pour wine and broth over chicken; sprinkle with salt, rosemary, thyme and pepper. Cover with foil.

2 Bake 25 minutes. Remove foil; bake an additional 25 minutes or until internal temperature reaches 170°F. If desired, baste with accumulated juices every 10 minutes.

3 Pour pan juices and garlic into large skillet; boil over high heat 5 minutes or until reduced by half. Strain. Serve chicken with juices.

Butterflied Chicken with Garlic

TIPS

* If green root is present in center, remove.

** Have the butcher butterfly chicken or, using kitchen shears, cut on either side of backbone. Remove and discard backbone. Place chicken breast-side up; press on breast bone to flatten slightly.

6 servings

PER SERVING: 325 calories, 17.5 g total fat (5 g saturated fat), 36 g protein, 2 g carbohydrate, 115 mg cholesterol, 700 mg sodium, 0 g fiber

Steakhouse-Marinated Top Round

Because top round is a less tender cut of meat, it's best to cook it to no more than medium-rare. The marinade also works well with flank, skirt or bottom round steak.

- ½ cup cider vinegar
- ¼ cup minced onion
- ¼ cup water
- 2 tablespoons paprika
- 1 tablespoon tomato paste
- 1 tablespoon minced garlic
- 1 tablespoon sugar
- 1 tablespoon lemon juice
- 1 tablespoon soy sauce
- 2 teaspoons dry mustard
- 1½ teaspoons crushed red pepper
- 1½ teaspoons salt
- 1 teaspoon Worcestershire sauce
- ⅛ teaspoon cayenne pepper
- 1 (2-lb.) beef top round steak (1½ inches thick)
- 2 tablespoons vegetable oil

1 Combine all ingredients except steak and oil in medium bowl. Place steak in shallow glass baking dish; pour marinade over steak. Cover and refrigerate 4 hours or overnight, turning occasionally and basting with marinade.

2 Heat grill. Remove steak from marinade; discard marinade. Brush steak with oil. Grill, covered, over medium-high heat or coals 8 minutes, turning once and rotating steak by 90 degrees to achieve square grill marks.

3 Reduce heat to medium; grill an additional 5 to 8 minutes for medium-rare, turning once. Cover loosely with foil; let stand 5 minutes before slicing.

6 servings

PER SERVING: 240 calories, 9.5 g total fat (2.5 g saturated fat), 34.5 g protein, 2 g carbohydrate, 85 mg cholesterol, 300 mg sodium, 5 g fiber

Greek Chicken Pot Pie

Greek Chicken Pot Pie

A tangy lemon-dill avgolemono sauce transforms an old-fashioned American pot pie into an impressive Greek specialty. I won't mislead you by suggesting that you can whip up this pie after work. However, because most or all of the preparation can be done in advance, it is ideal for casual entertaining.

FILLING

2	teaspoons olive oil
4	cups thinly sliced leeks
2	(14.5-oz.) cans reduced-sodium chicken broth
½	cup rice
4	medium carrots, cut into 1x¼-inch strips
¼	cup all-purpose flour
½	cup fresh lemon juice
1	egg
3½	cups shredded cooked chicken breasts
6	green onions, sliced
½	cup chopped fresh dill
¾	teaspoon salt
½	teaspoon freshly ground pepper

CRUST

	Olive oil nonstick cooking spray
⅓	cup unseasoned dry bread crumbs
14	sheets frozen phyllo dough, thawed
2	teaspoons butter, melted

1 Heat oil in large saucepan over medium heat until hot. Add leeks; sauté 3 to 4 minutes or until tender, stirring frequently. (If necessary, add a little water to prevent sticking.)

2 Add broth; bring to a boil. Add rice; boil 7 minutes. Add carrots; boil 3 minutes. Drain rice mixture; reserve broth.

3 Measure 2¼ cups reserved broth; add water if necessary. Place in large saucepan. Bring to a boil over medium heat.

4 Meanwhile, place flour in small bowl; gradually whisk in lemon juice. Beat egg in large bowl; set aside.

5 Slowly add lemon mixture to broth, whisking constantly. Bring to a boil; boil 1 to 2 minutes or until sauce thickens slightly.

6 Gradually add hot sauce to egg, whisking constantly.

7 In large bowl, combine rice mixture, chicken, sauce, green onions, dill, salt and pepper. (Filling can be made up to 24 hours before baking. Cover and refrigerate.)

8 Place oven rack in lower third of oven; heat to 375°F. Spray 12-inch tart pan* with cooking spray; sprinkle lightly with bread crumbs.

9 Place 1 sheet phyllo in tart pan. Spray with cooking spray; sprinkle with bread crumbs. Repeat with 7 sheets phyllo, angling each sheet to form a rough circle to cover bottom and sides of pan. Trim overhang to ½ inch; fold inside to form neat rim. Spread filling over phyllo.

10 To make ruffled top, place 1 sheet phyllo on work surface. Spray with cooking spray; sprinkle with bread crumbs. Cut phyllo in half lengthwise. Starting at long side, roll each piece into ½-inch-thick rope. Arrange over filling along edge of tart. Repeat with remaining 5 sheets phyllo to cover top of tart. Brush with butter.

11 Set tart pan on baking sheet. Bake 50 to 60 minutes or until crust is golden brown. Remove sides of tart pan; place on serving platter. (Pie can be baked up to 24 hours ahead. Cover and refrigerate. Reheat in 350°F. oven for 25 to 30 minutes or until filling is hot.)

TIP

* Recipe can be assembled in 13 × 9-inch pan. Bake as directed.

8 servings

PER SERVING: 375 calories, 7.5 g total fat (2 g saturated fat), 27 g protein, 48.5 g carbohydrate, 75 mg cholesterol, 675 mg sodium, 4 g fiber

Sea Scallops with Champagne Beurre Blanc

Beurre blanc ("white butter") is a French sauce traditionally served with fish. Here, champagne adds a subtle sweetness that beautifully complements the scallops. If you wish, steam 2 cups of julienned carrots, leeks and celery with the scallops. To serve, nestle the scallops on a bed of the vegetables before covering them with the champagne beurre blanc.

- ¼ cup minced shallots
- 2 cups brut champagne or other sparkling wine, chilled
- 1½ lb. trimmed cleaned sea scallops*
- ¼ cup whipping cream
- 1 teaspoon champagne vinegar or white wine vinegar
- ½ teaspoon salt
- ⅛ teaspoon freshly ground white pepper
- ½ cup cold unsalted butter, cut into chunks
  Fresh chervil or chives

Sea Scallops with Champagne Beurre Blanc

1 Choose a Dutch oven or large saucepan that will accommodate a steamer basket. Combine shallots and champagne in Dutch oven; bring to a boil over high heat. Cook about 10 minutes or until reduced to 1 cup.

2 Fit steamer basket in Dutch oven; place scallops in basket. Reduce heat to medium-low; cover and steam over simmering champagne 5 minutes or until scallops are cooked but still very tender.** (You may need to steam scallops in 2 batches, depending on size of Dutch oven and steamer basket.) Remove scallops from Dutch oven; cover loosely to keep warm. Remove basket from Dutch oven.

3 Over high heat, reduce champagne and scallop juices to ½ cup. Add cream, vinegar, salt and pepper; boil briefly to reduce slightly. Reduce heat to low; whisk cold butter into sauce a few chunks at a time. Do not let sauce boil. Strain sauce, if desired.

4 Arrange scallops on warm serving plates; spoon sauce over scallops. Garnish with chervil or chives.

TIPS

* This dish works best with large sea scallops. You may substitute an equal amount of shelled, deveined medium shrimp or make the recipe with half scallops and half shrimp.

** Test scallops for doneness like other fish and meat: Press them with your finger to measure the resistance. If a scallop feels very soft, it is still undercooked. A properly cooked scallop will have some "give," gently firm but not stiff. If you feel uncertain the first time you prepare them, buy a few extra scallops that can be cut in half for a peek.

4 servings

PER SERVING: 470 calories, 30 g total fat (17.5 g saturated fat), 135 mg cholesterol, 760 mg sodium, 0 g fiber

Beef and Black Bean Chili

This beefy chili is enriched by cooking black beans with smoked ham hocks and then adding the broth and ham to the chili mixture. Serve it in large mugs or crocks with a choice of garnishes, including chopped cilantro, sour cream and a variety of hot sauces.

1	lb. dried black beans
1	lb. smoked ham hocks
1½	tablespoons olive oil
2	lb. coarsely ground beef round (85% lean)
2½	cups chopped leeks
2	green bell peppers, chopped
2	jalapeño chiles, seeded, deveined, minced
2	large garlic cloves, minced
¼	cup chopped fresh oregano

2	teaspoons cumin seeds, toasted*
1½	teaspoons paprika
1½	teaspoons salt
½	teaspoon cayenne pepper
½	teaspoon black pepper
2	(10-oz.) cans diced tomatoes with green chiles
2	tablespoons red wine vinegar
4½	cups lower-sodium beef broth

1 Combine beans and ham hocks in large pot; add enough water to cover by 2 inches. Bring to a boil. Reduce heat to low; simmer, partially covered, 1¼ hours or until beans are barely tender. Remove ham hocks; remove meat and chop. Cool beans in cooking liquid. (Beans and ham can be made 3 days ahead. Cover and refrigerate separately.)

2 Heat oil in large pot over medium heat until hot. Cook beef in batches 5 minutes or until browned. Remove beef.

3 Add leeks, bell peppers and chiles; cook 5 minutes or until softened. Add beef, ham, garlic, oregano, cumin seeds, paprika, salt, cayenne pepper and black pepper. Stir in tomatoes and vinegar.

4 Drain beans, reserving cooking liquid; add beans to pot. Measure cooking liquid, adding enough broth to equal 8 cups; add to pot. Bring to a boil. Reduce heat to low; simmer, uncovered, 1½ hours or until beans are tender. Increase heat to medium-high during last 30 minutes of cooking; boil until of desired thickness. (Chili can be made 2 days ahead. Cover and refrigerate.)

TIP

* Toast cumin seeds in dry small skillet over medium-high heat 1 minute or until seeds turn reddish brown and become fragrant, stirring occasionally. Cool. Grind in spice grinder or with mortar and pestle.

8 (1¾-cup) servings

PER SERVING: 485 calories, 18 g total fat (6 g saturated fat), 38 g protein, 45 g carbohydrate, 80 mg cholesterol, 890 mg sodium, 14 g fiber

Beef and Black Bean Chili

Mexican Burgers

The patties are infused with intense seasonings and topped with layers of condiments—creamy guacamole, spicy salsa and flavored mayonnaise. The guacamole should be made right before serving, but the salsa and flavored mayonnaise can be made up to 8 hours ahead.

Mexican Burgers

1½	lb. ground beef chuck (85% lean)
¼	cup chopped cilantro
2	tablespoons thinly sliced green onion
1	pickled jalapeño chile, finely chopped, if desired
2	teaspoons minced garlic
2	teaspoons chili powder
1	teaspoon grated lime peel
¾	teaspoon salt
4	slices Monterey Jack cheese
4	Kaiser rolls or Mexican bolillo rolls, split
½	cup Jalapeño-Lime Mayonnaise (recipe follows)
2	cups shredded iceberg lettuce
½	cup Quick-Roasted Chile Salsa (recipe follows)
1	cup Quick Guacamole (recipe follows)

1 In medium bowl, gently mix together beef, cilantro, green onion, chile, garlic, chili powder, lime peel and salt. Shape into 4 (4½-inch) patties about ¾ inch thick.

2 Heat grill. Place burgers on gas grill over medium heat or on charcoal grill 4 to 6 inches from medium coals; cover grill. Grill 8 to 10 minutes or until thoroughly cooked and no longer pink in center, turning once. Top each burger with 1 slice cheese; grill 1 minute or until cheese has melted.

3 Spread each roll with 2 tablespoons of the Jalapeño-Lime Mayonnaise. Place lettuce on rolls; top with burgers, salsa and guacamole.

4 sandwiches

PER SANDWICH: 770 calories, 49 g total fat (16 g saturated fat), 43 g protein, 39.5 g carbohydrate, 140 mg cholesterol, 1270 mg sodium, 6 g fiber

JALAPEÑO-LIME MAYONNAISE

½	cup mayonnaise
2	tablespoons lime juice
2	teaspoons grated lime peel
1	tablespoon finely chopped pickled jalapeño chile

In small bowl, stir together all ingredients.

¾ cup

QUICK-ROASTED CHILE SALSA

1	large tomato, diced
2	tablespoons finely chopped red onion
2	tablespoons diced canned roasted green chiles
2	tablespoons chopped cilantro

In small bowl, stir together all ingredients.

1¼ cups

QUICK GUACAMOLE

1	large avocado
¼	cup diced tomato
¼	cup finely chopped red onion
2	teaspoons finely chopped seeded deveined jalapeño chile, if desired
½	teaspoon freshly ground pepper
¼	teaspoon salt

Place avocado in medium bowl; mash coarsely with fork or potato masher. (Do not overmash; texture should be quite lumpy.) Stir in all remaining ingredients.

1 cup

Chicken, Chorizo and Beaujolais Stew

3 Pour off all but 1 tablespoon drippings from skillet. Cook onions over medium heat 2 to 3 minutes or until they begin to brown. Add garlic; cook 30 to 60 seconds or until fragrant. Add to pot.

4 Add wine to skillet; bring to a boil, stirring to scrape up any browned bits from bottom of skillet. Stir in Kitchen Bouquet; pour into pot.

5 Add broth to pot; bring to a boil over medium heat. Reduce heat to low; simmer, partially covered, 20 minutes. Turn chicken breasts; simmer, partially covered, an additional 25 to 30 minutes or until chicken is no longer pink in center. Remove chicken, sausage and onions; cover loosely with foil.

6 Bring liquid in pot to a boil over medium-high heat. Whisk 3 tablespoons water and cornstarch to dissolve; whisk into hot liquid in pot. Boil several minutes to thicken slightly. Return chicken, sausage and onions to pot; stir to coat with sauce.

TIP

* Kitchen Bouquet is a browning and seasoning sauce used here to prevent the stew from taking on a purple hue from the wine. You can find it in the condiment and sauce aisle.

4 (2½-cup) servings

PER SERVING: 650 calories, 40 g total fat (12.5 g saturated fat), 46 g protein, 21 g carbohydrate, 145 mg cholesterol, 1275 mg sodium, 2.5 g fiber

Chicken, Chorizo and Beaujolais Stew

Coq au vin, a traditional dish from Burgundy, France, gets a Spanish-style twist with the addition of chorizo. Cooking the chicken in red wine gives it rich, deep flavor.

- 1 tablespoon canola oil
- 4 Spanish-style smoked chorizo sausage links, halved lengthwise, cut into 1½-inch pieces
- 4 bone-in skin-on chicken thighs
- 2 bone-in skin-on chicken breast halves, halved crosswise if large
- ½ teaspoon salt
- ¼ teaspoon pepper
- 1 (16-oz.) pkg. frozen pearl onions, thawed
- 1 tablespoon minced garlic
- 2 cups Beaujolais Nouveau or Beaujolais
- 1 teaspoon Kitchen Bouquet*
- 1 cup lower-sodium chicken broth
- 2 tablespoons cornstarch

1 Heat large skillet over medium heat until hot. Add oil; heat until hot. Cook sausage 3 to 4 minutes or until browned, stirring occasionally. Place in large pot.

2 Sprinkle chicken with salt and pepper. Cook in same skillet, in batches, 8 to 12 minutes or until well-browned, turning once. Place in pot, placing breasts on top of thighs.

Farmer's Pasta

Farmer's Pasta

This peasant-style pasta is a meal in itself. If the marriage of potatoes and pasta leaves you wondering, you will become a believer once you taste it.

Quick-Roasted Hoisin Salmon with Sesame Asparagus

 3 tablespoons extra-virgin olive oil
 2 boneless skinless chicken breast halves
 4 oz. pancetta, diced*
 3 large garlic cloves, minced
 2 portobello mushroom caps, sliced
 ½ cup dry white wine
 1 cup chicken broth
 5 new potatoes, unpeeled, each cut into 12 wedges
 2 red bell peppers, cut into ¾-inch pieces
 1 green bell pepper, cut into ¾-inch pieces
 ½ teaspoon salt
 ½ teaspoon freshly ground pepper
 1 tablespoon chopped fresh rosemary
 8 oz. penne (tube-shaped pasta)
 ⅓ cup (about 1.5 oz.) freshly grated Parmigiano-Reggiano cheese

1 Heat 1 tablespoon of the oil in large skillet or Dutch oven. Add chicken breasts; cook over medium heat 4 to 6 minutes or until golden brown and juices run clear. Remove from skillet. Slice diagonally into ½-inch strips; set aside.

2 Heat remaining 2 tablespoons oil in same skillet. Add pancetta; cook over medium heat until brown, stirring occasionally. Add garlic; cook briefly. Add mushrooms; cook 1 to 2 minutes.

3 Increase heat to high. Add wine; bring to a boil. Add broth, potatoes, bell peppers, salt and pepper. Bring to a boil. Reduce heat to medium-low; cover and simmer 5 minutes.

4 Remove cover; increase heat to medium-high. Add chicken and rosemary. Cook 3 to 5 minutes or until potatoes are tender and sauce is slightly thickened.

5 Meanwhile, cook penne according to package directions.

6 Drain penne; toss with sauce and cheese.

TIP

*Regular bacon can be substituted. Eliminate the oil for cooking and drain the bacon drippings.

4 servings

PER SERVING: 630 calories, 20 g total fat (5 g saturated fat), 32 g protein, 79.5 g carbohydrate, 45 mg cholesterol, 960 mg sodium, 6 g fiber

Quick-Roasted Hoisin Salmon with Sesame Asparagus

This Asian-inspired dish relies on hoisin sauce for a nice hit of flavor. Hoisin is a thick, sweet, reddish-brown sauce made with soybeans, chiles, garlic, vinegar and spices. It's typically used as a barbecue marinade. You can find it in Asian markets or in the Asian section of your grocery store.

 ¼ cup soy sauce
 ¼ cup dry sherry or chicken broth
 3 quarter-sized slices fresh ginger, minced
 2 garlic cloves, crushed
 4 (6-oz.) salmon fillets
 ¼ cup hoisin sauce
 1 lb. asparagus
 1 teaspoon dark sesame oil

1 Heat oven to 450°F. Line 15 × 10-inch baking pan with foil; spray with nonstick cooking spray. In shallow dish, stir together soy sauce, sherry, ginger and garlic. Add salmon, skin side up; let stand 10 minutes.

2 Remove salmon from marinade; discard marinade. Place salmon on one side of pan, skin side down. Spoon hoisin sauce over salmon. Add asparagus to other side of pan in single layer. Bake 5 to 8 minutes or until asparagus is crisp-tender. Remove asparagus; drizzle with sesame oil. Continue baking salmon 4 to 6 minutes or until it just begins to flake. Serve with asparagus.

4 servings

PER SERVING: 315 calories, 12 g total fat (3 g saturated fat), 40.5 g protein, 11.5 g carbohydrate, 110 mg cholesterol, 365 mg sodium, 2.5 g fiber

Roast Pork with Shallots and Chestnuts

Chestnuts make the perfect foil for a succulent pork loin roast. If fresh ones are difficult to find, use unsweetened whole canned chestnuts, or look for them cooked and vacuum-sealed in plastic.

Roast Pork with Shallots and Chestnuts

PORK

- 30 fresh chestnuts or 1 (10-oz.) can unsweetened whole chestnuts, drained
- 4 large garlic cloves, minced
- 2 tablespoons olive oil, divided
- 1 tablespoon dried thyme
- ¾ teaspoon salt
- ½ teaspoon freshly ground pepper
- ¼ teaspoon ground allspice
- 1 (3-lb.) single boneless pork loin
- 1 lb. shallots

SAUCE

- 2 teaspoons cornstarch
- 1 tablespoon water
- 1 cup port or cranberry juice
- 1 (14-oz.) can reduced-sodium beef broth
- ¼ teaspoon salt

1 If using fresh chestnuts, bring 2 quarts water to a boil in large saucepan. With small knife, make an "X" on one side of each chestnut. Drop into boiling water; boil 3 to 4 minutes or until shells begin to curl where cut. Drain. When cool enough to handle but still warm, peel with sharp knife. Slice chestnuts in half lengthwise. If using canned chestnuts, drain well.

2 Heat oven to 350°F. In small bowl, stir together garlic, 1 tablespoon of the oil, thyme, ¾ teaspoon salt, pepper and allspice.

3 Heat large skillet over medium-high heat until hot. Add remaining 1 tablespoon oil; heat until hot. Add pork; cook 10 minutes or until browned on all sides. Place on rimmed baking sheet. Add shallots to skillet; cook 2 to 3 minutes or until light brown, stirring occasionally. Place shallots around pork. (Reserve skillet with drippings.) Rub pork with garlic mixture.

4 Bake 30 minutes. Add chestnuts; bake 25 to 35 minutes or until internal temperature reaches 145°F. Place pork, shallots and chestnuts on platter; cover loosely with foil. Let stand 15 minutes.

5 Meanwhile, in small bowl, stir together cornstarch and water. Heat reserved skillet with drippings over medium-high heat until hot. Carefully add port, scraping up any browned bits from bottom of skillet. Boil 4 to 6 minutes or until port is reduced by half. Add broth; boil 3 to 5 minutes or until slightly reduced. Pour in enough of the cornstarch mixture to lightly thicken; boil 1 minute. Pour any juices from roasting pan into sauce. Add ¼ teaspoon salt; stir to combine. Serve sauce with roast.

8 servings

PER SERVING: 400 calories, 17.5 g total fat (5.5 g saturated fat), 40 g protein, 18 g carbohydrate, 110 mg cholesterol, 415 mg sodium, 3 g fiber

Citrus-Peppercorn-Spiked Tuna

Fresh tuna, with its meaty texture and flavor, is like steak—it's great on its own, but it also welcomes highly seasoned rubs and marinades. In this recipe, a sweet-hot rub adds zesty flavor with little effort.

- 1 tablespoon packed brown sugar
- 1 teaspoon grated lemon peel
- 1 teaspoon grated lime peel
- ½ teaspoon paprika
- 4 (6- to 8-oz.) tuna steaks (¾ inch thick)
- 1 teaspoon freshly ground pepper
- ¼ teaspoon salt
- 1 tablespoon canola oil

1 In small bowl, stir together brown sugar, lemon peel, lime peel and paprika. Sprinkle tuna with pepper and salt; sprinkle citrus mixture over tuna, pressing lightly into flesh.

2 Heat heavy large skillet over medium-high heat until hot. Add oil; heat until hot. Add tuna; cook 4 to 5 minutes for medium-rare or until of desired doneness, turning once.

4 servings

PER SERVING: 290 calories, 12 g total fat (2.5 g saturated fat), 40 g protein, 4 g carbohydrate, 65 mg cholesterol, 215 mg sodium, .5 g fiber

Shrimp and Sausage Gumbo

Filé powder, the ground dried leaves of the sassafras tree, is the traditional thickener for gumbos. Because too much cooking can make it stringy, it's added at the end. Ladle the gumbo around rice and pass hot pepper sauce for more zing.

- 7 tablespoons vegetable oil, divided
- 6 tablespoons all-purpose flour
- 8 oz. okra, thickly sliced
- 1 large onion, chopped
- 2 ribs celery, sliced
- 2 garlic cloves, minced
- 1 (14.5-oz.) can diced tomatoes with jalapeño chiles
- 1 (32-oz.) container lower-sodium chicken broth
- 8 oz. smoked andouille, chorizo or other smoked sausage, sliced
- 1 green bell pepper, coarsely chopped
- ¼ teaspoon salt
  Dash to ¼ teaspoon cayenne pepper
- 12 oz. shelled, deveined uncooked medium shrimp
- 2 tablespoons filé powder

1 To make roux, heat large skillet over medium-high to medium heat until hot. Add 6 tablespoons of the oil. Whisk in flour. Cook and stir 8 minutes or until mixture turns deep chocolate brown. (Be careful it doesn't become black and burned.) Remove from heat.

2 Heat remaining 1 tablespoon oil in large pot over medium-high heat until hot. Cook okra 8 minutes or until browned. (Okra will produce a slippery string-like substance at the beginning of cooking, which will disappear as it cooks and browns.) Add onion and celery; cook 3 minutes. Add garlic; cook 30 seconds or until fragrant.

3 Stir in roux until vegetables are coated; stir in tomatoes. Slowly stir in broth; bring to a boil. Add sausage, bell pepper, salt and cayenne pepper; bring to a boil. Reduce heat to medium; simmer 5 minutes. (Soup can be made to this point 2 days ahead. Cover and refrigerate.) Add shrimp; cook 1 minute or until shrimp turn pink. Stir in filé powder.

6 (about 1½-cup) servings

PER SERVING: 380 calories, 27 g total fat (6.5 g saturated fat), 17.5 g protein, 17.5 g carbohydrate, 105 mg cholesterol, 995 mg sodium, 3.5 g fiber

Citrus-Peppercorn-Spiked Tuna

Garlic-Parsley Stuffed Flank Steak

The filling combines the flavors of a traditional Italian gremolata—parsley, garlic and lemon zest—with a kick of fresh chile. Its bright, clean flavors complement the richness of the meat.

Garlic-Parsley Stuffed Flank Steak

BEEF

  1½ lb. beef flank steak

MARINADE

  ½ cup fresh lemon juice

  3 tablespoons olive oil

  1 teaspoon salt

  ½ teaspoon freshly ground pepper

STUFFING

  6 garlic cloves

  ½ teaspoon salt

  3 tablespoons olive oil

  2 tablespoons minced jalapeño chile

  ¾ cup chopped Italian parsley

  2 teaspoons grated lemon peel

  ¼ teaspoon freshly ground pepper

1 Have butcher butterfly flank steak, or with knife cut steak horizontally in half, leaving one edge attached so steak opens like book.

2 In large resealable plastic bag, combine all marinade ingredients; mix well. Add steak. Seal bag; refrigerate 3 to 6 hours to marinate.

3 Meanwhile, place garlic on cutting board; sprinkle with ½ teaspoon salt. Mash garlic and salt together with side of chef's knife to form paste.

4 Heat 3 tablespoons oil in small skillet over medium heat until hot. Add garlic mixture; cook 1 minute or until garlic is fragrant and begins to soften. Add jalapeño; cook 10 seconds. Place in small bowl; set aside to cool. Add parsley, lemon peel and pepper.

5 Heat grill. Remove steak from marinade; discard marinade. Open steak; spread stuffing over steak. Roll up steak (with the grain); secure with toothpicks every inch. Cut between toothpicks into 1-inch slices.

6 Place steak slices on gas grill over medium heat or on charcoal grill 4 to 6 inches from medium coals. Cook 10 to 14 minutes for medium-rare to medium, turning once. Remove toothpicks before serving.

4 servings

PER SERVING: 420 calories, 30.5 g total fat (8.5 g saturated fat), 31 g protein, 3.5 g carbohydrate, 90 mg cholesterol, 565 mg sodium, .5 g fiber

Grilled Lemon-Basil Salmon

By grilling the salmon skin-side up and then turning and covering the fillets with a fresh herb mixture, the topping stays on the fish, not on the grill.

  4 (5- to 6-oz.) salmon fillets (1 inch thick)

  ½ teaspoon freshly ground pepper

  ¼ teaspoon salt

  2 tablespoons minced fresh basil

  2 tablespoons chopped fresh chives

  1 tablespoon balsamic vinegar

  1 tablespoon grated lemon peel

  2 teaspoons extra-virgin olive oil

1 Heat grill. Sprinkle salmon with pepper and salt. In small bowl, stir together all remaining ingredients.

2 Oil grill grate well. Place salmon, skin-side up, on gas grill over medium heat or on charcoal grill 4 to 6 inches from medium coals; cover grill. Grill 6 minutes; turn and top with basil mixture. Grill 4 to 6 minutes or until salmon just begins to flake.

4 servings

PER SERVING: 225 calories, 10.5 g total fat (2.5 g saturated fat), 30 g protein, 1 g carbohydrate, 95 mg cholesterol, 230 mg sodium, .5 g fiber

Grilled Lemon-Basil Salmon

Spicy Pork Burgers with Asian Slaw

Enhance your burger's flavor from the ground up: use ground chuck for rich flavor, add herbs, seasonings and garlic right into the meat, and complete the ensemble with the perfect bun.

- 1½ lb. ground pork
- ½ lb. ground beef chuck
- ¼ cup chopped fresh cilantro
- 3 tablespoons chili sauce with garlic
- 2 tablespoons minced fresh ginger
- 1 tablespoon soy sauce
- 4 garlic cloves, minced
- 6 sandwich buns, split
  Asian Slaw (recipe follows)

1 In large bowl, combine ground pork, ground beef, cilantro, chili sauce, ginger, soy sauce and garlic; mix well. Shape mixture into 6 (4-inch) patties. Place on large plate. Refrigerate 30 minutes or up to 2 hours to blend flavors.

2 Heat grill. Place patties on gas grill over medium heat or on charcoal grill 4 to 6 inches from medium coals. Cook 8 to 10 minutes or until no longer pink in center, turning once.

3 Serve patties on buns, topped with Asian Slaw.

6 sandwiches

PER SANDWICH: 435 calories, 24 g total fat (8.5 g saturated fat), 31 g protein, 23 g carbohydrate, 95 mg cholesterol, 615 mg sodium, 2 g fiber

Spicy Pork Burgers with Asian Slaw

ASIAN SLAW

- 2 cups shredded savoy or napa cabbage
- 3 tablespoons sliced green onions
- 2 tablespoons grated carrots
- 2 tablespoons chopped fresh cilantro
- ¼ cup water
- 2 tablespoons rice wine vinegar
- ¼ teaspoon salt

1 In large bowl, combine cabbage, green onions, carrots and cilantro.

2 In small bowl, combine water, vinegar and salt; mix well. Add to cabbage mixture; toss to mix. Refrigerate 1 hour or up to 24 hours to blend flavors.

Potato-Parmesan-Crusted Fillet of Beef

Meat and potatoes are a marriage made in culinary heaven!

- ¾ lb. russet potatoes, peeled, coarsely shredded
- ¼ cup minced onion
- 2 tablespoons grated Parmesan cheese
- 1½ tablespoons all-purpose flour
- 1 egg, beaten
- ¾ teaspoon salt, divided
- ¾ teaspoon freshly ground pepper, divided
- 4 (6-oz.) beef tenderloin steaks, 1½ inches thick
- 1 tablespoon canola oil
- 1 tablespoon butter

1 Heat oven to 500°F. Place potatoes in clean kitchen towel; squeeze out as much liquid as possible. Place potatoes in large bowl with onion, cheese, flour and egg. In small bowl, stir together salt and pepper; sprinkle potatoes with ¾ teaspoon of the salt and pepper mixture. Toss to mix well.

2 Sprinkle steaks with remaining ¾ teaspoon salt and pepper mixture. Heat oil in large skillet over medium-high to high heat until hot. Add steaks; cook 2 minutes or until browned, turning once. Place on plate.

3 Pat scant ⅓ cup potato mixture on top of each steak to form crust. In clean large skillet, melt butter over medium heat. Increase heat to medium-high; add steaks, potato side down. Cook 2 minutes or until golden brown. Using spatula, carefully remove steaks and place, potato side up, on small rimmed baking sheet.

4 Bake 8 to 10 minutes for medium-rare or until of desired doneness. Let stand 5 minutes.

4 servings

PER SERVING: 435 calories, 20.5 g total fat (7.5 g saturated fat), 41 g protein, 19 g carbohydrate, 160 mg cholesterol, 620 mg sodium, 1.5 g fiber

Grilled T-Bone Steaks with Bourbon-Peppercorn Mop Sauce

Country table syrup, shelved near other syrups in the store, is a blend of sorghum syrup, molasses and corn syrup. The sweetness of the syrup combined with the smokiness of the bourbon and bite of the peppercorns make this an unusual and tasty alternative to standard barbecue sauces.

Grilled T-Bone Steaks with Bourbon-Peppercorn Mop Sauce

SAUCE

- 2 cups country table syrup (sorghum syrup) or mild molasses
- 1 teaspoon cracked black peppercorns
- 6 tablespoons smoky-style Kentucky bourbon whiskey, such as Knob Creek
- ¼ cup unsalted butter, chilled, cut up
- 1¼ teaspoons lemon juice

STEAKS

- 8 T-bone steaks (1 inch thick)
- 3 tablespoons vegetable oil
- 2 teaspoons kosher (coarse) salt
- 2 teaspoons freshly ground pepper

1 Heat grill. Place syrup and peppercorns in medium saucepan; bring to a boil over medium-high heat. Remove from heat; whisk in bourbon, butter and lemon juice. Reserve 1¼ cups; keep remaining sauce warm to brush over steaks during grilling.

2 Lightly brush steaks with oil; sprinkle with salt and pepper. Place on gas grill over medium heat or on charcoal grill 4 to 6 inches from medium coals; cover grill. Grill 6 to 8 minutes for medium-rare or until of desired doneness, generously brushing with warm sauce during last 3 to 4 minutes of grilling and turning several times. Serve reserved 1¼ cups sauce with steak.

8 servings

PER SERVING: 675 calories, 25.5 g total fat (10 g saturated fat), 44 g protein, 63.5 g carbohydrate, 130 mg cholesterol, 565 mg sodium, 0 g fiber

Pork Tenderloin with Tarragon-Mustard Sauce

Crème fraîche is an ideal ingredient choice when higher heat is used. Unlike sour cream, it will not curdle when boiled or baked.

- ¼ cup crème fraîche or whipping cream
- ¼ cup Dijon mustard
- 2 tablespoons minced fresh tarragon
- 2 (¾-lb.) pork tenderloins
- ¼ teaspoon salt
- ⅛ teaspoon freshly ground pepper
- 1 tablespoon canola oil
- ½ cup white wine

1 Heat oven to 400°F. In small bowl, stir together crème fraîche, mustard and tarragon.

2 Sprinkle pork tenderloins with salt and pepper. Heat large skillet over medium-high heat until hot. Add oil; heat until hot. Cook pork 4 to 6 minutes or until browned, turning once. Place pork in shallow roasting pan.

3 Place same skillet over high heat. Add wine; bring to a boil, scraping up browned bits from bottom of skillet. Pour wine mixture around pork in roasting pan. Brush pork with 2 tablespoons of the mustard mixture. Bake 15 to 25 minutes or until internal temperature reaches 145°F. Place on serving platter; cover loosely with foil.

4 Place roasting pan over low heat. Whisk remaining mustard mixture into pan juices. Slice tenderloin into medallions; pour sauce over pork.

5 servings

PER SERVING: 210 calories, 10 g total fat (3.5 g saturated fat), 26.5 g protein, 1.5 g carbohydrate, 85 mg cholesterol, 285 mg sodium, .5 g fiber

Creamy Spinach-Shrimp Linguine

Splurge a little with this rich, creamy pasta by purchasing authentic Parmigiano-Reggiano cheese, available in the imported cheese section of the supermarket or cheese shops. Because it's aged longer than most Parmesans, its flavor is deeper, nuttier and worth every penny.

- 8 oz. linguine
- 1 (9- to 10-oz.) bag baby spinach
- 1 tablespoon butter
- 12 oz. shelled, deveined uncooked medium shrimp
- 2 large garlic cloves, minced
- ¾ cup heavy whipping cream
- 2 tablespoons chopped fresh tarragon
- ¼ teaspoon salt
- ¼ teaspoon pepper
- ¾ cup freshly grated Parmigiano-Reggiano cheese, divided

1 Cook linguine according to package directions. Just before linguine is finished cooking, stir in spinach. Drain.
2 Melt butter in same pot over low heat. Stir in shrimp and garlic; increase heat to medium-high. Stir in cream, tarragon, salt and pepper; bring to a boil. Boil until shrimp turn pink. Add linguine, spinach and ½ cup of the cheese; toss well. Sprinkle with remaining ¼ cup cheese.

4 (1½-cup) servings

PER SERVING: 570 calories, 24.5 g total fat (14.5 g saturated fat), 33 g protein, 54.5 g carbohydrate, 195 mg cholesterol, 940 mg sodium, 4.5 g fiber

Big-Bowl Asian Chicken Soup

Chunks of chicken and mushrooms give this tasty soup main-dish heartiness. If you like a lot of spice, increase the crushed red pepper to ½ teaspoon. A spinach salad topped with sliced ripe mango or papaya makes a sweet accompaniment.

- 1 lb. boneless skinless chicken breast halves, cut into 1-inch pieces
- 3 tablespoons reduced-sodium soy sauce
- 4 oz. shiitake or button mushrooms (if using shiitakes, remove and discard stems)
- 1 tablespoon dark sesame oil*
- 2 garlic cloves, minced
- ¼ teaspoon crushed red pepper
- 1 (14-oz.) can reduced-sodium chicken broth
- 2 tablespoons seasoned rice vinegar
- 3 tablespoons cold water
- 1½ tablespoons cornstarch
- 2 cups packed sliced napa cabbage, bok choy or fresh spinach
- ¼ cup chopped fresh cilantro or thinly sliced green onions

1 In small bowl, stir together chicken and soy sauce. Cut mushrooms in half or, if large, into quarters.
2 Heat oil in large saucepan over medium-high heat until hot. Add chicken mixture, mushrooms, garlic and crushed red pepper; cook 2 minutes, stirring constantly. Add broth and vinegar; bring to a boil. Reduce heat to medium-low; simmer, uncovered, 2 minutes or until chicken is no longer pink
3 In another small bowl, stir together water and cornstarch; add to soup. Cook 1 minute or until soup has thickened slightly, stirring constantly. Stir in cabbage and cilantro; cook 2 minutes.

TIP

* Dark sesame oil is made from toasted sesame seeds. It has a rich, nutty sesame flavor. Look for it in the Asian section of the grocery store.

4 (1¼-cup) servings

PER SERVING: 210 calories, 7 g total fat (1.5 g saturated fat), 28.5 g protein, 7.5 g carbohydrate, 70 mg cholesterol, 695 mg sodium, 1 g fiber

Big-Bowl Asian Chicken Soup

Chicken Saté with Spicy Mango Dip

If you don't mind eating with your fingers, serve the skewers withi a leaf of Boston, Bibb or other tender lettuce. Put the chicken on the leaf, top it with the dip, roll it up and eat it like a wrap.

CHICKEN

- 4 boneless skinless chicken breast halves
- ¼ cup chopped cashews
- 4 teaspoons coriander seeds
- ½ teaspoon cumin seeds
- ¼ cup finely chopped onion
- 3 tablespoons vegetable oil
- 2 tablespoons tamarind paste or lime juice*
- 2 tablespoons soy sauce
- 4 teaspoons grated fresh ginger
- 1 tablespoon minced garlic
- 2 teaspoons sugar
- 2 teaspoons rice vinegar

DIP

- 1 mango, coarsely chopped
- 2 small red serrano chiles or 1 jalapeño chile, veins and seeds removed, chopped
- 3 tablespoons lime juice
- 2 tablespoons fish sauce**
- 2 teaspoons sugar
- 2 tablespoons chopped cilantro

1 Soak 16 (8-inch) wooden skewers in cold water 20 minutes. Slice each chicken breast lengthwise into 4 strips; thread onto skewers. Place in shallow glass or ceramic baking dish.

2 Place cashews, coriander seeds and cumin seeds in small skillet. Cook over medium heat 3 to 4 minutes or until light brown and fragrant, stirring frequently. Cool. Place in food processor; pulse until coarsely ground. (A mortar and pestle also can be used.) Place in medium bowl; stir in all remaining chicken ingredients. Spoon mixture over both sides of chicken skewers; cover and refrigerate 30 to 60 minutes.

3 Meanwhile, place all dip ingredients except cilantro in food processor or blender; process until smooth. Stir in cilantro.

4 Heat grill. Remove skewers from marinade; discard marinade. Place skewers on gas grill over medium heat or on charcoal grill 4 to 6 inches from medium coals; cover grill. Grill 3 to 5 minutes or until no longer pink, turning once. Serve skewers with mango dip.

TIPS

* Tamarind paste can be found in the Asian or Middle Eastern section of grocery stores or in specialty markets. Its sour taste is used as flavoring.

** Look for fish sauce in the Asian section of supermarkets.

4 servings

PER SERVING: 250 calories, 8 g total fat (1.5 g saturated fat), 28.5 g protein, 17 g carbohydrate, 75 mg cholesterol, 880 mg sodium, 2 g fiber

Chicken Saté with Spicy Mango Dip

Flat Iron Steaks Grilled with Chile-Orange Marinade

Flat iron steaks are one of the three most tender cuts of beef. They're also known as top blade steaks. Here, they acquire a fabulous smoky flavor from chopped chiles and chili powder.

MARINADE

- 1 cup orange juice
- ¼ cup lemon juice
- ¼ cup olive or vegetable oil
- 1 jalapeño chile, veins and seeds removed, chopped
- 1 tablespoon chopped chipotle chile in adobo sauce*
- 2 tablespoons soy sauce
- 2 teaspoons grated orange peel
- 2 teaspoons grated lemon peel
- 2 teaspoons minced garlic
- 2 teaspoons chili powder
- 2 teaspoons kosher (coarse) salt
- 1 teaspoon freshly ground pepper

STEAK

- 4 (6-oz.) boneless beef flat iron, chuck-eye or top round steaks (1 inch thick)

1 In small bowl, stir together all marinade ingredients. Place steaks in 1-gallon resealable plastic bag; pour in marinade. Seal bag; turn to coat steaks. Refrigerate at least 12 hours or up to 24 hours, turning occasionally.

2 Heat grill. Remove steaks from marinade; discard marinade. Pat steaks dry. Place on gas grill over medium heat or on charcoal grill 4 to 6 inches from medium coals; cover grill. Grill 8 to 12 minutes for medium-rare or until of desired doneness, turning once. Place on platter; cover loosely with foil. Let stand 5 minutes.

TIP

*Chipotle chiles are brown, dried, smoked jalapeño chiles with wrinkled skin. They come dried, pickled or canned in adobo sauce. Look for them in the Latin section of the supermarket.

4 servings

PER SERVING: 365 calories, 23 g total fat (8 g saturated fat), 35 g protein, 2.5 g carbohydrate, 105 mg cholesterol, 405 mg sodium, .5 g fiber

Country Pork Ribs with Hoisin Sauce and Shiitake Mushrooms

Today's country pork ribs are very meaty, surprisingly lean and an excellent choice for braising. Slow cooking produces beautiful mahogany-lacquered ribs. Serve with gingered mashed potatoes tossed with sliced green onions.

- 1 oz. dried shiitake mushrooms (about 1⅓ cups)
- 1 cup boiling water
- 2 tablespoons vegetable oil
- 3 lb. bone-in country-style pork ribs
- 1½ cups chopped onion
- 4 large garlic cloves, minced
- 1 tablespoon minced fresh ginger
- ½ cup apple cider
- ⅓ cup hoisin sauce
- 2 tablespoons soy sauce
- 2 teaspoons dark sesame oil
- 4 tablespoons sliced green onions, divided

1 Heat oven to 325°F. Place mushrooms in small bowl; add boiling water to cover. Let stand 10 to 20 minutes or until soft. Drain, reserving liquid (there should be about ½ cup). Remove and discard stems; slice mushrooms.

2 In large ovenproof skillet, heat oil over medium-high heat until hot. Add ribs in batches; cook 8 to 10 minutes or until browned on all sides. Place on plate.

3 Reduce heat to medium. Add onion to same skillet; cook 2 to 3 minutes or until onion begins to soften. Add garlic and ginger; cook 1 minute or until fragrant. Stir in apple cider, hoisin sauce, soy sauce and reserved mushroom liquid. Return ribs, any accumulated juices and mushrooms to skillet. Cover; place in oven. Bake 1 hour 15 minutes to 1 hour 30 minutes or until tender, turning ribs every 30 minutes.

4 Place ribs on platter; if necessary, skim off any accumulated fat from pan juices. Place skillet with pan juices over high heat; boil 4 to 5 minutes or until slightly thickened. Stir in sesame oil and 2 tablespoons of the green onions; pour over ribs. Sprinkle with remaining 2 tablespoons green onions.

4 servings

PER SERVING: 565 calories, 32.5 g total fat (9.5 g saturated fat), 45 g protein, 23.5 g carbohydrate, 115 mg cholesterol, 595 mg sodium, 3.5 g fiber

Rustic Pizza Crust

This bread-like pizza dough bakes on a hot baking stone, resulting in a golden, crisp outside crust with a tender, chewy middle. The dough is very easy to work with, but remember to allow at least 1 hour for rising. The dough can be mixed and kneaded by hand or with a stand mixer using the paddle attachment. It also can be made overnight and allowed to rise in the refrigerator. Or, to make the dough several hours ahead of time, just place it in a cool spot on the counter and let it rise slowly, punching down the dough as it doubles in size. As with any bread, the longer the dough rises, the more flavor it will have.

DOUGH

- ¾ cup warm water (110°F. to 115°F.)
- ½ teaspoon sugar
- 1 teaspoon active dry yeast
- 1 tablespoon extra-virgin olive oil
- 2 to 2¼ cups bread flour
- 1 teaspoon salt
- 1 to 2 tablespoons cornmeal

GARLIC OIL

- 1 large garlic clove
- Dash salt
- 1½ tablespoons extra-virgin olive oil

1 Place water, sugar and yeast in large bowl; let stand 5 to 10 minutes or until foamy. Add 1 tablespoon olive oil and 1 cup of the flour; stir to combine. Add 1 teaspoon salt; stir to combine. Slowly stir in enough of the remaining flour to form a soft dough.

2 On lightly floured surface, knead dough 6 to 8 minutes or until smooth and elastic. Place in greased medium bowl; cover with plastic wrap and clean towel. Let rise in warm place 1 hour or until doubled in size.

3 Meanwhile, place baking stone on bottom oven rack; heat oven to 475°F. for at least 45 minutes. To make garlic oil, smash garlic clove on cutting board with side of knife; sprinkle with dash salt. With knife, mash garlic and salt together to form paste; place in small cup. Stir in 1½ tablespoons oil.

4 Gently punch down dough to deflate; place on lightly floured surface. Roll into 14- to 16-inch round, making sure dough doesn't stick to surface during rolling. (Or divide dough in half; roll into 2 (10-inch) rounds.) Sprinkle cornmeal on pizza peel or rimless baking sheet. Place dough on peel; brush with garlic oil.

5 Top with desired sauce, toppings and cheese, shaking pizza occasionally to make sure it isn't sticking to peel. (If sticking occurs, sprinkle with additional cornmeal.) Slide pizza directly onto baking stone. Bake 9 to 12 minutes or until bottom of crust is brown and cheese is melted and bubbly.

1 (14- to 16-inch) pizza

PER ½ OF CRUST: 115 calories, 3 g total fat (.5 g saturated fat), 2.5 g protein, 18.5 g carbohydrate, 0 mg cholesterol, 220 mg sodium, .5 g fiber

Tomato-Basil Pizza Sauce

This simple pizza sauce is a snap to make and cooks in about 8 minutes. During tomato season, use about 2 cups chopped fresh plum tomatoes in place of the canned tomatoes.

- 1 tablespoon olive oil
- 2 medium garlic cloves, minced
- 1 (14.5-oz.) can diced tomatoes, undrained
- ¼ teaspoon salt
- ⅛ teaspoon freshly ground pepper
- 2 tablespoons coarsely chopped fresh basil or 2 teaspoons dried

1 Heat oil in medium saucepan over medium heat until hot. Add garlic; cook 30 seconds or until fragrant.

2 Stir in tomatoes, salt and pepper; cook 8 to 10 minutes or until slightly thickened, stirring and mashing tomatoes with potato masher until crushed. Stir in basil. Place in small bowl; cool to room temperature. (Sauce can be made up to 3 days ahead and refrigerated or up to 2 months ahead and frozen.)

1 cup

PER 2 TABLESPOONS: 25 calories, 2 g total fat (0 g saturated fat), .5 g protein, 2.5 g carbohydrate, 0 mg cholesterol, 150 mg sodium, .5 g fiber

Tomato-Olive Pizza with Fresh Mushrooms

Pizza toppings are limited only by your imagination. Use restraint, however, with the amount you pile on. A pizza heavy with sauce and a mountain of toppings will never develop the crisp and light crust that characterizes the best pizzas.

1	recipe Rustic Pizza Crust
½	cup Tomato-Basil Pizza Sauce
½	cup diced seeded fresh tomatoes
½	cup sliced mushrooms
⅓	cup sliced pitted Kalamata olives
3	tablespoons coarsely torn fresh basil, divided
2	tablespoons freshly grated Parmesan cheese
1	cup (4 oz.) shredded mozzarella cheese

Prepare pizza dough through Step 4. Spoon and spread Tomato-Basil Sauce over dough to within ½ inch of edge. Arrange tomatoes, mushrooms, olives and 2 tablespoons of the basil over sauce; sprinkle with Parmesan cheese and mozzarella. (Don't sprinkle cheese over ½-inch border.) Bake pizza according to directions in recipe. Sprinkle with remaining 1 tablespoon basil.

1 (12-slice) pizza

PER SLICE: 150 calories, 5 g total fat (1.5 g saturated fat), 6 g protein, 21 g carbohydrate, 5 mg cholesterol, 400 mg sodium, 1.5 g fiber

Tomato-Olive Pizza with Fresh Mushrooms

Molasses-Glazed Roast Turkey with Peppered Sherry Gravy

A molasses glaze brushed over the turkey during baking gives it a magnificent sheen. The onion and celery that are stuffed into the turkey cavity season it inside and out. If you're serving a larger crowd, choose a 15- to 16-pound bird and roast it about 30 minutes longer.

- 1 (12- to 14-lb.) turkey
- ½ teaspoon salt, divided
- ½ teaspoon freshly ground pepper, divided
- 1 large rib celery with leaves, cut into 1-inch pieces
- 1 medium onion, cut into 8 wedges
- 1 cup fresh sage
- 3 tablespoons unsalted butter, softened, divided
- 1 tablespoon molasses
- 1 teaspoon red wine vinegar
  Peppered Sherry Gravy (recipe follows)

1 Heat oven to 325°F. Sprinkle turkey cavity with ¼ teaspoon of the salt and pepper; stuff with celery, onion and sage. Place turkey on rack in roasting pan. Rub with 2 tablespoons of the butter; sprinkle with remaining ¼ teaspoon salt and pepper.

2 Bake 3 to 3¾ hours or until internal temperature of thickest part of thigh reaches 180°F., basting with drippings every 30 minutes after first hour of baking.

3 Meanwhile, in small saucepan, stir together remaining 1 tablespoon butter, molasses and vinegar; heat over low heat until butter is melted. Baste turkey with glaze during last hour of baking. Baste again about 10 minutes before turkey is done.

4 Remove turkey from pan, reserving drippings for gravy. Place turkey on cutting board; cover loosely with foil. Let stand 20 minutes before carving. Serve with Peppered Sherry Gravy.

8 servings

PER SERVING: 580 calories, 37 g total fat (12 g saturated fat), 49 g protein, 8.5 g carbohydrate, 170 mg cholesterol, 715 mg sodium, 0 g fiber

Molasses-Glazed Roast Turkey with Peppered Sherry Gravy

PEPPERED SHERRY GRAVY

For even more flavor, let the giblets from the turkey simmer in the chicken broth the day before you make the gravy. Strain them and discard.

- 6 tablespoons turkey drippings or butter
- 6 tablespoons all-purpose flour
- 5 cups reduced-sodium chicken broth
- ⅓ cup dry sherry or apple cider
- ¾ teaspoon freshly ground pepper
- ½ teaspoon salt

Pour drippings from turkey roasting pan into measuring cup; let stand 5 minutes. Spoon off 6 tablespoons of the fat; place in large saucepan. (Discard remaining fat.) Whisk in flour; cook over medium heat 3 to 4 minutes or until smooth, bubbly and golden, whisking constantly. Gradually whisk in broth and sherry. Bring to a simmer; cook 2 minutes, whisking constantly. Whisk in pepper and salt.

4 cups

Duck Breast with Red Pepper Jam

Although delicious tasting, duck breasts can be fatty unless the skin is browned thoroughly and rendered of most of its fat. Skillet roasting the breasts skin-side down makes that happen. Scoring the skin first facilitates the draining of fat while the meat cooks.

JAM

½ teaspoon vegetable oil

½ teaspoon minced garlic

½ teaspoon grated fresh ginger

2 large red bell peppers, finely chopped

2 tablespoons balsamic vinegar

2 tablespoons packed light brown sugar

¼ teaspoon salt

DUCK

4 boneless duck breast halves

1 tablespoon minced garlic

1 tablespoon minced fresh parsley

1 tablespoon minced fresh thyme

½ teaspoon salt

¼ teaspoon freshly ground pepper

1 Heat oil, ½ teaspoon garlic and ginger in medium nonstick skillet over medium-low heat 1 to 2 minutes or until fragrant. Add bell peppers; cook 10 minutes or until peppers are soft, stirring occasionally. Stir in vinegar, brown sugar and salt. Reduce heat to low; cook 15 to 20 minutes or until liquid is almost evaporated but mixture isn't dry. Cool. (Jam can be made up to 2 days ahead. Cover and refrigerate. Serve at room temperature.)

2 Score skin of duck breasts every ½ inch (do not cut into meat); rotate and score again, creating a crisscross pattern. In small bowl, stir together all remaining duck ingredients. Rub mixture over both sides of duck breasts, pushing mixture into cuts to season duck.

3 Heat oven to 425°F. Heat large nonstick skillet over medium-low heat until hot. Add duck, skin-side down. Cook 6 to 8 minutes or until skin is brown and fat is rendered, removing fat as it accumulates. Turn duck; place skillet in oven. Bake 4 to 5 minutes for medium-rare or until of desired doneness. Remove from oven; let stand 5 minutes.

4 Carve each breast across the grain into 4 or 5 slices; serve with jam.

4 servings

PER SERVING: 300 calories, 13 g total fat (3.5 g saturated fat), 32.5 g protein, 13.5 g carbohydrate, 90 mg cholesterol, 525 mg sodium, 2 g fiber

Peppered Beef Tenderloin with Whipped Mustard Butter

These spice-coated steaks are not for the timid. Underneath the crunchy pepper crust, however, lies meat that's wonderfully tender and juicy. A creamy whipped butter is served with the steaks to tame the assertive pepper taste.

¼ cup unsalted butter, softened

1 tablespoon Dijon mustard

1 teaspoon honey

¼ teaspoon grated lemon peel

1¼ teaspoons kosher (coarse) salt, divided

1 tablespoon cracked black peppercorns

1 tablespoon cracked white peppercorns

⅛ teaspoon crushed red pepper

4 beef tenderloin steaks (1½ inches thick)

2 teaspoons vegetable oil

1 In small bowl, stir together butter, mustard, honey, lemon peel and ¼ teaspoon of the salt until smoothly blended and of whipped consistency. Let stand at room temperature.

2 Heat oven to 425°F. In another small bowl, stir together black peppercorns, white peppercorns, crushed red pepper and remaining 1 teaspoon salt. Brush steaks with oil; sprinkle with peppercorn mixture, pressing evenly onto both sides.

3 Heat large ovenproof skillet over medium-high heat until hot. Add steaks; cook 4 minutes. Turn steaks; place skillet in oven. Bake 7 minutes for medium-rare or until of desired doneness. Serve steaks topped with mustard butter.

4 servings

PER SERVING: 405 calories, 25.5 g total fat (12 g saturated fat), 39 g protein, 4 g carbohydrate, 105 mg cholesterol, 640 mg sodium, 1 g fiber

Chicken-Spinach Lasagna with Artichokes

This creamy white lasagna is layered with an appealing combination of chicken, artichokes, mushrooms and spinach. Two kinds of cheese and a luscious white sauce add rich, satisfying flavor. Prepare the lasagna in advance for low-stress entertaining.

LASAGNA

- 2 tablespoons butter
- 2 large garlic cloves, minced
- 1½ teaspoons dried oregano
- 1 lb. boneless skinless chicken thighs, cut into ¾-inch pieces
- 1 (14-oz.) can quartered artichoke hearts, drained
- 8 oz. crimini mushrooms, coarsely chopped
- ¼ teaspoon salt
- ¼ teaspoon freshly ground pepper
- 12 no-boil lasagna noodles (from 9-oz. pkg.)
- 2 (9-oz.) pkg. frozen chopped spinach, thawed, squeezed dry
- 3 cups (12 oz.) shredded mozzarella cheese
- ¾ cup (3 oz.) freshly grated Parmesan cheese

SAUCE

- ½ cup butter
- ½ cup all-purpose flour
- 2 cups whipping cream
- 2 cups milk
- ¼ teaspoon salt
- ¼ teaspoon freshly ground pepper
- ⅛ teaspoon ground nutmeg

Chicken-Spinach Lasagna with Artichokes

1 Melt 2 tablespoons butter in heavy large skillet over medium heat. Add garlic and oregano; cook 30 seconds or until fragrant. Add chicken, artichoke hearts, mushrooms, ¼ teaspoon salt and ¼ teaspoon pepper; cook 6 to 8 minutes or until chicken is no longer pink and mushrooms are soft. Cool.

2 Melt ½ cup butter in large saucepan over medium heat. Whisk in flour; cook 3 to 4 minutes or until bubbly all over with nutty smell, whisking constantly. Whisk in all remaining sauce ingredients. Bring to a boil, whisking frequently; boil 1 to 2 minutes or until sauce has thickened.

3 Heat oven to 350°F. Spray 13 × 9-inch pan with non-stick cooking spray. Spread 1 cup of the sauce in pan. Top with 4 lasagna noodles; spread with 1 cup of the sauce. Sprinkle with one-half of the chicken mixture; top with one-half of the spinach. Sprinkle with 1 cup of the mozzarella cheese and ¼ cup of the Parmesan cheese. Repeat layering, starting with lasagna noodles. Top with remaining 4 noodles, remaining 1 cup sauce, 1 cup mozzarella cheese and ¼ cup Parmesan cheese. (Lasagna can be made to this point up to 8 hours ahead. Cover and refrigerate. It may need an additional 10 to 15 minutes baking time.)

4 Bake, uncovered, 45 to 55 minutes or until golden brown and bubbling. (Cover with foil during last 5 to 10 minutes if top is browning too quickly.) Let stand 15 minutes before cutting.

12 servings

PER SERVING: 525 calories, 34 g total fat (20 g saturated fat), 26 g protein, 30 g carbohydrate, 115 mg cholesterol, 590 mg sodium, 4.5 g fiber

Fennel-Roasted Pork Rib Roast

Fennel seeds and fresh fennel lend anise flavor to a tender pork roast. At the end, the pan juices are cooked down and blended with a touch of butter for a luscious sauce. Reserve some of the bright green frilly fronds from the fresh fennel for a beautiful garnish.

PORK

1	(6-lb.) bone-in center-cut pork loin roast
4	teaspoons kosher (coarse) salt
2	teaspoons fennel seeds, ground*
1	teaspoon freshly ground pepper
1	medium fennel bulb, halved, thinly sliced (2 cups)**
2	tablespoons sugar
1	tablespoon olive oil
2	cups reduced-sodium chicken broth, hot
1	cup hot water

SAUCE

¼	cup water
2	tablespoons cornstarch
¼	cup unsalted butter, cut up

1 Heat oven to 425°F. Place roast on cutting board so that rib bones point up. Starting at tips of ribs, cut loin away from bones until bottom of loin is reached. Leave loin connected to flat bones that roast is standing on.

2 In small bowl, stir together salt, fennel seeds and pepper. Sprinkle inside of loin with half of the salt mixture; replace meat on bones. Place roast on rimmed baking sheet, bone side down; sprinkle with remaining salt mixture. Bake pork 30 minutes.

3 Meanwhile, in medium bowl, stir together sliced fennel, sugar and oil. Reduce oven temperature to 325°F. Spread sliced fennel mixture over top of roast; bake 30 minutes. Pour broth and 1 cup hot water into baking sheet. Bake an additional 40 to 50 minutes or until internal temperature reaches 145°F. Place roast on cutting board; cover loosely with foil. Let stand 10 to 15 minutes.

4 Meanwhile, pour pan juices into small saucepan; bring to a boil over medium-high heat. In small bowl, whisk together ¼ cup water and cornstarch; whisk into juices in saucepan. Reduce heat to medium-low; cook 1 minute or until slightly thickened. Whisk in butter; remove from heat. Cover.

5 Cut loin from bones. Thinly slice loin; serve with sauce.

TIPS

* Grind fennel seeds using a spice grinder or mortar and pestle.

** Fennel is a vegetable with a bulbous base and long, feathery fronds that look similar to dill. It has a sweet, delicate, anise-like flavor. To use fennel, remove the fronds and save for garnish or discard. The bulb can be sliced or chopped.

8 servings

PER SERVING: 505 calories, 26.5 g total fat (10.5 g saturated fat), 55.5 g protein, 7.5 g carbohydrate, 170 mg cholesterol, 1040 mg sodium, 1 g fiber

Fennel-Roasted Pork Rib Roast

Spicy Pork Meatballs in Chile-Spiked Tomato Sauce

Don't be surprised if chili comes to mind when you dig into this pasta dish. The components have a hint of the Southwest to them, from the trio of spices that flavor the meatballs to the jalapeño-laced sauce.

Spiced Rib-Eye Steaks with Stout

- 1 large garlic clove
- 1½ teaspoons salt, divided
- 1 lb. ground pork
- ¼ cup fresh white bread crumbs
- 2 tablespoons red wine vinegar or garlic-flavored vinegar
- 1 tablespoon plus 1 teaspoon ancho chile powder, divided
- 2 teaspoons Mexican-style hot chili powder
- 2 teaspoons dried oregano, divided
- 1 (28-oz.) can peeled whole tomatoes
- 2 tablespoons olive oil
- 2 large jalapeño chiles, seeded, deveined, minced
- 1 teaspoon minced garlic
- 8 oz. gemelli or other twisted pasta

1 Mash garlic clove and 1 teaspoon of the salt with mortar and pestle or side of chef's knife until paste forms; place in large bowl. Mix in pork, bread crumbs, vinegar, 2 tablespoons water, 1 tablespoon of the ancho chile powder, hot chili powder and ½ teaspoon of the oregano until well-blended. Shape into 20 (1-inch) balls.

2 Puree tomatoes with juices in food processor. Heat oil in large skillet over medium-high heat until hot. Cook meatballs in batches 5 minutes or until browned on all sides. Remove meatballs.

3 Reduce heat to medium. Add chiles and minced garlic; cook and stir 1 minute. Add pureed tomatoes and remaining 1½ teaspoons oregano, 1 teaspoon ancho chile powder and ½ teaspoon salt; bring to a boil. Reduce heat to medium-low; cover and simmer 3 minutes. Add meatballs; cover and simmer 10 minutes or until cooked through, no longer pink in center and sauce thickens slightly.

4 Meanwhile, cook gemelli in large pot of boiling salted water according to package directions; drain. Toss with meatballs and sauce.

4 (1¾-cup) servings

PER SERVING: 595 calories, 25 g total fat (7 g saturated fat), 31.5 g protein, 61.5 g carbohydrate, 70 mg cholesterol, 1460 mg sodium, 7 g fiber

Spiced Rib-Eye Steaks with Stout

A steak right out of the Old West—bold with a dynamic blend of seasonings and stout.

- 4 teaspoons ground red chile powder*
- 1 teaspoon ground coriander
- 1 teaspoon cumin seeds
- ½ teaspoon freshly ground pepper
- 4 boneless beef rib-eye steaks (1 inch thick)
- ½ teaspoon kosher (coarse) salt
- 1 tablespoon olive oil
- 2 large garlic cloves, minced
- ½ cup Russian stout

1 In small nonstick skillet over medium heat, toast chile powder, coriander, cumin and pepper 1 to 1½ minutes or until mixture becomes fragrant, stirring constantly. Place on plate.

2 Sprinkle mixture over both sides of steaks. Sprinkle with salt.

3 Heat large heavy skillet over medium-high heat until hot. Add oil; heat until hot. Add steaks; cook 8 to 10 minutes for medium-rare, turning once.

4 Remove steaks from skillet; pour off drippings. Reduce heat to low. Add garlic; sauté briefly, being careful not to burn garlic. Increase heat to high; add stout and boil 2 to 3 minutes or until slightly thickened, scraping browned bits from bottom of skillet. Pour sauce over steaks.

TIP

*Ground red chile powder is made from dried red chiles. It can range from mild to hot. If it is unavailable, use chili powder, a combination of dried red chiles, garlic, oregano and other seasonings.

4 servings

PER SERVING: 320 calories, 15.5 g total fat (5 g saturated fat), 37 g protein, 3.5 g carbohydrate, 95 mg cholesterol, 290 mg sodium, 5 g fiber

Marinated Thai Chicken Breasts

To intensify the flavors of this dish, some of the fresh marinade is set aside and poured over the chicken right before serving. You also can try this marinade with pork ribs or thin-cut beef short ribs.

CHICKEN

- 4 boneless skinless chicken breast halves

MARINADE

- ¼ cup fish sauce*
- 3 tablespoons peanut or vegetable oil
- 3 tablespoons soy sauce
- 1 tablespoon dark sesame oil
- 1 tablespoon lime juice
- 1 tablespoon rice wine vinegar
- 2 teaspoons chili-garlic sauce or 1 teaspoon hot pepper sauce**
- 2 teaspoons grated lime peel
- ¼ cup finely chopped lemon grass***
- 1 tablespoon minced garlic
- 1 tablespoon minced ginger
- 1 tablespoon sugar

GARNISH

- ½ cup chopped fresh cilantro

1 Place chicken in large resealable plastic bag. In small bowl, stir together all marinade ingredients. Reserve 3 tablespoons of the marinade. Pour remaining marinade over chicken; seal bag. Refrigerate at least 1 hour or up to 4 hours.

2 Heat grill. Remove chicken from marinade; discard marinade. Place chicken on gas grill over medium-high heat or on charcoal grill 4 to 6 inches from medium-high coals. Grill 10 to 13 minutes or until chicken is no longer pink in center and juices run clear, turning once.

3 Place chicken on platter. Pour reserved 3 tablespoons marinade over chicken; garnish with cilantro.

TIPS

   * Look for fish sauce in the Asian section of supermarkets.

  ** Look for chili-garlic sauce (Sriracha brand is recommended) in the Asian section of supermarkets.

*** Lemon grass is an herb with long, thin, grass-like leaves; it's used extensively in Thai cooking. It adds a fragrant lemon flavor to dishes. If lemon grass is not available, use 1 tablespoon grated lemon peel.

4 servings

PER SERVING: 185 calories, 7 g total fat (1.5 g saturated fat), 27 g protein, 3 g carbohydrate, 65 mg cholesterol, 430 mg sodium, 0 g fiber

Marinated Thai Chicken Breasts

Grilled Lobster with Lime and Tarragon Butters

Lobster, with its natural richness, is a perfect candidate for the smokiness grilling imparts. It's easiest to first steam the lobster for a few minutes and then split it lengthwise, brush it with butter and grill. Complement the sweet meat with the tarragon-flavored or lime-spiked butter.

1 **cup unsalted butter**
2 **tablespoons chopped fresh tarragon**
1 **tablespoon lime juice**
1 **teaspoon grated lime peel**
4 **(2-lb.) lobsters**
8 **lime wedges**
   Tarragon sprigs

1 Melt butter in small saucepan over medium-low heat. Reduce heat to low; gently simmer 5 minutes, making sure butter doesn't begin to brown. Remove from heat; let stand 5 minutes. Gently spoon off frothy mixture on top; pour butter into glass measuring cup, leaving milky solids in pan. Divide butter between 2 small bowls. Stir tarragon into one bowl; stir lime juice and lime peel into second bowl. (Butter can be prepared up to 2 hours ahead. Keep at room temperature.)

2 Fill large pot with about 2 inches water; bring to a boil over high heat. Place lobsters in batches in pot; cover and steam 3 to 4 minutes or until shells turn mottled red. Place lobsters on rimmed baking sheet. Cool.

3 With large sharp knife, cleaver or kitchen shears, cut lobsters in half lengthwise, starting at the head. Remove and discard papery sac from head of lobster, grayish-green liver and vein running length of tail. (Lobster meat will be only partially cooked and look opaque.) Reserve any lobster juices to brush on grilled lobsters. (Lobsters can be prepared to this point up to 3 hours ahead. Cover and refrigerate.)

4 Heat grill. Brush cut sides of lobsters with some of one of the butters; place, cut-side up, on gas grill over medium heat or on charcoal grill 4 to 6 inches from medium coals; cover grill. Grill 5 minutes or until shells are lightly charred. Brush with any reserved lobster juices. Turn lobsters; grill an additional 3 to 5 minutes or until lobster meat is slightly firm and white.

5 Garnish lobsters with lime wedges and tarragon sprigs. Serve with warm flavored butters for dipping.

8 servings

PER SERVING: 300 calories, 21 g total fat (13 g saturated fat), 24.5 g protein, 2.5 g carbohydrate, 135 mg cholesterol, 450 mg sodium, .5 g fiber

Grilled Lobster with Lime and Tarragon Butters

Provençale Chicken

In Provence, chicken is often prepared with garlic, tomatoes and olives, hallmark ingredients of the region. Serve this dish with a rice pilaf, couscous or pasta tossed with olive oil.

- 2 tablespoons olive oil
- 3 cups sliced (½ inch) quartered onions (about 2 large)
- 2 medium fennel bulbs, fronds removed and discarded, bulbs quartered, sliced (½ inch)
- 1 tablespoon minced garlic
- 1 (28-oz.) can diced tomatoes, drained
- 1 (6-oz.) jar pitted Kalamata olives, drained
- ½ cup chopped fresh basil
- 8 boneless skinless chicken breast halves
- ½ teaspoon salt
- ¼ teaspoon freshly ground pepper
- 2 medium yellow squash, sliced (¼ inch)
- 2 teaspoons cornstarch
- 2 teaspoons water

1 Heat oil in large skillet over medium-high heat until hot. Add onions and fennel; cook 6 to 8 minutes or until onions are tender and mixture begins to brown. Add garlic; cook 30 to 60 seconds or until fragrant. Place in large bowl; cool 30 minutes or until room temperature.

2 Stir tomatoes, olives and basil into onion mixture. Sprinkle chicken breasts with salt and pepper; place in single layer in 13 × 9-inch glass baking dish. Top with vegetable mixture. (Chicken can be made to this point up to 8 hours ahead. Cover and refrigerate. Increase baking time 10 minutes.)

3 Heat oven to 350°F. Bake, uncovered, 40 minutes. Arrange squash over vegetables. Cover and bake an additional 15 to 20 minutes or until chicken is no longer pink in center and juices run clear. Place chicken and vegetables on large platter.

4 Pour cooking juices (you should have about 1 cup) into small saucepan. Bring to a boil over medium-high heat. In small bowl, whisk together cornstarch and water; whisk into cooking juices. Cook 1 to 2 minutes or until thickened. Serve with chicken.

8 servings

PER SERVING: 245 calories, 8.5 g total fat (1.5 g saturated fat), 29 g protein, 14 g carbohydrate, 65 mg cholesterol, 485 mg sodium, 4 g fiber

Italian Sausage Meatball Rigatoni with Vodka-Tomato Sauce

Rich and flavorful pork sausage and beef meatballs make an ideal pairing for a creamy, mildly spicy vodka sauce. Rigatoni, large tubular-shaped pasta, are a nice size and shape for catching enough sauce for each bite. Garnish the pasta with chopped fresh Italian parsley.

- ½ cup fresh white bread crumbs
- ½ cup milk
- ¾ lb. bulk mild Italian sausage
- ¾ lb. ground beef (85% lean)
- 1 medium onion, coarsely grated
- 1 cup grated Parmesan cheese, divided
- ¼ cup chopped fresh parsley
- 1 teaspoon salt, divided
- ½ teaspoon crushed red pepper, divided
- 12 oz. rigatoni
- ¼ cup butter
- 2 large garlic cloves, minced
- ⅔ cup vodka or chicken broth
- 1 cup canned crushed tomatoes
- ¾ cup whipping cream
- ¼ teaspoon black pepper

1 Heat oven to 425°F. Combine bread crumbs and milk in large bowl; let stand 5 minutes. Mix in sausage, ground beef, onion, ½ cup of the cheese, parsley, ½ teaspoon of the salt and ¼ teaspoon of the crushed red pepper until well-blended. Shape into 24 (1¾-inch) balls. Place on rimmed baking sheet. Bake 10 to 15 minutes or until cooked through and no longer pink in center. Cover loosely with foil.

2 Cook rigatoni in large pot of boiling salted water according to package directions; drain.

3 Meanwhile, melt butter in medium saucepan over medium-low heat. Cook garlic 30 seconds or until fragrant. Stir in vodka; reduce until slightly thickened, about 5 minutes. Add tomatoes, cream, remaining ½ teaspoon salt, remaining ¼ teaspoon crushed red pepper and black pepper; bring to a boil. Simmer 5 minutes. Spoon sauce over rigatoni; sprinkle with remaining ½ cup cheese. Top with meatballs.

6 (1¾-cup) servings

PER SERVING: 775 calories, 41 g total fat (20.5 g saturated fat), 36 g protein, 58 g carbohydrate, 125 mg cholesterol, 1590 mg sodium, 4 g fiber

Grilled Lamb Chops with Roasted Tomatoes and Sheep's Milk Cheese

In Greece, the favorite way to season lamb is the simplest, with a little extra-virgin Greek olive oil, garlic and lemon juice. Topping these lamb chops with roasted tomatoes and sheep's milk cheese lends a slightly sweet and rich note to every tender bite.

LAMB

- ½ cup extra-virgin olive oil
- ½ cup fresh lemon juice
- 4 garlic cloves, minced
- 2 tablespoons dried marjoram or oregano
- 1 tablespoon dried rosemary
- 3 (1½-lb.) racks of lamb, cut into individual chops (about 24)
- ½ teaspoon kosher (coarse) salt
- ½ teaspoon freshly ground pepper

TOMATOES

- 6 large ripe but firm tomatoes, cut into 8 wedges
- ½ teaspoon kosher (coarse) salt
- ¼ teaspoon freshly ground pepper
- 2 tablespoons sugar
- 2 tablespoons extra-virgin olive oil
- 2 tablespoons balsamic vinegar

GARNISH

- 4 oz. firm aged sheep's milk cheese, such as Greek kefalograviera or kefalotyri, or Gruyère cheese, shaved*
- 4 cups fresh arugula leaves

1 In large bowl or resealable plastic bag, whisk together ½ cup oil, lemon juice, garlic, marjoram and rosemary. Add lamb chops; toss to coat. Cover and refrigerate at least 1 hour or up to 3 hours.

2 Meanwhile, heat oven to 400°F. Place tomatoes, skin-side down, on lightly oiled rimmed baking sheet. Sprinkle with ½ teaspoon salt, ¼ teaspoon pepper and sugar; drizzle with 2 tablespoons oil and vinegar. Bake 30 to 35 minutes or until tomatoes are wrinkled and just beginning to char. Cool, saving accumulated juices.

3 Heat grill. Remove lamb from marinade; discard marinade. Sprinkle lamb with ½ teaspoon salt and ½ teaspoon pepper. Brush grill grate with oil. Place lamb on gas grill over medium heat or on charcoal grill 4 to 6 inches from medium coals; cover grill. Grill 6 minutes for medium-rare or until of desired doneness, turning once.

4 Place tomatoes in center of serving plates; arrange lamb over tomatoes. Top with cheese. Arrange arugula around lamb; drizzle with reserved tomato juices.

TIP

*Shave cheese with vegetable peeler.

8 servings

PER SERVING: 330 calories, 21.5 g total fat (7 g saturated fat), 24 g protein, 10.5 g carbohydrate, 80 mg cholesterol, 315 mg sodium, 2 g fiber

Grilled Lamb Chops with Roasted Tomatoes and Sheep's Milk Cheese

Roasted Mustard Pork Loin with Fresh Plum Compote

The crusty brown exterior of this pork loin is flecked with sage and mustard seeds, making a stunning presentation. For the compote, any flavorful variety of plums will work. Depending on the plums' juiciness, however, you may need to adjust the amount of time they're simmered to obtain the desired consistency.

MEAT AND GLAZE

- 2 large garlic cloves, chopped
- 1¼ teaspoons freshly ground pepper
- 1¼ teaspoons kosher (coarse) or sea salt
- 1 teaspoon mustard seeds
- 1 (3-lb.) single boneless pork loin
- ⅔ cup plum preserves
- ⅔ cup dry red wine or cranberry juice
- 2 tablespoons chopped fresh sage

COMPOTE

- 2 tablespoons unsalted butter
- 3 tablespoons chopped shallots
- 1½ lb. fresh plums (about 4 large), cut into eight wedges (5 cups)
- ¾ cup dry red wine or cranberry juice, divided
- 2 tablespoons chopped fresh sage
- ½ teaspoon kosher (coarse) salt
- ¼ teaspoon freshly ground pepper

1 Heat oven to 400°F. In small bowl, stir together garlic, 1¼ teaspoons pepper, 1¼ teaspoons salt and mustard seeds. Rub mixture over pork. Place pork on rack in shallow roasting pan; bake 45 minutes.

2 Meanwhile, place preserves and ⅔ cup wine in small saucepan. Simmer over medium-high heat 5 to 7 minutes or until slightly thickened and reduced by half. Stir in 2 tablespoons sage. Brush pork with glaze; bake an additional 25 to 30 minutes or until internal temperature reaches 145°F., lightly brushing with glaze every 10 to 15 minutes.

Roasted Mustard Pork Loin with Fresh Plum Compote

3 To make compote, melt butter in medium saucepan over medium heat. Add shallots; cook 3 minutes or until softened. Stir in plums and ¾ cup wine. Reduce heat to medium; cook 18 to 20 minutes or until plums are very soft, stirring frequently. Stir in 2 tablespoons sage, ½ teaspoon salt and pepper; simmer 5 minutes.

4 Place pork on cutting board. Cover loosely with foil; let stand 10 minutes. Slice pork into thick slices; spoon warm compote over each serving.

8 servings

PER SERVING: 440 calories, 17 g total fat (6.5 g saturated fat), 39 g protein, 30.5 g carbohydrate, 115 mg cholesterol, 425 mg sodium, 3 g fiber

Mint Pesto-Stuffed Chicken Breasts

Mint and parsley take the place of traditional basil in the springy pesto that's tucked inside these chicken breasts. Don't be concerned if a little of the pesto leaks out; it will flavor the braised vegetables and broth in the pan, which are served with the chicken.

PESTO

- 6 tablespoons toasted slivered almonds*
- 2 garlic cloves
- ¾ teaspoon kosher (coarse) salt
- 1½ cups loosely packed fresh Italian parsley
- ¾ cup loosely packed fresh mint
- 6 tablespoons extra-virgin olive oil
- ½ cup (2 oz.) freshly grated Parmigiano-Reggiano cheese

CHICKEN

- 8 boneless skinless chicken breast halves
- 3 cups sliced leeks (½ inch)
- 2 cups reduced-sodium chicken broth
- 1½ lb. thin carrots (about 6), peeled, sliced (¼ inch)
- ¼ cup butter
- 1¼ teaspoons kosher (coarse) salt, divided
- 2 teaspoons chopped fresh marjoram
- ½ teaspoon freshly ground pepper

Mint Pesto-Stuffed Chicken Breasts

1 Place almonds, garlic and ¾ teaspoon salt in food processor; process until ground. Add parsley and mint; process until finely chopped. With processor running, pour in oil; process until almost smooth. Add cheese; pulse until blended.

2 Make horizontal slit in chicken breasts to create pockets, being careful not to cut through the other side. Stuff each pocket with pesto. (Chicken can be made to this point up to 1 day ahead. Cover and refrigerate.)

3 Heat oven to 375°F. Place leeks, broth, carrots, butter and ½ teaspoon of the salt in deep large ovenproof skillet; bring to a boil over medium-low heat.** Simmer 15 minutes or until vegetables are soft and liquid is reduced by about half. Stir in marjoram. (Vegetables can be made to this point up to 1 day ahead. Cover and refrigerate.)

4 Arrange chicken over vegetables; sprinkle with remaining ¾ teaspoon salt and pepper. Spoon some of the vegetables over chicken. (If chicken and vegetables have been made ahead, bring to a simmer on stovetop before baking.)

5 Cover and bake 30 to 35 minutes or until chicken is no longer pink in center.

TIPS

*To toast almonds, place on baking sheet; bake at 375°F. for 4 to 6 minutes or until light golden brown. Cool.

**If you don't have a skillet large enough to hold all the chicken, use 1 or 2 shallow baking dishes large enough to hold the chicken breasts comfortably. Cook vegetables in skillet first, and then transfer them, along with broth, to dish; arrange chicken on top. Cover tightly.

8 servings

PER SERVING: 410 calories, 24.5 g total fat (7.5 g saturated fat), 33 g protein, 15 g carbohydrate, 95 mg cholesterol, 820 mg sodium, 4 g fiber

Marinated Beef Tenderloin with Roasted Shallots and Port Reduction

The port-wine marinade, flavored with orange and lemon, adds an almost sangria-like taste to the beef. The marinade is then transformed by reduction to become a rich, smooth velvety sauce.

MARINADE

- 3 cups port
- ½ medium orange, sliced
- ½ medium lemon, sliced
- 3 garlic cloves, minced
- 1 tablespoon chopped fresh sage
- 1 bay leaf
- Dash allspice

BEEF AND SAUCE

- 1 (2-lb.) center-cut beef tenderloin
- 12 large shallots, peeled, quartered
- 1 tablespoon plus 1 teaspoon olive oil
- 1 teaspoon kosher (coarse) salt
- ½ teaspoon freshly ground pepper
- 1½ cups beef broth
- 2 tablespoons unsalted butter, softened

Marinated Beef Tenderloin with Roasted Shallots and Port Reduction

1 In large resealable plastic bag, combine all marinade ingredients. Place beef and shallots in bag; seal bag. Refrigerate 24 hours, turning bag occasionally.

2 Heat oven to 425°F. Spray shallow roasting pan with nonstick cooking spray. Remove beef from marinade; pat dry with paper towels. Strain marinade, reserving liquid. Remove shallots from marinade ingredients; set shallots aside. Discard remaining marinade ingredients. Pat shallots dry with paper towels; place in medium bowl. Add 1 teaspoon of the oil; toss to coat.

3 Heat large skillet over medium-high heat until hot. Add remaining 1 tablespoon oil; heat until hot. Add tenderloin; cook 4 to 6 minutes or until browned on all sides, turning occasionally. (Tenderloin can be browned up to 4 hours ahead. Cover and refrigerate until ready to bake. Immediately skip to step 6 and make sauce.)

4 Place tenderloin in roasting pan; set unwashed skillet aside. Sprinkle tenderloin with salt and pepper. Arrange shallots around beef.

5 Bake 20 to 25 minutes or until internal temperature reaches 130°F. for medium rare or until of desired doneness. Remove from oven. Cover loosely with foil; let stand 15 minutes before slicing.

6 Meanwhile, heat same skillet over high heat until hot. Add reserved marinade; bring to a boil, scraping browned bits from bottom of skillet. Add broth; return to a boil. Boil over high heat until slightly thickened and syrupy, stirring once or twice. (Liquid will be reduced to about ⅔ cup.) Reduce heat to medium; whisk in butter just until melted. Serve immediately. (Sauce can be made up to 4 hours ahead. If making ahead, reheat and whisk in butter immediately before serving.)

7 To serve, cut tenderloin in half lengthwise. Cut each half crosswise into ⅜-inch-thick slices. Mound shallots in center of each dinner plate. Arrange sliced beef over shallots. Drizzle sauce around shallots and beef.

6 servings

PER SERVING: 375 calories, 17.5 g total fat (7 g saturated fat), 35 g protein, 18.5 g carbohydrate, 95 mg cholesterol, 615 mg sodium, 1.5 g fiber

Meltingly Tender Pot Roast

This traditional-style pot roast is cooked smothered in onions, giving it a sweet, caramelized taste. Roasted carrots and Yukon Gold potatoes cook alongside the meat, making this a one-pot meal. For the best flavor, make sure to brown the brisket on all sides.

- 1 tablespoon olive oil
- 1 (2½- to 2¾-lb.) beef brisket (flat-cut or first-cut)
- 2 teaspoons dried thyme
- ½ teaspoon salt
- ½ teaspoon freshly ground pepper
- 1 tablespoon butter
- 4 large onions, halved, sliced (½ inch)
- 4 large garlic cloves, minced
- ¾ cup reduced-sodium beef broth
- ¾ cup red wine or additional beef broth
- 1 tablespoon Worcestershire sauce
- 4 medium carrots, cut into 2-inch pieces
- 4 medium Yukon Gold potatoes (1¾ lb.), unpeeled, quartered, or halved if small

Grilled Pork Tenderloin Spiedini

1 Heat oven to 350°F. Heat heavy large pot over medium-high heat until hot. Add oil; heat until hot. Add brisket; cook 5 to 7 minutes or until browned, turning once. Place on plate; sprinkle both sides with thyme, salt and pepper.

2 Melt butter in pot over medium heat. Add onions; stir to coat with butter. Cover and cook 5 minutes or until wilted. Uncover; increase heat to medium-high. Cook 5 minutes or until onions start to brown, stirring occasionally. Add garlic; cook 30 seconds or until fragrant, stirring constantly. Stir in broth, wine and Worcestershire sauce.

3 Return brisket to pot; spoon onions over brisket. Cover; bake 1 hour. Turn brisket; spoon onions over brisket. Arrange carrots and potatoes around brisket. Cover; bake an additional 1 hour or until brisket and vegetables are tender when pierced with knife.

4 Place brisket on cutting board; cover loosely with foil. Let stand 10 to 15 minutes. Thinly slice brisket; serve with onions, potatoes and carrots. Spoon any accumulated pan juices over brisket.

6 servings

PER SERVING: 440 calories, 14.5 g total fat (5.5 g saturated fat), 37.5 g protein, 40.5 g carbohydrate, 70 mg cholesterol, 345 mg sodium, 6.5 g fiber

Meltingly Tender Pot Roast

Grilled Pork Tenderloin Spiedini

Spiedini are grilled Italian meat skewers. They're typically made with quail wrapped in fresh bay leaves, chunks of mild sausage and pieces of country bread, but skewers of pork also are popular. Because pork tenderloin is lean and prone to drying out, it's first soaked in a salt brine to improve the juiciness and infuse flavor.

 2 **cups water**
 2 **tablespoons plus ½ teaspoon kosher (coarse) salt, divided**
 2 **tablespoons packed light brown sugar**
 ¼ **cup chopped fennel fronds**
 2 **tablespoons minced garlic, divided**
 1 **tablespoon fennel seeds, crushed**
 1 **tablespoon Pernod or other anise-flavored liqueur, if desired**
1½ **teaspoons freshly ground pepper, divided**
 2 **(1-lb.) pork tenderloins, sliced crosswise into 1-inch pieces**
 3 **tablespoons olive oil**
    Fresh sage leaves
 1 **red onion, cut into 1½-inch wedges**
 1 **fennel bulb, cut into 8 wedges**

1 Bring water to a boil in medium saucepan. Stir in 2 tablespoons of the salt and brown sugar until dissolved. Stir in fennel fronds, 1 tablespoon of the garlic, fennel seeds, Pernod and 1 teaspoon of the pepper; simmer 1 minute. Refrigerate until cold (about 45°F.).

2 Place pork in large resealable plastic bag; pour in brine. Seal bag; refrigerate 1 to 2 hours. Remove pork; discard brine.

3 Heat grill. In small bowl, stir together oil and remaining 1 tablespoon garlic, ½ teaspoon salt and ½ teaspoon pepper.

4 Thread 6 (12- to 14-inch) flat metal skewers with pork, sage leaves, onion and fennel. Brush skewers with garlic-flavored oil. Place on gas grill over medium heat or on charcoal grill 4 to 6 inches from medium coals; cover grill. Grill 10 to 12 minutes or until pork is slightly pink in center.

6 servings

PER SERVING: 285 calories, 12.5 g total fat (3 g saturated fat), 35 g protein, 6 g carbohydrate, 95 mg cholesterol, 375 mg sodium, 2 g fiber

Spicy Lentil and Bean Chili

If you like your chili spicy, this vegetarian version may become a favorite. If you prefer it less spicy, replace one or both of the cans of chile-spiked tomatoes with unseasoned diced tomatoes. As accompaniments, serve grated pepper Jack or cheddar cheese, coarsely chopped fresh cilantro, chopped green onions and reduced-fat sour cream.

Spicy Lentil and Bean Chili

 2 **teaspoons extra-virgin olive oil**
 1 **cup chopped onion**
 1 **cup diced carrots**
 3 **garlic cloves, minced**
 5 **teaspoons chili powder**
 4 **teaspoons ground cumin**
 1 **teaspoon dried oregano**
 4 **cups reduced-sodium chicken or vegetable broth**
 ¾ **cup brown lentils, rinsed**
 2 **(10-oz.) cans diced tomatoes with green chiles**
 2 **(14.5-oz.) cans dark red kidney beans, drained, rinsed**
 ¼ **teaspoon freshly ground pepper**

1 Heat oil in Dutch oven or large pot over medium heat until hot. Add onion and carrots; cook, stirring frequently, 3 to 5 minutes or until softened. Add garlic, chili powder, cumin and oregano; cook and stir 30 seconds. Add broth and lentils; bring to a simmer. Reduce heat to medium-low; cover and simmer 25 minutes.

2 Add tomatoes, beans and pepper; return to a simmer. Cook, covered, 10 to 15 minutes or until lentils are tender. Spoon into bowls.

8 (about 1¼-cup) servings

PER SERVING: 220 calories, 3 g total fat (.5 g saturated fat), 14.5 g protein, 36.5 g carbohydrate, 0 mg cholesterol, 625 mg sodium, 10.5 g fiber

Grilled Leg of Lamb with Almonds

Spices, herbs and a healthy dose of garlic infuse the yogurt-based marinade and sauce with delicious, full-bodied flavor. The indirect method of cooking the meat on the grill gives it ample time to absorb the smoky notes from the fire.

3 cups plain yogurt, divided	1½ teaspoons cayenne pepper
24 medium garlic cloves	¾ teaspoon black peppercorns
¾ cup slivered almonds	6 tablespoons finely chopped fresh mint
3 (3-inch) cinnamon sticks, broken into smaller pieces	3 tablespoons finely chopped fresh cilantro
3 teaspoons salt	3½ lb. boneless leg of lamb, rolled, tied
1½ teaspoons cardamom seeds	
1½ teaspoons cumin seeds	

1 Place 1½ cups of the yogurt, garlic, almonds, cinnamon sticks, salt, cardamom seeds, cumin seeds, cayenne pepper and peppercorns in blender; blend until almost smooth (marinade will feel slightly grainy). Stir in mint and cilantro. Place ½ cup of the marinade in medium bowl; stir in remaining 1½ cups yogurt. Cover and refrigerate until ready to serve.

2 Place lamb in shallow baking dish or 2-gallon resealable plastic bag. Spoon remaining marinade over outside of lamb and into center of roll. Cover and refrigerate 24 hours.

3 When ready to grill, set up grill as follows. For charcoal grills: Heat 40 to 60 coals in center of grill to medium heat. Divide coals, placing half on each side of grill, leaving center open. Place drip pan between piles of coals. Place grates on grill 4 to 6 inches from coals. For gas grills: Light two outside sections, leaving middle section unlit (three-burner grill). Or light one side and leave other side unlit (two-burner grill). Place drip pan on unlit side. Heat on high until hot. Reduce heat to medium.

4 Remove lamb from marinade; discard marinade. Place lamb over drip pan. Cover and grill 1 hour to 1 hour 15 minutes or until thermometer inserted in thickest section of lamb reaches 140°F. for medium-rare or until of desired doneness. Adjust grill as needed to keep temperature around 350°F.

5 Remove lamb from grill; let stand 20 to 30 minutes before slicing. Serve with reserved yogurt sauce.

8 servings

PER SERVING: 355 calories, 15 g total fat (5.5 g saturated fat), 46 g protein, 7 g carbohydrate, 140 mg cholesterol, 600 mg sodium, .5 g fiber

Grilled Leg of Lamb with Almonds

Italian Tuscan Vegetable Soup

This soup is based on the Italian soup la ribollita, which was reheated and stretched over many meals. It's packed with root vegetables, chard and beans and topped with crunchy garlic toasts. Although any type of chard can be used, look for a red-stemmed or rainbow variety for color. The stems cook longer than the leaves, so they're added first.

SOUP

- 2 tablespoons olive oil
- 2 large onions, chopped
- 2 medium leeks, halved, sliced
- 2 large carrots, sliced
- 2 parsnips, chopped
- 2 small turnips, chopped
- 1 bunch Swiss chard
- 6 large garlic cloves, minced
- 6 red new potatoes, unpeeled, diced (¾ inch)
- 2 (32-oz.) containers lower-sodium chicken or vegetable broth
- 1½ tablespoons dried basil
- 1 teaspoon salt
- ½ teaspoon pepper
- 1 (15- or 19-oz.) can cannellini beans, drained, rinsed

GARLIC TOASTS

- 1½ teaspoons olive oil
- 1 small garlic clove, minced
- 8 slices ciabatta bread
- ½ cup grated Parmigiano-Reggiano cheese

1 Heat 2 tablespoons oil in large pot over medium-high heat until hot. Add onions, leeks, carrots, parsnips and turnips; stir to combine. Place circle of parchment paper or foil on top of vegetables; cover and reduce heat to medium. Cook 5 to 8 minutes or until vegetables have begun to sweat and are glistening.

2 Meanwhile, diagonally slice chard stems to equal 1 cup. Coarsely chop chard leaves to equal 3 cups. (Reserve remaining chard for another use.)

Italian Tuscan Vegetable Soup

3 Remove cover and paper from pot. Add 6 garlic cloves; cook 30 seconds or until fragrant. Stir in potatoes. Add broth, basil, salt and pepper; bring to a boil. Reduce heat to medium-low; simmer 15 to 20 minutes or until vegetables are almost tender.

4 Stir in beans and chard stems; cook 4 minutes. Add chard leaves; cook 3 to 4 minutes or until tender. (Soup can be made to this point 2 days ahead. Cover and refrigerate.)

5 Before serving, heat broiler. Combine 1½ teaspoons oil and 1 garlic clove; brush over both sides of bread. Place on baking sheet. Broil 1 to 2 minutes or until light golden brown, turning once. Top each serving with 1 garlic toast; sprinkle with 1 tablespoon of the cheese.

8 (about 1½-cup) servings

PER SERVING: 340 calories, 7 g total fat (2 g saturated fat), 16 g protein, 55 g carbohydrate, 5 mg cholesterol, 1260 mg sodium, 9 g fiber

Grilled Shrimp with Chile-Tomato Topping

Pretty, spicy and bursting with flavor, these shrimp skewers are a natural choice for entertaining. But they're quick enough to make on weeknights. The shrimp marinate for just 30 minutes, which is about the time you need to prepare the topping.

Grilled Shrimp with Chile-Tomato Topping

SHRIMP

- 1½ lb. shelled, deveined uncooked medium shrimp
- 3 tablespoons rice wine, white wine or chicken broth
- 3 tablespoons hoisin sauce
- 2 tablespoons finely grated onion
- 1 tablespoon minced garlic
- ¼ teaspoon salt
- ¼ teaspoon freshly ground pepper
- 2 tablespoons olive oil

TOPPING

- 2 tablespoons olive oil
- ¼ cup minced shallots
- 3 serrano chiles, veins and seeds removed, minced
- 1 tablespoon minced garlic
- 1 cup diced seeded peeled tomatoes (about 3 medium)*
- ¼ cup white wine or chicken broth
- 1 tablespoon tomato paste
- ½ teaspoon chopped fresh thyme
- ⅛ teaspoon salt
- ⅛ teaspoon freshly ground pepper

1 Place all shrimp ingredients except oil in medium bowl; toss to combine. Cover and refrigerate 30 minutes. Meanwhile, soak 4 (12-inch) wooden skewers in cold water 20 minutes.

2 Meanwhile, heat 2 tablespoons oil in large skillet over medium-high heat until hot. Add shallots, chiles and 1 tablespoon garlic; cook 1 to 2 minutes or until shallots soften and garlic is fragrant. Add tomatoes, white wine, tomato paste, thyme, ⅛ teaspoon salt and ⅛ teaspoon pepper; bring to a boil. Reduce heat to medium; cook 4 to 5 minutes or until thickened, stirring occasionally. (Topping can be made up to 1 day ahead. Cover and refrigerate. Reheat before serving.)

3 Heat grill. Remove shrimp from marinade; discard marinade. Thread shrimp onto skewers. Brush with oil. Brush grill grate with oil. Place skewers on gas grill over medium heat or on charcoal grill 4 to 6 inches from medium coals; cover grill. Grill 4 to 5 minutes or until shrimp turn pink, turning once. Serve topping spooned over shrimp.

TIP

* To peel tomatoes, cut small "X" in bottom of each tomato. Place in large pot of boiling water 30 to 60 seconds or until skins become loose; place in large bowl of ice water. Skins should slip off with help of paring knife.

4 servings

PER SERVING: 230 calories, 10 g total fat (1.5 g saturated fat), 27.5 g protein, 7 g carbohydrate, 240 mg cholesterol, 475 mg sodium, 1.5 g fiber

Mediterranean Herb-Roasted Chicken

Whole leg portions are the tastiest part of the bird, and one per person is just enough to satisfy. If you can't find entire legs, purchase separate thighs and drumsticks. Potatoes, onions, zucchini and mini sweet bell peppers roast alongside the chicken, making this a complete meal in a pan.

5 teaspoons chopped fresh rosemary	3 medium red potatoes, cut into 8 wedges each
4 teaspoons chopped garlic	2 medium onions, cut into 1-inch wedges
½ teaspoon salt	4 whole chicken legs
3 tablespoons lemon juice	1 (4-oz.) pkg. multi-colored mini sweet bell peppers, halved, or 1 red bell pepper, cut into 1-inch wedges
1 tablespoon olive oil	
1½ teaspoons dried thyme	1 medium zucchini, halved lengthwise, cut into 2-inch pieces
½ teaspoon dried savory or oregano	
¼ teaspoon pepper	

1 Heat oven to 375°F. Finely chop rosemary, garlic and salt together; place in small bowl. Stir in lemon juice, oil, thyme, savory and pepper.

2 Spray bottom of wide shallow roasting pan with cooking spray. Scatter potatoes and onions in pan; add chicken. Spoon 2 tablespoons of the herb mixture over chicken and vegetables in pan; toss to coat. Place chicken on top of potatoes and onion.

3 Bake 45 minutes. Remove from oven; baste with accumulated juices. Scatter peppers and zucchini around chicken; spoon remaining herb mixture over chicken and all vegetables. Bake 20 to 30 minutes or until chicken is browned and no longer pink in center.

4 servings

PER SERVING: 455 calories, 19 g total fat (5 g saturated fat), 33.5 g protein, 38 g carbohydrate, 105 mg cholesterol, 415 mg sodium, 6 g fiber

Mediterranean Herb-Roasted Chicken

Eight-Treasure Fried Rice

In Chinese tradition, eight is a lucky number. It's represented here by the delicious "treasures" that comprise the dish: eggs, shrimp, shiitake mushrooms, edamame, sausage or ham, pineapple, cashews and cilantro.

4 cups cooked long-grain rice, chilled	1 cup diced Chinese smoked sausage or ham
3 tablespoons vegetable oil, divided	¾ cup well-drained canned pineapple tidbits or diced fresh pineapple
3 eggs, well-beaten	
¼ cup chopped onion	¾ cup dry-roasted salted cashews
1 lb. shelled, deveined uncooked medium shrimp	½ cup thinly sliced green onions
6 oz. shiitake or crimini mushrooms (remove stems from shiitakes), sliced	½ cup purchased stir-fry sauce
	⅓ cup chopped cilantro
¾ cup frozen shelled edamame or petite peas, thawed	2 tablespoons dark sesame oil

1 Break up rice into individual grains, using your hands to crumble it gently.

2 Heat 1 tablespoon of the vegetable oil in large nonstick skillet over high heat until hot. Add eggs; tilt or swirl pan to cover bottom with eggs. (Lift cooked edges and tilt pan to allow uncooked egg to run underneath.) When set, gently turn eggs; cook 10 seconds. Place on cutting board; cool. Roll up; cut crosswise into ⅛-inch-wide ribbons. Fluff to loosen.

3 Heat remaining 2 tablespoons vegetable oil in same skillet over medium heat until hot. Cook onion 15 seconds or until shiny and fragrant. Add shrimp; cook 1 to 2 minutes or until shrimp just begins to turn pink. Add mushrooms and edamame; cook 1 minute or until mushrooms are shiny and softened and shrimp turn pink.

4 Add rice; toss to combine. Add egg ribbons, sausage, pineapple, cashews, green onions and stir-fry sauce; cook 2 to 3 minutes or until rice is tender and all ingredients are heated through. Stir in cilantro and sesame oil.

6 (1⅔-cup) servings

PER SERVING: 600 calories, 31 g total fat (6.5 g saturated fat), 29 g protein, 52 g carbohydrate, 235 mg cholesterol, 1110 mg sodium, 3 g fiber

Eight-Treasure Fried Rice

Tequila-Chile-Marinated Pork Chops

Tequila-Chile-Marinated Pork Chops

To prevent overcooking, use thick-cut pork chops, at least 1 inch thick. This marinade is also excellent with country spareribs, flank steak or butterflied leg of lamb.

PORK

4   bone-in rib pork chops (1 inch thick)

MARINADE

2   jalapeño chiles, finely chopped

1   cup chopped fresh cilantro

1   tablespoon grated lime peel

1   tablespoon minced garlic

1   tablespoon ground chipotle chile pepper or chili powder

1   tablespoon chopped fresh oregano or 1 teaspoon dried

2½   teaspoons salt

1½   teaspoons ground cumin

1   teaspoon freshly ground pepper

½   teaspoon ground allspice

¼   cup fresh lime juice

¼   cup vegetable or olive oil

3   tablespoons tequila or water

1 Place pork in large resealable plastic bag. In small bowl, stir together all marinade ingredients. Pour over pork; seal bag. Refrigerate overnight, turning bag occasionally.

2 Heat grill. Remove pork from marinade, leaving as much marinade on as possible; discard remaining marinade. Place pork on gas grill over medium heat or on charcoal grill 4 to 6 inches from medium coals. Grill 7 to 10 minutes or until no longer pink in center, turning once.

Place on serving platter; loosely tent with foil. Let stand 5 minutes.

4 servings

PER SERVING: 310 calories, 16.5 g total fat (5 g saturated fat), 36.5 g protein, 1.5 g carbohydrate, 105 mg cholesterol, 435 mg sodium, .5 g fiber

Beef Tenderloin Steaks with Caesar Butter

This rich, super-tender cut of steak needs little except a generous sprinkling of kosher salt and freshly ground black pepper. A pat of melting butter—spiked with the flavors of a Caesar salad—adds a final punch. The leftover butter can be wrapped tightly and frozen.

CAESAR BUTTER

- 1 anchovy fillet, finely chopped
- 2 tablespoons finely chopped Italian parsley
- 2 tablespoons freshly grated Parmesan cheese
- 1 teaspoon Dijon mustard
- 1 teaspoon grated lemon peel
- 1 teaspoon minced garlic
- 1 teaspoon freshly ground pepper
- ¼ teaspoon kosher (coarse) salt
- ¼ teaspoon Worcestershire sauce
- ½ cup unsalted butter, cut up, softened

STEAKS

- 4 (6-oz.) beef tenderloin steaks (1½ inches thick)
- 1 tablespoon olive oil
- 2 teaspoons chopped fresh rosemary
- ½ teaspoon kosher (coarse) salt
- ½ teaspoon freshly ground pepper

1 In small bowl, stir together all Caesar butter ingredients except butter. Stir in butter until mixture is well-blended. Spread 12-inch sheet of plastic wrap on work surface; scrape butter onto plastic wrap. Shape and roll into log 1½ to 2 inches thick. Refrigerate. (Butter can be prepared and refrigerated up to 2 weeks ahead or frozen up to 2 months ahead.)

2 Heat grill. Brush both sides of steaks with oil; sprinkle with rosemary, ½ teaspoon salt and ½ teaspoon pepper. Place steaks on gas grill over medium heat or on charcoal grill 4 to 6 inches from medium coals; cover grill. Grill 12 to 15 minutes for medium-rare or until of desired doneness, turning once.

3 Top each steak with 1 (¼-inch) slice butter; let stand 5 minutes.

4 servings

PER SERVING: 405 calories, 27.5 g total fat (12.5 g saturated fat), 37.5 g protein, 1 g carbohydrate, 130 mg cholesterol, 390 mg sodium, .5 g fiber

Beef Tenderloin Steaks with Caesar Butter

Mexican Pork Stew

Traditional Mexican posole is made from dried hominy kernels that require lengthy soaking and cooking. This version relies on canned hominy to cut preparation time. Add a burst of freshness by garnishing each serving with thinly sliced green onions and radishes, chopped cilantro, lime wedges and hot sauce.

Mexican Pork Stew

- 2   tablespoons vegetable oil
- 2   lb. boneless pork shoulder, cubed (1½ inches)
- 2   medium onions, chopped
- 4   large garlic cloves, minced
- 4   cups reduced-sodium chicken broth, divided
- 2   teaspoons dried oregano (Mexican preferred)
- ½   teaspoon freshly ground pepper
- 1   lb. tomatillos, husks removed, halved or quartered (4 cups), or 3 (11-oz.) cans, drained
- 4   serrano chiles, seeded
- ½   teaspoon toasted cumin seeds*
- 2   (15.5-oz.) cans yellow or white hominy, drained, rinsed
- ½   teaspoon salt

1 Heat oil in large pot over medium heat until hot. Add pork in batches; cook 6 to 8 minutes or until browned. Add onions and garlic; cook 5 minutes or until softened. Add 3 cups of the broth; bring to a simmer. Stir in oregano and pepper. Reduce heat to low; cover and cook 1 hour or until meat is almost tender.

2 Meanwhile, place tomatillos and remaining 1 cup broth in large saucepan. Bring to a simmer over medium heat; cover and cook 10 minutes or until tender. (If using canned tomatillos, eliminate cooking step.) Place in blender, along with chiles and cumin seeds; blend until smooth.

3 Stir tomatillo mixture, hominy and salt into pork; simmer, uncovered, 30 minutes.

TIP

* Toast cumin seeds in dry small skillet over medium-high heat 1 minute or until seeds turn reddish brown and become fragrant, stirring occasionally. Cool.

6 (1⅔-cup) servings

PER SERVING: 480 calories, 24.5 g total fat (7.5 g saturated fat), 37.5 g protein, 25.5 g carbohydrate, 95 mg cholesterol, 855 mg sodium, 5.5 g fiber

Santa Fe Stuffed Chicken

The cooking method used here serves two purposes: Broiling the chicken allows it to brown, while baking it covered helps the chicken retain its moisture and juices.

¾	teaspoon chili powder
¾	teaspoon cumin
½	teaspoon salt
¼	teaspoon paprika
½	cup unseasoned dry bread crumbs
2	tablespoons butter

¼	cup chopped celery
¼	cup chopped onion
½	cup corn
1	oz. (¼ cup) shredded Monterey Jack cheese
2	tablespoons chopped fresh cilantro
4	chicken breast halves, bone-in with skin

1 Spray 12 × 8-inch baking dish with nonstick cooking spray. In small bowl, combine chili powder, cumin, salt and paprika; mix well. Reserve 1 teaspoon seasoning mixture; set aside. To remaining seasoning mixture, add bread crumbs; mix well.

2 In medium skillet, melt butter over medium heat. Add celery and onion; cook 5 to 7 minutes or until vegetables are tender. Add corn, cheese, cilantro and bread crumb mixture; mix well.

3 Loosen skin from each chicken breast to form pocket between skin and meat. Fill each pocket with about ½ cup corn mixture; secure opening with toothpick. Place skin side up in baking dish. Sprinkle chicken with reserved seasoning mixture.

4 Broil 4 to 6 inches from heat 5 to 7 minutes or until skin is brown.

5 Remove baking dish from oven; cover with foil. Heat oven to 350°F. Bake 35 to 45 minutes or until juices run clear.

4 servings

PER SERVING: 360 calories, 18.5 g total fat (8 g saturated fat), 33 g protein, 15 g carbohydrate, 100 mg cholesterol, 570 mg sodium, 1.5 g fiber

Santa Fe Stuffed Chicken

Sicilian Grilled Swordfish

Sicily is an island whose food has been shaped by many cultures. The influence of two of them, ancient Greek and Moorish, are reflected in this recipe's use of exotic spices, lemon and mint.

RUB

- ½ cup chopped onion
- 4 garlic cloves
- 2 tablespoons olive oil
- 1 tablespoon grated lemon peel
- 1 tablespoon lemon juice
- 2 teaspoons paprika
- 2 teaspoons kosher (coarse) salt
- 1 teaspoon ground cumin
- 1 teaspoon ground coriander
- 1 teaspoon fennel seeds, ground
- 1 teaspoon freshly ground pepper
- ⅛ teaspoon ground cinnamon

FISH

- 4 (6-oz.) swordfish steaks (1 inch thick)

SAUCE

- 1 tablespoon olive oil
- 3 garlic cloves, thinly sliced
- 1 cup diced seeded peeled tomatoes
- ½ cup sliced pitted Kalamata olives
- 2 tablespoons capers
- ⅛ teaspoon hot pepper sauce
- ⅛ teaspoon salt
- ⅛ teaspoon freshly ground pepper
- 1 tablespoon chopped fresh mint

1 Place all rub ingredients in blender; blend until coarse paste forms. Rub generously over swordfish; place in shallow glass baking dish. Cover and refrigerate 30 to 60 minutes.

2 Meanwhile, heat 1 tablespoon oil in large saucepan over medium heat until hot. Add 3 garlic cloves; sauté 1 minute or until softened. Increase heat to medium-high. Add tomatoes; cook 4 to 6 minutes or until juices evaporate. Stir in all remaining ingredients except mint; cover and remove from heat. Add mint right before serving.

3 Heat grill; oil grill grate. Place swordfish on gas grill over medium heat or on charcoal grill 4 to 6 inches from medium coals; cover grill. Grill 7 to 9 minutes or until fish just begins to flake. Serve with warm sauce.

4 servings

PER SERVING: 320 calories, 19.5 g total fat (3.5 g saturated fat), 27.5 g protein, 9.5 g carbohydrate, 80 mg cholesterol, 1195 mg sodium, 3 g fiber

Roast Rack of Lamb with Blackberry Crust

A bountiful crop of blackberries inspired Member Pat Goodwin to create this recipe. The sweetness of the berries combines well with the mild flavor of the lamb.

- 2 (1- to 1¼-lb.) racks of lamb, frenched
- ½ teaspoon kosher (coarse) salt
- ½ teaspoon freshly ground pepper
- ¼ cup blackberry preserves
- ¼ cup stone-ground Dijon mustard
- 1 tablespoon lemon juice
- 1 cup fine fresh bread crumbs
- 1½ teaspoons chopped fresh tarragon
- 1 teaspoon butter, melted

1 Heat oven to 425°F. Line rimmed baking sheet with foil. Trim fat well from rack of lamb. Sprinkle lamb with salt and pepper; place on baking sheet.

2 In small bowl, whisk together preserves, mustard and lemon juice. In another small bowl, stir together bread crumbs and tarragon. Spoon mustard mixture over top of lamb; press bread crumb mixture into mustard mixture. Drizzle butter over bread crumbs.

3 Bake 35 to 45 minutes or until bread crumbs are lightly browned and internal temperature reaches 135°F. for medium-rare or until of desired doneness. Let stand 3 to 5 minutes. Cut between bones into chops.

6 servings

PER SERVING: 170 calories, 7 g total fat (2.5 g saturated fat), 12 g protein, 13.5 g carbohydrate, 40 mg cholesterol, 465 mg sodium, .5 g fiber

Slow-Cooked Chicken, Butternut Squash and Wild Rice Stew

Slow-Cooked Chicken, Butternut Squash and Wild Rice Stew

Wild rice imbues this homey, slow-cooker stew with an appealing nuttiness. If you prefer your rice fully open, cook the dish for the longer period of time; the chicken will hold up well during extended cooking. If you can't find boneless, skinless chicken thighs, use bone-in ones but remove the skin.

1½ lb. butternut squash, peeled, cubed (1 inch) (about 3 cups)
1 (8-oz.) pkg. sliced mushrooms
1 cup chopped celery
¾ cup chopped onion
1 large garlic clove, minced
6 boneless skinless chicken thighs, halved
1 cup cubed Canadian bacon, ham or smoked turkey

1 cup wild rice
4 cups lower-sodium chicken broth
1 teaspoon dried thyme
1 teaspoon salt
¼ teaspoon pepper
½ cup crème fraîche or whipping cream
3 tablespoons cornstarch

1 Place squash, mushrooms, celery, onion and garlic in 4- to 5-quart slow cooker. Top with chicken and bacon; sprinkle with rice. Stir in broth, thyme, salt and pepper.

2 Cook 5½ to 6½ hours on low or until rice is almost tender. Increase heat to high. Combine crème fraîche and cornstarch; stir into mixture in slow cooker. Cover and cook on high 30 minutes or until thickened, chicken is no longer pink in center and rice is tender.

6 (1¾-cup) servings

PER SERVING: 395 calories, 14 g total fat (6.5 g saturated fat), 29 g protein, 40.5 g carbohydrate, 80 mg cholesterol, 1175 mg sodium, 4 g fiber

Lamb Chops with Green Olive Tapenade

These chops are stuffed with a delectable green olive tapenade that's simple to prepare and more flavorful than the store-bought varieties. Use mild green olives, such as Picholine from Provence, or regular green olives that have been rinsed. Be sure not to overfill the chops with the tapenade; it's meant to be more of a flavoring than a stuffing. The tapenade also can be used as a spread for crackers or a dip for raw vegetables.

4 lamb rib chops (1½ inches thick)
½ cup Green Olive Tapenade, divided (recipe follows)
2 teaspoons olive oil, divided
½ teaspoon salt
½ teaspoon freshly ground pepper

1 To create a pocket, make small horizontal slit in chops, taking care not to cut past bone. Fill each pocket with 1 teaspoon of the tapenade. (Do not overfill.)
2 Brush chops with 1 teaspoon of the oil; sprinkle with salt and pepper. Heat remaining 1 teaspoon oil in heavy large nonstick skillet over medium-high heat until hot. Add chops, being careful not to overcrowd. Cook 4 to 6 minutes or until browned, turning once. Reduce heat to medium. Cover; cook 4 to 6 minutes or until lamb is pink in center for medium-rare or until of desired doneness, turning once.
3 Place chops on platter; top with remaining tapenade. Cover loosely with foil; let stand 5 minutes.

4 servings

PER SERVING: 385 calories, 27 g total fat (7 g saturated fat), 32.5 g protein, 2.5 g carbohydrate, 105 mg cholesterol, 770 mg sodium, 1.5 g fiber

GREEN OLIVE TAPENADE

3 tablespoons toasted slivered almonds*
1 garlic clove
½ cup pitted green olives, such as Picholine**
2 anchovy fillets
1 tablespoon capers
1 tablespoon extra-virgin olive oil

1 Place almonds in food processor; process until finely ground. Place in small bowl.
2 With food processor running, add garlic; process until chopped. Add olives, anchovies, capers and oil; pulse until very finely chopped (do not overprocess). Add ground almonds; pulse 2 or 3 times to blend. (Tapenade also can be made by hand.)

TIPS

* To toast almonds, place on baking sheet; bake at 375°F. for 4 to 6 minutes or until light golden brown. Cool.
** Remove pits from olives by pressing olives with side of knife until olives split.

Lamb Chops with Green Olive Tapenade

Braised Chicken with Orange and Ginger

Braised Chicken with Orange and Ginger

This easy braise gets its bright flavor from a triple hit of orange in the form of grated peel, juice and chunks of fruit. You can make it ahead and warm it just before serving, or serve it at room temperature.

- 6 bone-in chicken breast halves
- 1 teaspoon salt
- ½ teaspoon pepper
- 3 tablespoons olive oil
- 1 cup chopped onion
- ¼ cup minced fresh ginger
- 2 garlic cloves, minced
- 1 cup orange juice
- 1 cup lower-sodium chicken broth
- 2 tablespoons chopped fresh thyme
- 1 teaspoon dried oregano
- 1 orange, peeled, cut into chunks
- 1 tablespoon grated orange peel

1 Sprinkle chicken with salt and pepper. Heat oil in large skillet over medium-high heat until hot. Cook chicken in batches 5 to 6 minutes or until browned on all sides. Remove chicken.

2 Add onion, ginger and garlic; cook over medium heat 4 minutes or until onion is soft, stirring occasionally. Add orange juice, broth, thyme and oregano; bring to a boil, scraping up any browned bits from bottom of skillet.

3 Return chicken to skillet; reduce heat to medium-low. Cover and simmer 30 minutes or until chicken is no longer pink in center. Stir in orange and orange peel.

6 servings

PER SERVING: 300 calories, 14.5 g total fat (3 g saturated fat), 29 g protein, 13 g carbohydrate, 75 mg cholesterol, 590 mg sodium, 2 g fiber

Moroccan Roast Chicken with Squash and Onions

Roasting squash and small whole onions alongside spice-rubbed chicken makes a deliciously simple dinner. The pan juices are imbued with the taste of cilantro, giving them exceptional flavor. Serve the chicken with couscous.

- 3 cups cubed butternut squash (¾ inch), about 1½ lb.
- 2 cups frozen small whole onions, thawed
- 4 teaspoons extra-virgin olive oil, divided
- ½ teaspoon salt, divided
- ¼ teaspoon freshly ground pepper, divided
- 2 teaspoons honey
- 2 teaspoons lemon juice
- 2 teaspoons paprika
- ½ teaspoon ground cumin
- 1 lb. boneless skinless chicken thighs
- 12 fresh cilantro sprigs
- ¼ cup coarsely chopped fresh cilantro

1 Heat oven to 450°F. Spray large roasting pan with nonstick cooking spray.

2 In large bowl, combine squash, onions, 2 teaspoons of the oil, ¼ teaspoon of the salt and ⅛ teaspoon of the pepper; toss to coat.

3 In small bowl, stir together remaining 2 teaspoons oil, honey and lemon juice until smooth. Stir in paprika, cumin, remaining ¼ teaspoon salt and remaining ⅛ teaspoon pepper. Rub over chicken thighs.

4 Place cilantro sprigs in center of roasting pan; place chicken thighs over cilantro sprigs. Surround chicken with squash mixture. Bake, uncovered, 35 to 40 minutes or until chicken is no longer pink in center, juices run clear and vegetables are tender, turning vegetables twice. Serve sprinkled with chopped cilantro.

4 servings

PER SERVING: 305 calories, 14 g total fat (3.5 g saturated fat), 26 g protein, 21 g carbohydrate, 70 mg cholesterol, 365 mg sodium, 3 g fiber

Chunky Pork and White Bean Chili

This mild chili has a full, deep pork flavor. The beans and marinated pork need to sit overnight, so don't wait until the last minute to start preparing the recipe.

MARINADE

- 2 tablespoons red wine vinegar
- 1 tablespoon minced shallots
- 1 tablespoon ground cumin
- 2 teaspoons salt
- 1 teaspoon chili powder
- 1 teaspoon freshly ground black pepper
- 1 teaspoon packed light brown sugar
- ½ teaspoon cayenne pepper

CHILI

- 3 lb. boneless country-style pork ribs or boneless Boston butt, cut into ¾-inch pieces
- 1 lb. dried white navy beans
- 9 cups reduced-sodium chicken broth, divided
- 2 tablespoons olive oil
- 2 cups chopped onions
- 1 cup deli baked ham, cut into ½-inch pieces
- ¾ cup chopped carrots
- ½ cup chopped celery
- ¾ cup chopped red bell pepper
- 2 tablespoons chopped garlic
- 2 bay leaves
- 1 tablespoon chili powder
- 1 teaspoon dried oregano
- ½ teaspoon cayenne pepper
- 1 cup finely chopped green onions

1 In large resealable plastic bag, combine all marinade ingredients. Add pork; toss to coat with marinade. Seal bag. Refrigerate overnight. Place beans in large bowl; add enough water to cover by 2 inches. Let stand at room temperature overnight.

2 Drain and rinse beans. Place in large heavy pot or Dutch oven; add 6 cups of the broth. Bring to a boil. Reduce heat to medium-low to low; simmer 45 minutes, skimming and discarding any foam that forms.

3 Meanwhile, heat oil in large skillet over medium-high heat until hot. Remove pork from marinade. Cook pork in batches 5 minutes or until browned on all sides. Remove from skillet.

4 To same skillet, add onions, ham, carrots and celery; cook over medium heat 10 minutes or until vegetables are soft, stirring occasionally and scraping up any browned bits from bottom of skillet. Add bell pepper and garlic; cook 2 minutes.

5 After beans have cooked 45 minutes, add vegetable mixture, reserved pork with any accumulated juices, bay leaves, 1 tablespoon chili powder, oregano, ½ teaspoon cayenne pepper and remaining 3 cups broth (beans and meat should be covered by 1 inch liquid). Cook 1¼ hours or until pork and beans are tender. To thicken chili, use potato masher to mash beans to desired consistency. Cook an additional 15 minutes; stir in green onions. (Chili can be made up to 2 days ahead. Cover and refrigerate.)

10 (scant 1½-cup) servings

PER SERVING: 500 calories, 20 g total fat (6.5 g saturated fat), 44 g protein, 36 g carbohydrate, 90 mg cholesterol, 1100 mg sodium, 8.5 g fiber

Moroccan Roast Chicken with Squash and Onions

Short Ribs Jambalaya

While many ingredients in a Louisiana jambalaya are subject to variation, rice is essential. This one-pot dish features tender, boneless short ribs, which imbue the rice with a rich, meaty flavor. The finished jambalaya should be moist but not soupy. Have hot sauce available for those who prefer it spicy.

2	lb. boneless beef short ribs
4	teaspoons Creole or Cajun seasoning
½	teaspoon freshly ground pepper
2	tablespoons vegetable oil
1	onion, chopped
1	green bell pepper, chopped
½	cup chopped celery
2	large garlic cloves, minced

1	(28-oz.) can diced tomatoes, drained
4	cups reduced-sodium beef broth, divided
2	bay leaves
2	teaspoons chopped fresh thyme
2	cups long-grain white rice
8	green onions, thinly sliced
¼	cup chopped fresh parsley

1 Heat oven to 350°F. Cut ribs into 2-inch pieces. In small bowl, stir together Creole seasoning and pepper; sprinkle over ribs.

2 Heat oil in heavy large pot or Dutch oven over medium-high heat until hot. Add ribs in batches; cook 3 to 4 minutes or until browned, turning once. Place on plate.

3 Reduce heat to medium. Add onion, bell pepper, celery and garlic; cook 8 to 10 minutes or until softened, stirring occasionally. Return ribs and any accumulated juices to pot; add tomatoes, 2 cups of the broth, bay leaves and thyme. Increase heat to medium-high; bring to a boil.

4 Cover pot; place in oven. Bake 1½ hours or until meat is tender, stirring halfway through.

5 Remove from oven; return pot to stovetop. Uncover and stir in remaining 2 cups broth; bring to a boil over medium-high heat. Stir in rice, green onions and parsley; cover and return to oven. Bake 30 minutes or until rice is tender and liquid is absorbed. Let stand, covered, 5 minutes.

8 (1½-cup) servings

PER SERVING: 515 calories, 22 g total fat (7.5 g saturated fat), 29.5 g protein, 49.5 g carbohydrate, 90 mg cholesterol, 535 mg sodium, 2.5 g fiber

Short Ribs Jambalaya

Grilled Pork Tenderloin with Sage Butter, Potatoes and Plums

This is a grilled version of a classic Alsatian combination of roasted pork, potatoes and plums. A sage butter topping adds a fresh, rich accent. When choosing wine to pair with the pork, select a fruity Riesling, which will match the sweetness of the dish. Stir-fried cabbage makes a delicious accompaniment.

¾ cup unsalted butter, softened
3 tablespoons minced fresh sage
2 tablespoons minced shallots
½ teaspoon anise seeds, finely crushed*
1¼ teaspoons salt, divided

½ teaspoon freshly ground pepper, divided
2 (1-lb.) pork tenderloins
1½ lb. red new potatoes, unpeeled, quartered
6 medium plums, halved

1 In small bowl, stir together butter, sage, shallots and anise seeds until blended. Stir in ½ teaspoon of the salt and ¼ teaspoon of the pepper. (Butter can be prepared up to 2 days ahead. Cover and refrigerate. Bring to room temperature before using.)

2 Heat grill. Rub each tenderloin with 1 tablespoon of the sage butter; sprinkle each with ¼ teaspoon salt and ⅛ teaspoon pepper. Place potatoes on double thickness of foil or in foil pan. Sprinkle with remaining ¼ teaspoon salt; top with 3 tablespoons of the sage butter. Cover completely with foil to seal.

3 Place tenderloins on gas grill over medium heat or on charcoal grill 4 to 6 inches from medium coals. Place foil-wrapped potatoes on grill next to meat, if room allows; cover grill. Grill pork 15 to 20 minutes or until internal temperature reaches 145°F., turning once. Grill potatoes 20 minutes or until tender, turning once. (To test potatoes for tenderness, punch through foil wrap with knife or cake tester.) Keep potatoes wrapped in foil; warm meat in 200°F. oven while grilling plums.

4 Place plum halves, cut-side down, on grill; cover grill. Grill 8 to 10 minutes or until soft, turning once.

5 Carve pork into thick slices; top with sage butter. Serve with grilled potatoes and plums.

TIP

* Finely crush anise seeds using a mortar and pestle or spice grinder.

6 servings

PER SERVING: 520 calories, 29 g total fat (16.5 g saturated fat), 36.5 g protein, 28 g carbohydrate, 155 mg cholesterol, 570 mg sodium, 4 g fiber

Grilled Pork Tenderloin with Sage Butter, Potatoes and Plums

Indian-Spiced Grilled Chicken

The highly spiced yogurt marinade not only flavors the chicken but also protects the tender meat by forming a crusty, caramelized coating during grilling. If you don't have all these seasonings on hand, you can substitute a good-quality garam masala, an Indian spice mix that contains most of them.

- 1 cup regular or low-fat plain yogurt (do not use nonfat)
- 2 tablespoons lemon juice
- 1 teaspoon ground turmeric
- 1 teaspoon ground cumin
- ¾ teaspoon ground coriander
- ½ teaspoon salt
- ½ teaspoon ground cardamom
- ½ teaspoon ground cinnamon
- ¼ teaspoon ground ginger
- ¼ teaspoon ground cloves
- ½ teaspoon cayenne pepper
- 4 large garlic cloves, minced
- 1 small onion, finely chopped
- 4 boneless skinless chicken breast halves

1 In shallow glass or ceramic baking dish or in resealable plastic bag, stir together yogurt, lemon juice, turmeric, cumin, coriander, salt, cardamom, cinnamon, ginger, cloves and cayenne pepper. Stir in garlic and onion.

2 Place chicken breasts between 2 sheets of plastic wrap; with flat side of meat mallet, pound to flatten chicken to ½ inch. Place chicken in marinade, turning to coat both sides. Refrigerate at least 1 hour or up to 2 hours.

3 Heat grill. Remove chicken from marinade; discard marinade. Oil grill grates. Place chicken on gas grill over medium-high heat or on charcoal grill 4 to 6 inches from medium-high coals; cover grill. Grill 8 to 10 minutes or until no longer pink in center, turning once.

4 servings

PER SERVING: 180 calories, 5 g total fat (2 g saturated fat), 28 g protein, 3.5 g carbohydrate, 75 mg cholesterol, 230 mg sodium, .5 g fiber

Spinach-Mushroom Lasagna

For even more mushroom flavor, add a few dry porcini mushrooms to the sauce.

- 9 lasagna noodles
- 2 tablespoons extra-virgin olive oil
- 1 lb. spinach, stems removed, chopped
- 1½ teaspoons salt
- 1¼ teaspoons freshly ground pepper
- 2 eggs
- 2 lb. ricotta cheese
- ¼ cup (1 oz.) freshly grated Parmigiano-Reggiano cheese
- 2 cups sliced mushrooms
- 1 onion, finely chopped
- 2 garlic cloves, minced
- 1 lb. plum tomatoes, chopped
- ⅓ cup red wine
- 1½ cups (6 oz.) shredded mozzarella cheese

1 Heat oven to 400°F. Grease 13×9-inch pan. Cook lasagna noodles according to package directions.

2 Meanwhile, heat 1 tablespoon of the oil in large skillet over medium heat until hot. Add spinach; cook 5 minutes. Stir in ¼ teaspoon each of the salt and pepper. Set aside.

3 In medium bowl, combine eggs, ricotta and Parmigiano-Reggiano cheeses. Stir in ¾ teaspoon of the salt and ½ teaspoon of the pepper. Set aside.

4 Heat remaining 1 tablespoon oil in large saucepan over medium heat until hot. Add mushrooms, onion and garlic; cook about 5 minutes or until onion is transparent.

5 Reduce heat to low. Add tomatoes, wine, remaining ½ teaspoon each of the salt and pepper; cook 10 minutes or until sauce is slightly thickened.

6 To assemble, arrange 3 cooked lasagna noodles over bottom of greased pan. Spoon and spread ⅓ of ricotta mixture over noodles. Top with ⅓ each of the spinach, sauce and mozzarella. Repeat layers twice. Cover pan with foil.

7 Bake 45 minutes or until hot and lightly browned. Let stand 10 minutes before serving.

12 servings

PER SERVING: 270 calories, 13 g total fat (6.5 g saturated fat), 18 g protein, 20.5 g carbohydrate, 70 mg cholesterol, 600 mg sodium, 2 g fiber

Salads

Apple, Walnut and Blue Cheese Salad

The nuts can be toasted and the vinaigrette prepared a day ahead, making this salad easy to assemble at serving time. Using slightly bitter greens balances the richness of the cheese and sweetness of the apples.

VINAIGRETTE

- ¼ cup vegetable oil
- ¼ cup walnut oil
- ¼ cup cider vinegar
- 2 tablespoons finely chopped shallot
- 1 tablespoon honey Dijon mustard
- ½ teaspoon freshly ground pepper
- ¼ teaspoon salt
- ¼ teaspoon apple pie spice

SALAD

- 12 cups torn slightly bitter greens (such as frisée, escarole and/or curly endive)
- 4 medium Golden Delicious apples, thinly sliced
- ¾ cup chopped toasted walnuts*
- 1 cup (4 oz.) Maytag blue or Roquefort cheese, coarsely crumbled

1 In small bowl, whisk all vinaigrette ingredients until well-blended. (Vinaigrette can be made up to 1 day ahead. Cover and refrigerate. Bring to room temperature and whisk before using.)

2 In large bowl, toss greens with enough vinaigrette to lightly coat. Divide among 8 salad plates, mounding in centers. Arrange apple slices around greens. Sprinkle with walnuts and cheese; drizzle with remaining vinaigrette. Serve immediately.

TIP

* To toast walnuts, spread on baking sheet; bake at 375°F. for 4 to 6 minutes or until lightly browned. Cool.

8 servings

PER SERVING: 295 calories, 25 g total fat (5 g saturated fat), 5.5 g protein, 15.5 g carbohydrate, 10 mg cholesterol, 300 mg sodium, 4 g fiber

Mediterranean Rice and Fennel Salad

Rice salads are ideal for a buffet because they hold their flavor and texture so well and actually taste best at room temperature. This one, full of color and crunch, gets an extra layer of flavor from the basmati rice, a nutty, aromatic grain worth seeking out.

SALAD

- 3 cups cooked basmati rice
- 2 cups frozen corn kernels, blanched*
- 1 large fennel bulb, diced**
- ½ cup chopped fennel fronds
- 1 large red bell pepper, diced
- 1 cup crumbled feta cheese
- ½ cup coarsely chopped pitted Kalamata olives
- ½ cup chopped fresh basil

VINAIGRETTE

- ¼ cup lemon juice
- 3 tablespoons tarragon vinegar or white wine vinegar
- 1½ teaspoons Dijon mustard
- 1½ teaspoons honey
- 1½ teaspoons dried tarragon
- 1 teaspoon grated lemon peel
- ½ teaspoon salt
- ¼ teaspoon pepper
- 6 tablespoons extra-virgin olive oil

1 Toss all salad ingredients in large bowl.

2 Whisk all vinaigrette ingredients except oil in small bowl; whisk in oil. Stir into salad. Serve at room temperature. (Salad can be made 1 day ahead. Cover and refrigerate.)

TIPS

* Place corn in pot of boiling water; return to a boil. Immediately drain; run under cold water to cool.

** Fennel is a vegetable with a bulbous base and long, feathery fronds that look similar to dill. It has a sweet, anise-like flavor.

12 (¾-cup) servings

PER SERVING: 320 calories, 10.5 g total fat (3 g saturated fat), 7 g protein, 49.5 g carbohydrate, 10 mg cholesterol, 855 mg sodium, 2.5 g fiber

Greens with Cherries and Walnuts

Contrasting flavors and textures make this salad irresistibly good. It partners well with a variety of grilled meats and seafood.

VINAIGRETTE

- ¼ cup finely chopped shallots
- ¼ cup white wine vinegar
- 1 tablespoon Dijon mustard
- ¾ teaspoon salt
- ½ teaspoon freshly ground pepper
- ½ cup light or regular olive oil
- 2 tablespoons walnut oil

SALAD

- 16 cups mixed salad greens
- 2 cups fresh cherries, pitted, halved
- 1 cup coarsely chopped toasted walnuts*
- 1 cup (4 oz.) crumbled Maytag blue or other blue-veined cheese

1 In small bowl, whisk together shallots, vinegar, mustard, salt and pepper. Whisk in olive oil and walnut oil until blended. Let stand 15 minutes. (Vinaigrette can be made up to 6 hours ahead.)

2 In large bowl, toss greens with enough vinaigrette to lightly coat. Add cherries and nuts; toss. Sprinkle with cheese.

TIP

* To toast walnuts, spread on baking sheet; bake at 375°F. for 4 to 6 minutes or until lightly browned. Cool.

8 (2-cup) servings

PER SERVING: 340 calories, 31 g total fat (6 g saturated fat), 7.5 g protein, 12.5 g carbohydrate, 10 mg cholesterol, 500 mg sodium, 4 g fiber

Asian Shredded Salad

Asian Shredded Salad

This variation on coleslaw combines many of the flavors of Southeast Asia. It's possible to substitute standard cabbage and chard leaves for the Asian greens. Make the salad a few hours before serving it so the flavors blend.

DRESSING

- ¾ cup mayonnaise
- 2 tablespoons rice vinegar
- 2 teaspoons minced fresh ginger
- 1 teaspoon hot pepper sauce
- ¼ teaspoon salt

SALAD

- 8 cups thinly sliced Chinese (napa) cabbage
- 2½ cups thinly sliced baby pac choi
- 1 cup chopped fresh cilantro
- 1 cup chopped green onions
- ½ cup chopped Thai basil, plus sprigs for garnish
- 2 tablespoons minced crystallized ginger
- ½ cup dry-roasted peanuts or cashews

1 In small bowl, whisk together all dressing ingredients.

2 In large bowl, combine all salad ingredients except peanuts. Pour dressing over salad; toss. Refrigerate 2 to 3 hours. Sprinkle peanuts over salad. Garnish with basil sprigs.

16 (½-cup) servings

PER SERVING: 115 calories, 10.5 g total fat (1.5 g saturated fat), 2 g protein, 4 g carbohydrate, 5 mg cholesterol, 155 mg sodium, 1 g fiber

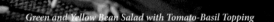

Green and Yellow Bean Salad with Tomato-Basil Topping

Green and Yellow Bean Salad with Tomato-Basil Topping

Make this colorful salad to showcase the first young, tender beans of the season. Basil brings out the flavor of the beans, and tomatoes lend color and a welcome full-bodied taste.

VINAIGRETTE

- ¼ cup fresh lemon juice
- 2 tablespoons finely chopped fresh tarragon
- 1 teaspoon minced garlic
- ½ teaspoon sugar
- ¼ teaspoon salt
- ¼ teaspoon freshly ground pepper
- 1½ teaspoons olive oil
- ½ teaspoon Dijon mustard

SALAD

- ¾ lb. yellow wax beans
- ¾ lb. green beans

TOPPING

- 2 tomatoes, seeded, chopped
- ½ cup chopped fresh basil

1 In small bowl, combine all vinaigrette ingredients; stir until blended. Set aside.

2 Place yellow wax beans and green beans in steamer basket; place basket over boiling water. Cover and steam 8 to 12 minutes or just until beans are tender.

3 Place hot beans in large bowl. Pour vinaigrette over beans; toss well to coat. Let stand at room temperature up to 30 minutes before serving.

4 Meanwhile, combine tomatoes and basil. Just before serving, sprinkle tomato mixture over beans. Serve at room temperature.

8 servings

PER SERVING: 40 calories, 1 g total fat (0 g saturated fat), 1.5 g protein, 8 g carbohydrate, 0 mg cholesterol, 90 mg sodium, 3 g fiber

Spring Herb Salad with Champagne Vinaigrette

Champagne vinegar adds a crisp note to this delicate combination of fresh herbs and greens. Combine the salad and dressing just before serving.

- ¼ cup extra-virgin olive oil
- 1 teaspoon Dijon mustard
- 1 tablespoon minced shallots
- 2 tablespoons champagne vinegar or white wine vinegar
- ¼ teaspoon salt
- ¼ teaspoon freshly ground pepper
- 6 cups torn Boston or Bibb lettuce
- 1 cup fresh Italian parsley leaves
- ½ cup mixed baby greens
- ½ cup fresh chervil sprigs
- ¼ cup coarsely chopped chives

In large bowl, whisk together oil, mustard and shallots. Whisk in vinegar, salt and pepper. Add lettuce, parsley, baby greens, chervil and chives; toss well.

6 servings

PER SERVING: 95 calories, 9.5 g total fat (1.5 g saturated fat), 1 g protein, 2.5 g carbohydrate, 0 mg cholesterol, 125 mg sodium, 1.5 g fiber

Greek Summer Bread Salad

This colorful dish is a version of one of the best-known Greek dishes, the "village salad." The jalapeño and pepperoncini chiles give a pleasant amount of heat to the vegetables, while capers and feta contribute a salty flavor.

½ cup plus 2 tablespoons extra-virgin olive oil, divided
1 garlic clove, crushed
2 (6-inch) pita breads*
⅛ teaspoon salt
2 medium tomatoes, cut into ½-inch pieces
1 cup chopped red onion
1 large green bell pepper, diced
1 medium cucumber, peeled, cut into ½-inch pieces
1 jalapeño chile, veins and seeds removed, very finely chopped

3 pepperoncini, thinly sliced
2 tablespoons capers (preferably large), rinsed, drained
⅔ cup crumbled Greek feta cheese
½ cup Greek anthotyro cheese, fresh myzithra cheese or additional feta cheese**
1 teaspoon freshly ground pepper
1 teaspoon dried basil, divided
1 teaspoon dried oregano, divided
⅓ cup cracked green olives, pitted, halved***

1 Heat 2 tablespoons of the oil in large nonstick skillet over low heat until hot. Add garlic; cook 2 minutes or until it starts to brown. Remove garlic. Increase heat to medium-high. Cook pita breads, one at a time, in skillet 1 to 2 minutes or until golden brown, turning once. Remove from skillet; cool. Cut into bite-sized pieces; place in bottom of large serving bowl. Sprinkle with salt.

2 Layer tomatoes, onion, bell pepper, cucumber, jalapeño, pepperoncini and capers in bowl.

3 In small bowl, stir together feta cheese, anthotyro cheese, pepper, ½ teaspoon of the basil and ½ teaspoon of the oregano. Sprinkle over salad. Top with olives; drizzle with remaining ½ cup oil. Sprinkle with remaining ½ teaspoon basil and ½ teaspoon oregano; toss just before serving.

TIPS

* Look for pita bread without pockets.

** Anthotyro and myzithra are fresh sheep's milk cheeses, similar to Italian ricotta cheese made with sheep's milk. The flavor is distinctive and nutty, and very different from the ricotta cheese widely available in supermarkets. These cheeses can be found in ethnic markets. If they are not available, substitute farmer's cheese or use additional feta cheese.

*** Remove pits from olives by pressing olives with side of knife until olives split.

8 (1¼-cup) servings

PER SERVING: 70 calories, 5 g total fat (3 g saturated fat), 3.5 g protein, 3 g carbohydrate, 15 mg cholesterol, 405 mg sodium, .5 g fiber

Walnut-Endive Salad

A simple mustard vinaigrette accents this salad that combines mixed greens, radicchio and Belgian endive.

¼ cup extra-virgin olive oil
1 tablespoon red wine vinegar
½ tablespoon Dijon mustard
½ teaspoon salt
⅛ teaspoon pepper

4 cups mixed salad greens
1 head Belgium endive, thinly sliced
1 small head radicchio, thinly sliced
⅓ cup chopped toasted walnuts*

Whisk oil, vinegar, mustard, salt and pepper in large bowl. Add all remaining ingredients; toss gently.

TIP

* To toast walnuts, place on baking sheet; bake at 375°F. for 4 to 6 minutes or until pale brown and fragrant. Cool.

6 (½-cup) servings

PER SERVING: 135 calories, 13 g total fat (2 g saturated fat), 2 g protein, 3.5 g carbohydrate, 0 mg cholesterol, 245 mg sodium, 1.8 g fiber

Mixed Greens with Hazelnuts and Goat Cheese

Creamy goat cheese and crunchy hazelnuts grace a salad that's simple yet elegant. The mustard-spiked vinaigrette is a perfectly delicious complement to the mixed greens.

Mixed Greens with Hazelnuts and Goat Cheese

VINAIGRETTE

- 2 tablespoons heavy whipping cream
- 1 tablespoon Dijon mustard
- 1 tablespoon tarragon vinegar
- ¼ teaspoon salt
- ⅛ teaspoon freshly ground pepper
- ⅓ cup canola oil
- 2 tablespoons minced shallots

SALAD

- 2 thin slices red onion, halved
- 9 cups mixed salad greens
- 6 oz. soft goat cheese, crumbled
- ¾ cup toasted skinned hazelnuts, coarsely chopped*

1 In small bowl, whisk together cream, mustard, vinegar, salt and pepper. Whisk in oil; stir in shallots.

2 Soak onion slices in small bowl of ice water 15 minutes. Drain; pat dry.

3 To serve, toss greens in large bowl with enough vinaigrette to lightly coat; divide among 8 salad plates. Arrange onion slices over greens; sprinkle with cheese and hazelnuts.

TIP

* To skin hazelnuts, place nuts on baking sheet. Bake at 350°F. for 7 to 9 minutes or until slightly darker in color and skins begin to crack. Place on kitchen towel; cool slightly. Briskly rub hazelnuts with towel until skins flake off. Some stubborn skins may remain, which is okay.

8 (1-cup) servings

PER SERVING: 240 calories, 23 g total fat (5 g saturated fat), 7 g protein, 5 g carbohydrate, 15 mg cholesterol, 215 mg sodium, 2.5 g fiber

Walnut-Pear Salad with Cranberry Vinaigrette

A really fabulous dressing sets off this lovely harvest salad of pears and cranberries. Cranberry juice gives it a nice sweet-tart character, while walnut oil lends depth and wonderful nutty notes.

VINAIGRETTE

- ¼ cup thawed frozen cranberry juice concentrate
- 3 tablespoons red wine vinegar
- 2 teaspoons Dijon mustard
- ½ teaspoon salt
- ½ teaspoon freshly ground pepper
- 5 tablespoons walnut oil

SALAD

- 12 cups mixed salad greens
- ⅓ cup coarsely chopped walnuts, toasted*
- ¼ cup dried cranberries
- 1 red pear, unpeeled, sliced

1 In small bowl, whisk together all vinaigrette ingredients except oil. Slowly whisk in oil. Let stand at room temperature at least 15 minutes or refrigerate up to 24 hours; bring to room temperature before using.

2 Place all salad ingredients in large bowl. Toss with enough vinaigrette to lightly coat.

TIP

* To toast walnuts, place on baking sheet; bake at 375°F. for 4 to 6 minutes or until pale brown and fragrant. Cool.

8 (1½-cup) servings

PER SERVING: 165 calories, 12 g total fat (1 g saturated fat), 2 g protein, 14.5 g carbohydrate, 0 mg cholesterol, 205 mg sodium, 2.5 g fiber

Fennel, Red Pepper and Pine Nut Salad

Chop all the salad ingredients ahead of time, toss them in a bowl and refrigerate until serving time. When you're ready to eat, simply mix in the dressing and top the salad with the toasted nuts.

DRESSING

- ¼ cup extra-virgin olive oil
- 1 tablespoon red wine vinegar
- 1 tablespoon white balsamic vinegar
- 1½ teaspoons Dijon mustard
- ¼ teaspoon salt
- ¼ teaspoon pepper
- 1 garlic clove, minced

1 Combine all dressing ingredients in small jar; cover and shake to emulsify. (Dressing can be made 1 day ahead. Cover and refrigerate.)

2 Toss all salad ingredients except nuts in large bowl. Toss with dressing; sprinkle with nuts.

SALAD

- 8 oz. romaine lettuce, torn into bite-size pieces (8 cups)
- 1 fennel bulb, sliced
- ½ cup chopped fennel fronds
- 1 large red bell pepper, sliced
- 3 green onions, sliced diagonally
- ½ cup toasted pine nuts*

TIP

*Toast pine nuts in dry skillet over medium heat, stirring constantly, or microwave on high 1 to 3 minutes or until lightly browned.

8 (1¾-cup) servings

PER SERVING: 140 calories, 13 g total fat (1.5 g saturated fat), 2.5 g protein, 6 g carbohydrate, 0 mg cholesterol, 115 mg sodium, 2.5 g fiber

Gorgonzola-Balsamic Greens with Pepper-Glazed Pecans

Sweet, sour, spicy and salty flavors come together in this salad. The peppered pecans and Gorgonzola cheese lend upscale flair to a classic mixed greens salad.

PECANS

- ¼ cup sugar
- ½ teaspoon freshly ground black pepper
- ¼ teaspoon salt
- ⅛ teaspoon cayenne pepper
- 2 tablespoons butter
- 1½ cups pecan halves
- 1 tablespoon balsamic vinegar

1 In medium bowl, stir together sugar, black pepper, ¼ teaspoon salt and cayenne pepper. Melt butter in large skillet over medium heat. Stir in pecans; cook and stir 2 minutes. Add 1 tablespoon balsamic vinegar; cook 1 minute or until vinegar has evaporated. Remove from heat. Add to spice mixture; toss to coat. Cool to room temperature.

SALAD

- 2 tablespoons balsamic vinegar
- 1 teaspoon Dijon mustard
- ¼ teaspoon salt
- 6 tablespoons canola oil
- 12 cups torn mixed salad greens
- 8 oz. Gorgonzola cheese, crumbled

2 In another small bowl, whisk together 2 tablespoons vinegar, mustard and ¼ teaspoon salt. Whisk in oil. Just before serving, in large bowl, toss greens with enough of the vinaigrette to lightly coat. Place on platter. Sprinkle with cheese; top with pecans.

8 (1¼-cup) servings

PER SERVING: 385 calories, 35 g total fat (9 g saturated fat), 9 g protein, 12 g carbohydrate, 30 mg cholesterol, 580 mg sodium, 3.5 g fiber

Red Potato
Salad with
Feta and
Olives

Warm Salad of Greens, Mushrooms and Cambozola Cheese

Cambozola is a wonderfully rich, creamy, blue-veined, triple-crème cheese that marries components of Camembert and Gorgonzola. If you can't find it, substitute another German cheese, such as smoky Bruder Basil, mild Butterkäse or tangy Paladin Bavarian Blue, or use a domestic creamy blue cheese.

- 8 tablespoons olive oil, divided
- 8 oz. mixed sliced mushrooms, such as button, shiitake or crimini (if using shiitake, remove and discard stems)
- ⅓ cup thinly sliced green onions
- ½ teaspoon salt
- ½ teaspoon freshly ground pepper
- 3 tablespoons red wine vinegar
- 10 cups lightly packed mixed greens with arugula
- 4 oz. Cambozola cheese, cut into 8 pieces

1 Heat 4 tablespoons of the oil in medium skillet over medium heat until hot. Add mushrooms and green onions; cook 3 minutes or until lightly softened, stirring frequently. Sprinkle with salt and pepper; stir in remaining 4 tablespoons oil and vinegar. (Mushroom mixture can be made to this point up to 1 hour ahead. Cover and store at room temperature. Reheat before using.)

2 Divide greens among 8 salad plates. With slotted spoon, place warm mushroom mixture on top of greens. Lightly drizzle with oil and vinegar mixture; top with piece of cheese.

8 (1½-cup) servings

PER SERVING: 180 calories, 17 g total fat (4 g saturated fat), 5 g protein, 3.5 g carbohydrate, 10 mg cholesterol, 285 mg sodium, 1.5 g fiber

Red Potato Salad with Feta and Olives

Member Simon Kaplan got this recipe right the first time he tried it. The Greek salad and potato salad combine well, and the mustard gives it a nice bite.

- 3 lb. red potatoes, unpeeled
- 4 oz. feta cheese, crumbled
- ¼ cup pitted Kalamata olives, coarsely chopped
- ¼ cup sliced green onions
- ½ cup mayonnaise
- ¼ cup coarse-ground mustard
- ¼ cup milk
- ¼ teaspoon salt

1 Place potatoes in large pot; add enough water to cover by 1 inch. Bring to a boil over medium-high heat. Reduce heat to medium-low; simmer 18 to 20 minutes or until tender when pierced with knife. Drain; cool.

2 Peel potatoes using small knife. Cut into ¾-inch pieces; place in large bowl. Add cheese, olives and green onions.

3 In medium bowl, whisk together mayonnaise, mustard, milk and salt. Add to potato mixture; stir gently until evenly coated.

16 (½-cup) servings

PER SERVING: 140 calories, 7.5 g total fat (2 g saturated fat), 2.5 g protein, 16.5 g carbohydrate, 10 mg cholesterol, 275 mg sodium, 1.5 g fiber

Warm New Potato and Spring Pea Salad

The bright, springy flavor of tarragon is the first thing you'll notice as you bite into this salad. It's a marvelous accent for the potatoes and peas. Buy the freshest potatoes available; their natural sugars turn to starch as they age, diminishing their flavor.

- 1 lb. tiny red and/or Yukon gold potatoes, unpeeled, halved (if large, cut into 1-inch pieces)
- ½ cup coarsely chopped red onion
- 1 cup fresh shelled or frozen petite peas
- 2 tablespoons tarragon vinegar or white wine vinegar
- 2 teaspoons Dijon mustard
- ⅓ cup extra-virgin olive oil
- 2 tablespoons chopped fresh tarragon
- ½ teaspoon salt
- ½ teaspoon pepper

1 Cook potatoes in large pot of boiling salted water 10 to 12 minutes or until tender. Drain; return to pot, along with onion.

2 Meanwhile, cook peas in small saucepan of boiling salted water 3 to 4 minutes or until tender and bright-green. Drain; cool under cold running water.

3 Whisk vinegar and mustard in small bowl. Slowly whisk in oil, tarragon, salt and pepper.

4 Toss warm potato mixture gently with vinaigrette; stir in peas just before serving. Serve warm or at room temperature.

4 (1-cup) servings

PER SERVING: 285 calories, 18.5 g total fat (2.5 g saturated fat), 4 g protein, 28 g carbohydrate, 0 mg cholesterol, 640 mg sodium, 5 g fiber

Tossed Greens with Balsamic Vinaigrette and Romano Cheese

Pecorino Romano is an aged Italian sheep's milk cheese that lends excellent, sharp flavor to this salad. For an attractive presentation, use a vegetable peeler to shave large curls of the cheese. White balsamic vinegar blends white wine vinegar with the concentrated musts of white grapes. It's made in a similar way to regular balsamic vinegar, but it's not aged in barrels for a long period of time. If necessary, you can substitute white wine vinegar.

VINAIGRETTE

- 1 tablespoon white balsamic vinegar
- ⅛ teaspoon sugar
- ⅛ teaspoon kosher (coarse) salt
  Dash freshly ground pepper
- ¼ cup extra-virgin olive oil

SALAD

- 8 cups packed mixed spring greens (about 10 oz.)
- ½ cup pine nuts, toasted*
- 2 oz. (½ cup) shaved Pecorino Romano cheese

1 In small bowl, whisk together all vinaigrette ingredients except oil. Slowly whisk in oil.

2 In large bowl, toss greens with enough of the vinaigrette to lightly coat. Divide among 8 salad plates; top with pine nuts and cheese.

TIP

* Toast pine nuts in dry skillet over medium heat, stirring constantly, or microwave on high 1 to 3 minutes or until lightly browned.

8 (1-cup) servings

PER SERVING: 155 calories, 14.5 g total fat (2.5 g saturated fat), 4 g protein, 3 g carbohydrate, 5 mg cholesterol, 125 mg sodium, 1.5 g fiber

Warm New Potato and Spring Pea Salad

Roasted Butternut Squash Salad

If there's any squash left over, roast and mash it and use it in soups or muffins. Serve this robust salad as a first course or as a side dish to roast pork or chicken.

SALAD

- 3 cups thickly sliced (½ inch) peeled halved butternut squash
- 1 tablespoon plus 2 teaspoons vegetable oil, divided
- ¼ cup packed brown sugar
- 2 teaspoons water
- ¼ teaspoon freshly ground pepper
- ½ cup walnut halves
- 6 cups torn romaine lettuce
- 1 cup (4 oz.) crumbled Gorgonzola cheese

VINAIGRETTE

- 1 tablespoon port or cranberry juice
- 1 teaspoon balsamic vinegar
- ½ teaspoon Dijon mustard
- ¼ teaspoon dried thyme
- ⅛ teaspoon salt
- ⅛ teaspoon freshly ground pepper
- 1 tablespoon minced shallots
- 2 tablespoons walnut or olive oil

1 Heat oven to 400°F. In shallow 15×10-inch baking pan, toss squash with 2 teaspoons of the vegetable oil. Bake 45 minutes or until golden brown, turning halfway through.

2 In small bowl, whisk together port, balsamic vinegar, mustard, thyme, salt and ⅛ teaspoon pepper; whisk in shallots. Slowly whisk in walnut oil until blended.

3 In medium skillet, stir together remaining 1 tablespoon vegetable oil, brown sugar, water and ¼ teaspoon pepper. Cook over medium heat, without stirring, until mixture is bubbling. Stir in nuts; cook an additional 30 seconds or until nuts are light brown. Turn out onto parchment paper; separate nuts with fork. When cool, break apart.

4 When squash is roasted, in large bowl, toss lettuce with vinaigrette. Place lettuce on serving platter. Top with squash; sprinkle with cheese and candied walnuts. Serve immediately.

6 (1⅓-cup) servings

PER SERVING: 280 calories, 19.5 g total fat (5 g saturated fat), 6.5 g protein, 22.5 g carbohydrate, 20 mg cholesterol, 330 mg sodium, 3.5 g fiber

Roasted Butternut Squash Salad

Bulgur Salad with Pine Nuts and Raisins

Sweet and savory ingredients meet up in a grain-rich salad that pairs well with grilled chicken or lamb. Serve it as is or over slices of grilled eggplant or ripe, juicy tomatoes.

- 1½ cups water
- 1 cup bulgur wheat
- ¼ cup raisins
- 1 teaspoon salt
- 1 teaspoon ground cumin
- ¼ teaspoon ground cinnamon
- ¼ teaspoon saffron threads, crushed
- ¼ teaspoon cayenne pepper
- 1 tablespoon extra-virgin olive oil
- 1 cup chopped fresh Italian parsley
- ½ cup pine nuts
- ¼ cup finely chopped fresh basil

1 Bring water to a boil in large saucepan over high heat. Reduce heat to medium; add bulgur wheat, raisins, salt, cumin, cinnamon, saffron and cayenne pepper. Cook and stir 1 minute.

2 Remove from heat; cover and let stand 15 minutes. Fluff bulgur with fork; place in medium bowl.

3 Refrigerate 30 minutes or until cool. Stir in oil until blended. Gently stir in parsley, pine nuts and basil.

8 (generous ½-cup) servings

PER SERVING: 140 calories, 6.5 g total fat (1 g saturated fat), 4.5 g protein, 19 g carbohydrate, 0 mg cholesterol, 305 mg sodium, 4 g fiber

Corn, Bean and Tomato Salad

A light basil-imbued vinaigrette tops this vegetable-intensive salad. Finish it with grilled chicken or cooked shrimp for a main course.

SALAD

2	medium ears corn
1	cup diagonally halved green beans
3	cups arugula or mixed salad greens
1	cup coarsely chopped fresh Italian parsley
¾	cup grape tomatoes, halved

VINAIGRETTE

1½	tablespoons chopped fresh basil and/or fresh tarragon
1	tablespoon minced shallots
1	tablespoon rice vinegar
¾	teaspoon lemon juice
½	teaspoon Dijon mustard
¼	teaspoon salt
⅛	teaspoon pepper
3	tablespoons extra-virgin olive oil

1 Cook corn in large pot of boiling salted water 10 minutes or until tender, adding beans during last minute. Cool quickly under cold running water. Cut corn kernels off cob (you should have about 1 cup).

2 Whisk all vinaigrette ingredients except oil in small bowl; slowly whisk in oil. Toss arugula and parsley in large bowl with enough vinaigrette to very lightly coat. Toss corn, beans and tomatoes with enough vinaigrette to lightly coat; arrange over greens.

6 (1-cup) servings

PER SERVING: 100 calories, 7 g total fat (1 g saturated fat), 2 g protein, 9 g carbohydrate, 0 mg cholesterol, 205 mg sodium, 2 g fiber

Southern Greens with Hot Bacon Vinaigrette

Any combination of young bitter greens, such as dandelion, collard, watercress or spinach, can be used. Be sure to wash the greens thoroughly; many varieties can be sandy.

8	slices bacon
¼	cup chopped shallots
2	garlic cloves, finely chopped
¼	cup white wine vinegar or champagne vinegar
½	teaspoon freshly ground pepper
1	lb. young greens, such as dandelion, collard or spinach (about 10 cups)*
½	cup toasted pecan halves**

1 Cook bacon in large skillet over medium-high heat 10 minutes or until crisp. Place on paper towels to drain, leaving about ¼ cup drippings in skillet. Coarsely crumble bacon.

2 Add shallots and garlic to skillet. Cook and stir over medium heat 2 minutes or until shallots are just softened. Stir in vinegar and pepper.

3 Place greens in large bowl. Just before serving, toss with enough of the hot vinaigrette to lightly coat greens; toss quickly to mix and barely wilt greens. Divide among 8 serving plates; sprinkle with crumbled bacon and pecans.

TIPS

* Remove stems from greens and discard; coarsely chop greens.

** To toast pecan halves, spread on baking sheet; bake at 375°F. for 4 to 6 minutes or until light golden brown.

8 servings

PER SERVING: 155 calories, 14.5 g total fat (4 g saturated fat), 4.5 g protein, 4 g carbohydrate, 10 mg cholesterol, 145 mg sodium, 2.5 g fiber

Strawberry-Walnut Salad with Warm Goat Cheese

Strawberry-Walnut Salad with Warm Goat Cheese

To get the most kudos at a dinner party, toast the walnuts while the cheese heats and serve both warm. This is truly a sublime marriage!

SALAD

- 2 tablespoons chopped toasted walnuts, ground*
- 4 oz. ash-ripened or plain goat cheese log, cut crosswise into 4 pieces
- 4 cups slightly packed tornBoston or Bibb lettuce
- 1½ cups halved small strawberries
- ½ cup toasted walnut halves*

VINAIGRETTE

- ¼ cup extra-virgin olive oil
- 2 tablespoons lemon juice
- 1 teaspoon walnut oil
- 1 tablespoon minced Italian parsley
- 1 tablespoon grated lemon peel
- ¼ teaspoon salt
- ⅛ teaspoon freshly ground pepper

1 Heat oven to 375°F. Line baking sheet with parchment paper. Place ground walnuts in shallow bowl. Press edges of cheese rounds into nuts, coating all sides. Place on baking sheet; refrigerate until right before serving.

2 In medium bowl, whisk together all vinaigrette ingredients.

3 Immediately before serving, bake cheese 5 minutes or until warm and slightly soft. (Cheese should be warm but still hold its shape.)

4 Meanwhile, in large bowl, toss lettuce with enough vinaigrette to lightly coat. Place on serving platter or individual salad plates. Arrange strawberries and walnut halves around plate over salad. Place cheese rounds on top of salad. Serve immediately.

TIP

*To toast walnuts, spread on baking sheet; bake at 375°F. for 4 to 6 minutes or until lightly browned. Cool. To grind, place in food processor; pulse until finely ground.

4 servings

PER SERVING: 330 calories, 30.5 g total fat (7 g saturated fat), 7 g protein, 10 g carbohydrate, 25 mg cholesterol, 250 mg sodium, 3 g fiber

Summer Salad with Buttermilk-Dill Dressing

Fresh dill combines beautifully with tangy buttermilk in this creamy dressing.

DRESSING

- 6 tablespoons mayonnaise
- ¼ cup buttermilk
- 1 tablespoon finely chopped sweet onion
- 1 tablespoon chopped fresh dill
- ¼ teaspoon salt
  Dash pepper

SALAD

- 5 cups mixed salad greens
- 2 small tomatoes, chopped
- ½ cucumber, halved lengthwise, sliced
- ½ sweet onion, sliced
- 2 tablespoons chopped fresh dill
- ½ cup crumbled blue cheese

1 Blend all dressing ingredients in blender until smooth. (Dressing can be made 1 day ahead. Cover and refrigerate.)

2 Toss greens in large bowl with enough dressing to lightly coat; place on platter. Arrange tomatoes, cucumber, sliced onion and 2 tablespoons dill over greens; sprinkle with cheese. Drizzle with dressing.

4 (2-cup) servings

PER SERVING: 245 calories, 21.5 g total fat (6 g saturated fat), 6 g protein, 8.5 g carbohydrate, 20 mg cholesterol, 540 mg sodium, 2.5 g fiber

Tossed Orange-Walnut Salad with Balsamic Dressing

This leafy green salad is brimming with the bright flavor of fresh citrus and the nutty crunch of toasted walnuts. Mix things up a bit by substituting radicchio for some of the mixed greens or using attractive blood oranges instead of the navel variety.

Tossed Orange-Walnut Salad with Balsamic Dressing

DRESSING

1	tablespoon balsamic vinegar
2	teaspoons grated orange peel
¼	teaspoon salt
⅛	teaspoon freshly ground pepper
2	tablespoons extra-virgin olive oil

SALAD

3	cups torn Boston lettuce
3	cups mixed baby greens
2	navel oranges, cut into segments, segments halved
1	cup walnut halves, toasted*

1 In small bowl, whisk together vinegar, orange peel, salt and pepper. Whisk in oil.

2 In large bowl, combine lettuce and baby greens; toss with enough dressing to lightly coat. Divide among 6 salad plates; top with orange segments and walnuts.

TIP

* To toast walnuts, place on baking sheet; bake at 375°F. for 4 to 6 minutes or until lightly browned. Cool.

8 (1¼-cup) servings

PER SERVING: 135 calories, 11.5 g total fat (1 g saturated fat), 3 g protein, 7 g carbohydrate, 0 mg cholesterol, 80 mg sodium, 2.5 g fiber

Vine-Ripened Tomato and Corn Platter

For all its simplicity, this salad is a winner every time. Try to find the ripest tomatoes around, preferably from a farmers' market or roadside produce stand.

4	ears corn
8	large tomatoes, sliced (¼ inch)
1	small Vidalia onion, halved, thinly sliced
4	green onions, chopped
3	tablespoons extra-virgin olive oil

3	tablespoons balsamic vinegar
1	teaspoon salt
½	teaspoon freshly ground pepper
¾	cup (3 oz.) crumbled feta cheese
¼	cup chopped fresh basil

1 Cook corn in large saucepan of boiling salted water 3 minutes. Place in bowl of ice water to stop cooking. When cool, drain and pat dry. With knife, cut kernels from cobs.

2 Arrange tomato slices on large platter. Top with corn, Vidalia onion and green onions. (Salad can be made to this point up to 3 hours ahead. Cover and refrigerate. Serve at room temperature.)

3 Drizzle salad with oil and vinegar. Sprinkle with salt, pepper, cheese and basil.

12 servings

PER SERVING: 115 calories, 5.5 g total fat (1.5 g saturated fat), 3.5 g protein, 15.5 g carbohydrate, 5 mg cholesterol, 295 mg sodium, 2.5 g fiber

Grilled Corn and Black Bean Salad

Grilling the corn and peppers brings out their natural sweetness and gives this salad a deliciously robust, toasty quality.

 4 large ears sweet corn
 2 large red bell peppers
 ½ cup vegetable oil
 ¼ cup cider vinegar
 2 tablespoons lime juice
 1 teaspoon sugar
 ½ teaspoon kosher (coarse) salt
 2 (15-oz.) cans black beans, drained, rinsed
 ½ cup finely diced sweet onion
 ¼ cup chopped cilantro

1 Heat grill. Remove all but 2 layers of husk from corn; remove silk. Place corn and peppers on gas grill over medium-high heat or on charcoal grill 4 to 6 inches from medium-high coals; cover grill. Grill 15 minutes, turning every 5 minutes to grill all sides. Cool 10 minutes. When cool enough to handle, remove remaining husks from corn; cut off kernels (you should have about 3 cups). Remove skin, veins and seeds from peppers; cut into small dice.

2 In large bowl, whisk together oil, vinegar, lime juice, sugar and salt until blended. Add corn, peppers, beans, onion and cilantro; stir to coat well. Cover and refrigerate at least 30 minutes to allow flavors to blend. (Salad can be made up to 1 day ahead. Cover and refrigerate.)

8 (about 1-cup) servings

PER SERVING: 305 calories, 15 g total fat (2 g saturated fat), 8.5 g protein, 38.5 g carbohydrate, 0 mg cholesterol, 385 mg sodium, 8 g fiber

White Bean Salad

Bean salads in Greece almost always have pungent, raw onions added, usually the red variety. Lemon and parsley give this version a lively taste. And capers, also an island staple, add a pleasant saltiness. Be sure you don't overcook the beans; they should be slightly crunchy, not mushy.

 1 cup dried navy or cannellini beans or
  1 (15- or 19-oz.) can
 1 bay leaf
 ½ cup chopped fresh Italian parsley
 ⅓ cup fresh lemon juice
 3 tablespoons capers, rinsed, drained
 1 medium red onion, finely chopped
 ½ teaspoon cayenne pepper
 ¼ teaspoon salt
 ½ cup extra-virgin olive oil

1 If using dried beans, place beans in large saucepan of cold water. Bring to a boil over medium-high heat; boil 3 minutes. Remove from heat; cover and let stand 1 hour. Drain; return beans to saucepan with enough cold water to cover. Bring to a boil. Add bay leaf. Reduce heat to low; simmer, uncovered, 1 hour or until beans are tender but not mushy. Drain; rinse under cold water. Remove bay leaf. (If using canned beans, drain and rinse with cold water.)

2 In large bowl, stir together beans, parsley, lemon juice, capers, onion, cayenne pepper and salt. Add oil; toss to coat. Let stand 1 hour. Drain slightly before serving. Serve cold or at room temperature. Store in refrigerator.

8 (½-cup) servings

PER SERVING: 215 calories, 14 g total fat (2 g saturated fat), 5.5 g protein, 18 g carbohydrate, 0 mg cholesterol, 165 mg sodium, 4.5 g fiber

Side Dishes

Broccoli Florets with Lemon Crumbs

Lemon peel, shallots and garlic perfume panko—light and airy Japanese bread crumbs—in this crispy topping for broccoli. Slightly toasted fresh white bread crumbs can be substituted for the panko.

10	cups broccoli florets (about 3 lb.)
1	tablespoon butter
1	large shallot, minced
1	large garlic clove, minced
½	cup panko*
2	teaspoons grated lemon peel
½	teaspoon salt, divided
¼	teaspoon pepper, divided
1	tablespoon olive oil
2	tablespoons lemon juice

1 Cook broccoli in large pot of boiling salted water 3 minutes or until crisp-tender. Drain; cool under cold running water. Drain well. (Broccoli can be prepared 8 hours ahead. Cover and refrigerate.)

2 Melt butter in small skillet over medium-low heat. Add shallot and garlic; cook and stir 3 minutes or until softened. Add panko; cook and stir 2 minutes or until panko begins to color. Place in small bowl; stir in lemon peel, ¼ teaspoon of the salt and ⅛ teaspoon of the pepper. (Bread crumbs can be prepared 8 hours ahead. Store at room temperature.)

3 Just before serving, heat oil in large nonstick skillet over medium-high heat until hot. Cook broccoli 4 minutes or until heated through and slightly browned. Sprinkle with remaining ¼ teaspoon salt and ⅛ teaspoon pepper. Stir in lemon juice; sprinkle with bread crumbs.

TIP

* Panko are coarse bread crumbs usually found next to other bread crumbs in the supermarket.

8 (1-cup) servings

PER SERVING: 75 calories, 3.5 g total fat (1 g saturated fat), 3 g protein, 9.5 g carbohydrate, 5 mg cholesterol, 215 mg sodium, 2.5 g fiber

Porcini, Fennel and Apple Stuffing

Be sure to use a firm-textured, flavorful white bread for this stuffing. Day-old bread is best, but if the bread is fresh, tear it into small pieces, spread it on a baking sheet and dry it overnight on the counter.

1	oz. dried porcini mushrooms
1	cup boiling water
6	tablespoons unsalted butter
2	medium onions, chopped
1	small fennel bulb, fronds removed and discarded, bulb chopped
1	medium tart apple, peeled, diced
4	cups cubed day-old hearty white bread
1½	cups quartered whole chestnuts in water (from 7.4-oz. jar or 10-oz. can), drained
2	tablespoons chopped fresh thyme
1	teaspoon salt
½	teaspoon freshly ground pepper

1 Place mushrooms in small bowl; pour in 1 cup boiling water. Let stand 30 minutes or until mushrooms are tender. Drain through cheesecloth-lined sieve into small dish, reserving soaking liquid.

2 Heat oven to 325°F. Melt butter in large pot or Dutch oven over medium-high heat. Add onions and fennel; cook, stirring frequently, 4 minutes or until just softened. Stir in apple and mushrooms; cook 2 minutes or until apples begin to soften. Stir in bread, chestnuts, thyme, salt and pepper; toss to mix well. (If stuffing seems dry, add some of the reserved mushroom liquid.)

3 Reserve about 3 cups stuffing for stuffing Crown Roast of Pork. Spoon remaining stuffing into shallow 6-cup baking dish.* (Stuffing can be made to this point up to 1 day ahead. Cover and refrigerate. Bring to room temperature before using.) Bake, uncovered, 45 to 55 minutes or until hot and lightly browned on top.

TIP

* If not baking stuffing in Crown Roast of Pork, place all stuffing in 9-inch square baking pan and continue as directed in recipe.

8 servings

PER SERVING: 185 calories, 10 g total fat (5.5 g saturated fat), 3 g protein, 23 g carbohydrate, 25 mg cholesterol, 405 mg sodium, 3 g fiber

Buttermilk-Parsley Mashed Potatoes with Bacon

This side dish is a completely new take on traditional mashed potatoes. It's based on the Irish peasant dish colcannon, which is a baked mixture of mashed potatoes and cabbage. In this version, parsley is sautéed with bacon, replacing the cabbage and adding marvelous herb flavor. There's no need to remove all the stems from the parsley; just wash the bunches, cut off most of the stems and pull out any very large stems before chopping.

2½	lb. Yukon Gold potatoes, peeled, cut into 2-inch pieces
1	tablespoon plus 1 teaspoon kosher (coarse) salt, divided
2	teaspoons vegetable oil
4	oz. bacon, diced
2	cups lightly packed very coarsely chopped fresh parsley
½	cup hot water
1	cup chopped green onions
¾	cup buttermilk
¼	cup unsalted butter
¼	teaspoon freshly ground pepper

Buttermilk-Parsley Mashed Potatoes with Bacon

1 Heat oven to 375°F. Butter shallow 2- to 3-quart glass or ceramic baking dish.

2 Place potatoes in large pot with enough cold water to cover; add 1 tablespoon of the salt. Bring to a boil over medium-high heat; boil 15 minutes or until tender. Drain. Reserve pot.

3 Meanwhile, heat oil in large skillet over medium heat until hot. Add bacon; cook until nearly crisp, stirring frequently. Pour off half of the drippings. Add parsley and hot water; cook 5 minutes or until liquid evaporates and parsley is tender. Add green onions; cook 30 seconds.

4 Place buttermilk, butter, remaining 1 teaspoon salt and pepper in same pot used to cook potatoes; bring to a simmer over medium heat. (Buttermilk will look curdled). Add potatoes; mash with potato masher. Stir in parsley mixture.

5 Spread potatoes in baking dish, leaving top uneven so potato peaks brown. (Potatoes can be prepared to this point up to 1 day ahead. Cover and refrigerate. Increase baking time 10 to 15 minutes.) Bake 30 minutes or until browned on edges and peaks.

8 (¾-cup) servings

PER SERVING: 230 calories, 11 g total fat (5.5 g saturated fat), 3 g protein, 28.5 g carbohydrate, 20 mg cholesterol, 740 mg sodium, 3.5 g fiber

Baby Baked Potato Fans

These thinly cut potatoes fan open as they bake. The trick is to use chopsticks as a guide to make sure you don't cut too far through the potatoes. They're easy to prepare, but you may want to purchase a few extra potatoes for cutting practice.

12	small new potatoes
¼	cup olive oil, divided
3	tablespoons butter, melted
1½	tablespoons chopped fresh thyme
½	teaspoon coarse salt
¼	teaspoon pepper

1 Heat oven to 400°F. Tape 2 wooden chopsticks or dowels to cutting board, leaving a space between them the width of the potatoes. Place 1 new potato between chopsticks; thinly slice (⅛ inch) without cutting through bottom. (Chopsticks stop knife from cutting too far.) Rub potato with 1 teaspoon of the oil; place on foil-lined rimmed baking sheet. Repeat with remaining potatoes.

2 Brush potatoes with butter, pressing lightly on potatoes to fan open (be careful not to press too hard). Sprinkle with thyme, salt and pepper. Bake 30 to 40 minutes or until tender and golden brown.

4 servings

PER SERVING: 310 calories, 22.5 g total fat (7.5 g saturated fat), 2.5 g protein, 26.5 g carbohydrate, 25 mg cholesterol, 265 mg sodium, 3.5 g fiber

Butternut Squash with Walnut Crumb Topping

A take-off on the colonial dessert called brown betty, this recipe layers squash, onions, apples and buttered bread crumbs for a marvelous side dish. The walnuts provide a satisfying crunch.

Butternut Squash with Walnut Crumb Topping

1	cup unseasoned dry bread crumbs
½	cup finely chopped walnuts
1	teaspoon dried sage
1	teaspoon salt, divided
¼	teaspoon white pepper, divided
	Dash nutmeg
¼	cup butter, melted
1¼	lb. butternut squash, peeled, halved lengthwise, sliced (⅛ inch) (about 3 cups)
1	large Granny Smith apple, peeled, halved lengthwise, thinly sliced
1	medium onion, halved, thinly sliced
2	tablespoons canola oil

1 Heat oven to 425°F. Spray 9-inch deep-dish pie pan or 2-quart glass or ceramic baking dish with nonstick cooking spray.

2 In medium bowl, stir together bread crumbs, walnuts, sage, ½ teaspoon of the salt, ⅛ teaspoon of the pepper and nutmeg. Add melted butter; stir with fork to blend well. Sprinkle half of the crumb mixture over bottom of pan.

3 In large bowl, toss squash, apple, onion, remaining ½ teaspoon salt and remaining ⅛ teaspoon pepper with oil to coat; spread over crumbs in pan. Top with remaining crumb mixture. Cover pan tightly with foil; bake 40 minutes or until squash is just tender. Remove foil; reduce oven temperature to 350°F. Bake an additional 15 to 20 minutes or until crumbs are well-browned and squash is fork-tender.

8 servings

PER SERVING: 220 calories, 15 g total fat (4 g saturated fat), 3.5 g protein, 20.5 g carbohydrate, 15 mg cholesterol, 450 mg sodium, 2 g fiber

Twice-Baked Potatoes with Butternut Squash

Because potatoes are on the menu at her home at least four times a week, member Eve LaTorre wanted to devise a way to make them a little bit different. Her solution: mashing russets with butternut squash to create a filling for twice-baked potatoes.

1	(2¾-lb.) butternut squash	1	teaspoon salt
4	large russet potatoes	¾	teaspoon dried sage
¼	cup butter	¼	teaspoon pepper

1 Pierce squash all over with knife. Place on microwave-safe plate; cover and microwave on high 10 to 14 minutes or until tender, turning every 5 minutes.

2 Pierce potatoes all over with knife. Place on microwave-safe plate; cover and microwave on high 15 to 20 minutes or until tender, turning every 5 minutes.

3 Cut squash in half lengthwise; remove and discard seeds. Remove cooked squash; place in large bowl (you should have about 2½ cups). Cut potatoes in half; remove flesh, keeping skins intact and reserving. Place flesh in bowl with squash; mash until smooth. Add butter, salt, sage and pepper; mash until blended.

4 Heat broiler. Fill potato skins with squash mixture; broil 6 to 8 minutes or until hot. (Potatoes can be made 1 day ahead. Cover and refrigerate. Heat oven to 350°F.; bake 30 minutes or until hot.)

8 servings

PER SERVING: 220 calories, 6 g total fat (3.5 g saturated fat), 4.5 g protein, 39.5 g carbohydrate, 15 mg cholesterol, 355 mg sodium, 4.5 g fiber

Tomato-Zucchini Gratin

This hearty gratin gets a nice, salty bite from Kalamata olives and crunch from an herb-laced bread crumb topping.

- 1 lb. tomatoes (about 3 medium), seeded, sliced (½ inch)
- 2 small zucchini, thinly sliced
- 1 teaspoon salt, divided
- ¾ cup fresh bread crumbs*
- ½ cup (2 oz.) lightly packed shredded Emmantaler or Gruyère cheese
- 1½ teaspoons herbes de Provence**
- 1½ teaspoons minced garlic
- ⅛ teaspoon freshly ground pepper
- 10 pitted Kalamata olives, quartered
- 5 teaspoons olive oil

1 Heat oven to 425°F. Spray 6-cup gratin or shallow ceramic or glass baking dish with nonstick cooking spray.

2 Arrange tomato and zucchini slices in single layer on paper towel-lined baking sheet. Sprinkle with ¾ teaspoon of the salt. Let stand 10 to 20 minutes. (Vegetables will begin to release moisture.) Pat gently with paper towels to dry.

3 Meanwhile, in medium bowl, toss together bread crumbs, cheese, herbes de Provence, garlic, remaining ¼ teaspoon salt and pepper until well-blended.

4 Layer tomato and zucchini slices alternately in gratin dish; top with olives. Sprinkle with bread crumb mixture; drizzle with oil.

5 Bake 18 to 20 minutes or until bread crumbs are browned and slightly crisp and gratin is heated through. Serve immediately.

TIPS

* To make fresh bread crumbs, tear day-old whole-grain or white bread into pieces; place in food processor. Pulse 30 to 60 seconds or until coarse crumbs form. One bread slice yields about ¾ cup crumbs.

** Herbes de Provence can be found in the spice aisle of the grocery store. If you can't find it, substitute 1½ teaspoons dried basil, marjoram, rosemary, sage and/or thyme.

4 servings

PER SERVING: 170 calories, 12 g total fat (3.5 g saturated fat), 6.5 g protein, 11 g carbohydrate, 15 mg cholesterol, 785 mg sodium, 2 g fiber

Apple and Sausage Dressing

It's much easier and quicker to bake the dressing outside the bird. Plus, when you bake it in a shallow dish, you get a lot more of the prized crusty top.

- 1 lb. bulk pork sausage
- ¼ cup unsalted butter
- 1½ cups coarsely chopped celery with leaves
- 1½ cups coarsely chopped onion
- 1 large tart apple, peeled, coarsely chopped
- ¼ cup coarsely chopped fresh sage
- 2 tablespoons chopped fresh thyme
- ½ teaspoon salt
- ½ teaspoon freshly ground pepper
- 1 cup reduced-sodium chicken broth, divided
- 8 cups cubed day-old hearty bread (¾ inch)

1 Heat oven to 325°F. Heat large skillet over medium-high heat until hot. Add sausage, breaking into small pieces; cook until browned and no longer pink, stirring frequently. Place on paper towel-lined plate.

2 Melt butter in same skillet. Reduce heat to medium. Add celery and onion; cook 4 minutes or until just softened, stirring frequently. Add apple; cook and stir 1 minute. Stir in sage, thyme, salt and pepper. Stir in ½ cup of the broth; cook 1 minute, scraping up any browned bits from bottom of skillet. Add sausage, bread and enough of the remaining ½ cup broth to lightly coat bread.

3 Place in 13 × 9-inch baking pan. (Dressing can be prepared to this point up to 1 day ahead. Cover and refrigerate.) Bake, uncovered, 1 hour or until top is golden brown and crusty.

8 (¾-cup) servings

PER SERVING: 270 calories, 15 g total fat (6.5 g saturated fat), 10 g protein, 25.5 g carbohydrate, 40 mg cholesterol, 640 mg sodium, 4 g fiber

Lemon Cream Scones

These delicate, buttery scones are extremely tender. The key to keeping them that way is to handle the dough as little as possible. Take a cue from the British and serve them with Lemon Cream, a tangy whipped cream reminiscent of clotted cream from Cornwall; or top them with a sweet raspberry jam.

    2¼   cups all-purpose flour
    ⅓   cup plus 2 teaspoons sugar, divided
    1   tablespoon baking powder
    ¼   teaspoon salt
    ½   cup unsalted butter, chilled, cut up
    ¾   cup plus 1 tablespoon whipping cream, divided
    2   egg yolks
    1   tablespoon grated lemon peel
         Lemon Cream (recipe follows)

1 Heat oven to 400°F. Line baking sheet with parchment paper. In large bowl, whisk together flour, ⅓ cup of the sugar, baking powder and salt. With pastry blender or 2 knives, cut in butter until butter is size of blueberries.

2 In small bowl, whisk together ¾ cup of the cream, egg yolks and lemon peel. Pour into flour mixture; stir with fork until evenly moistened. With hands, quickly and gently press together to form dough. On lightly floured surface, pat into 7-inch round 1 inch thick. With 2½-inch round cutter, cut into 8 rounds, pressing together dough scraps as necessary. Place on baking sheet.

3 Lightly brush top of scones with remaining 1 tablespoon cream; sprinkle with remaining 2 teaspoons sugar. Bake 15 to 18 minutes or until toothpick inserted in center comes out clean. Cool on wire rack 10 minutes. Serve warm or at room temperature with Lemon Cream.

8 scones

PER SCONE: 430 calories, 28 g total fat (17 g saturated fat), 5.5 g protein, 40 g carbohydrate, 135 mg cholesterol, 280 mg sodium, 1 g fiber

LEMON CREAM

    ½   cup whipping cream
    1   tablespoon sugar
    ½   cup sour cream
    1   teaspoon grated lemon peel

In medium bowl, beat whipping cream and sugar at medium-high speed until soft peaks form. Fold in sour cream and lemon peel.

Braised Tarragon Carrots

The addition of chopped herbs turns a simple carrot side dish into a fresh-tasting accompaniment for turkey. Other herbs, such as thyme, marjoram or mint, can stand in quite nicely for the tarragon.

    2   lb. baby-cut carrots, halved lengthwise if large
    6   tablespoons reduced-sodium chicken broth
    ¼   cup unsalted butter
    ¼   cup chopped fresh tarragon
    2   tablespoons chopped fresh chives
    ¾   teaspoon salt
    ¼   teaspoon freshly ground pepper

1 Place carrots, broth and butter in medium saucepan. Cover and bring to a boil over medium heat. Reduce heat to medium-low; simmer 12 to 15 minutes or until carrots are just tender.

2 Stir in all remaining ingredients; cover and cook 1 minute.

8 (¾-cup) servings

PER SERVING: 100 calories, 6 g total fat (3.5 g saturated fat), 1.5 g protein, 11.5 g carbohydrate, 15 mg cholesterol, 325 mg sodium, 3.5 g fiber

Braised Tarragon Carrots

Lemon-Garlic Vegetables

The lemon flavor in this dish brightens a rather simple pairing of vegetables, while letting their fresh flavors shine through.

- 1 **lemon**
- 5 **tablespoons butter**
- 1 **tablespoon chopped garlic**
- 1½ **cups baby carrots**
- 1½ **cups red pearl onions, peeled***
- 1½ **cups cauliflower florets**
- 1½ **cups broccoli florets**
- ½ **teaspoon salt**
- ⅛ **teaspoon freshly ground pepper**

1 With vegetable peeler, remove outer layer of peel from lemon, avoiding bitter white pith beneath peel; place peel in small saucepan. Add butter and garlic. Heat over low heat until butter is melted; simmer 5 minutes. (Do not brown butter or garlic; remove from heat occasionally if necessary.) Remove from heat; let stand 15 minutes. Strain; discard lemon peel and garlic. Skim off any foam or particles from surface; let remaining particles settle to bottom. Pour off clear butter, leaving milky residue on bottom. Cover and refrigerate until ready to serve. (Butter can be prepared up to 3 days ahead.)

2 Fill large saucepan half full with water; bring to a boil over medium heat. Add carrots; boil 5 minutes. Add peeled onions; boil 3 minutes. Add cauliflower and broccoli; boil 3 minutes or until vegetables are crisp-tender. Drain thoroughly. Run cold water over vegetables to stop cooking; drain well. (Vegetables can be prepared to this point up to 1 day ahead. Cover and refrigerate.)

3 To serve, melt lemon-garlic butter in large skillet over medium heat. Add vegetables; cook 1 to 2 minutes or until heated through. (If vegetables have been refrigerated, cook 5 minutes or until heated through.) Sprinkle with salt and pepper.

TIP

* To peel pearl onions, place in boiling water and boil 3 minutes. Drain; rinse with cold water to cool. Cut off root end and squeeze opposite end (onion should pop right out of its skin).

6 (scant 1-cup) servings

PER SERVING: 105 calories, 8 g total fat (5 g saturated fat), 2 g protein, 8 g carbohydrate, 20 mg cholesterol, 220 mg sodium, 2.5 g fiber

Cranberry-Port Relish

Cranberry-Port Relish

Thanksgiving would not be complete without this traditional relish. For variation, add nuts, but note that the relish must be eaten right away so the nuts stay crisp.

- 3 **cups fresh or frozen cranberries**
- 1½ **cups tawny port**
- 1¼ **cups sugar**
- 1 **cup golden raisins**
- 1 **medium onion, finely chopped**
- 2 **tablespoons cider vinegar**
- 1 **teaspoon ground ginger**
- 1 **teaspoon cinnamon**
- ½ **teaspoon nutmeg**

1 In large saucepan, combine all ingredients; mix well. Bring to a boil over medium-high heat, stirring occasionally.

2 Reduce heat to medium low; simmer uncovered about 30 minutes or until cranberries have popped and liquid has slightly thickened. Cool to room temperature. Cover and store in refrigerator.

3½ cups

PER 1/4 CUP: 135 calories, 0 g total fat (0 g saturated fat), 5 g protein, 33 g carbohydrate, 0 mg cholesterol, 5 mg sodium, 1.5 g fiber

Crunchy Whole Wheat Parmesan Bread

To make this pull-apart-style loaf, the dough is cut into squares but left intact before it's baked. Parmesan cheese sprinkled over the top provides a savory-salty note in every bite. Make the dough by hand, as instructed, or prepare it in a stand mixer with a paddle or dough hook.

BREAD

- 1¼ cups lukewarm water (85°F. to 95°F.)
- 1 (¼-oz.) pkg. active dry yeast (2¼ teaspoons)
- 1½ cups whole wheat flour
- 2 tablespoons olive oil
- 1½ teaspoons salt
- 1½ cups bread flour, divided
- ¼ cup (1 oz.) freshly shredded Parmesan cheese

TOPPING

- 1 egg white, beaten until foamy
- 1 tablespoon olive oil
- ½ cup (2 oz.) freshly shredded Parmesan cheese

1 Place water in large bowl; sprinkle with yeast. Let stand 30 seconds; stir until blended. Let stand 5 minutes or until yeast is foamy. Stir in whole wheat flour, 2 tablespoons oil and salt until batter is smooth. Slowly stir in 1 cup of the bread flour and ¼ cup cheese to form soft dough. (Dough will be sticky.) Cover; let stand 15 minutes.

2 Turn dough out onto lightly floured surface; knead 8 minutes or until dough is smooth and springy, using additional ½ cup bread flour as needed to keep dough from sticking.

3 Lightly oil clean large bowl. Place dough in bowl; turn to coat with oil. Cover; let rise in warm place 1 hour or until doubled in size. (Or cover and refrigerate at least 2 hours or up to 24 hours.)

4 Gently punch dough down; turn out onto lightly greased baking sheet. With greased hands, shape into 12-inch flat round loaf. Cover with clean towel; let rise in warm place 45 to 60 minutes or until loaf is almost doubled in size.

5 Meanwhile, place oven rack in lower third of oven. Heat oven to 375°F. With sharp knife (dip knife in flour to avoid sticking), cut dough all the way through into 2-inch squares. (Leave loaf whole; do not separate into squares.) Lightly brush top with egg white.

6 Bake 35 minutes or until light brown on top and pale brown on bottom. Brush with 1 tablespoon oil; sprinkle with ½ cup cheese. Bake 5 minutes or until cheese is melted and bottom of bread is light brown. Remove from pan; cool completely on wire rack.

1 (32-piece) loaf

PER PIECE: 65 calories, 2 g total fat (.5 g saturated fat), 2.5 g protein, 9 g carbohydrate, 0 mg cholesterol, 155 mg sodium, 1 g fiber

Spinach- and Feta-Stuffed Whole Wheat Baguettes (top), and Crunchy Whole Wheat Parmesan Bread (bottom)

Spinach- and Feta-Stuffed Whole Wheat Baguettes

Slicing into these baguettes reveals a swirl of spinach, herbs and cheese. Vinegar is added to give the loaves a bit of sourdough flavor. Reduce the heat as soon as the baguettes are placed in the oven to produce crusty bread without overbrowning.

BREAD

- 1½ cups lukewarm water (85°F. to 95°F.)
- 1 (¼-oz.) pkg. active dry yeast (2¼ teaspoons)
- 2 tablespoons sugar
- 2 cups whole wheat flour
- 1 tablespoon white vinegar
- 1 teaspoon salt
- 1½ cups bread flour

FILLING

- 2 tablespoons butter or olive oil
- ½ cup finely chopped onion
- 1 garlic clove, minced
- 1 tablespoon finely chopped parsley
- ½ teaspoon salt
- 2 cups lightly packed fresh baby spinach
- 1 cup (4 oz.) crumbled feta cheese

1 Place water in large bowl; sprinkle with yeast and sugar. Let stand 30 seconds; stir until blended. Let stand 5 minutes or until yeast is foamy. Stir in whole wheat flour, vinegar and 1 teaspoon salt until batter is smooth. Cover; let stand 15 minutes. Slowly stir in 1 cup of the bread flour to form soft dough. (Dough will be sticky.) Cover; let stand 15 minutes.

2 Turn dough out onto lightly floured surface; knead 5 to 10 minutes or until smooth and springy, using additional ½ cup bread flour as needed to keep dough from sticking.

3 Lightly oil clean large bowl. Place dough in bowl; turn to coat with oil. Cover; let rise in warm place 1 hour or until doubled in size. (Or cover and refrigerate at least 2 hours or up to 24 hours.)

4 Meanwhile, melt butter in small skillet over medium heat. Add onion and garlic; cook 2 to 3 minutes or until soft. Remove from heat; stir in parsley and ½ teaspoon salt.

5 Lightly grease baking sheet or line with parchment paper. Turn dough out onto floured surface; divide in half.

Pat or roll each half into 12-inch square. Spread each square with half of the onion mixture; layer with half of the spinach. Sprinkle each with half of the cheese.

6 Tightly roll each dough square into log, enclosing filling. Pinch edges to seal. Place loaves, seam sides down, on baking sheet. Cover with clean towel; let rise in warm place 45 minutes or until doubled in size.

7 Meanwhile, heat oven to 500°F. Spray loaves with water. With sharp knife, make 4 (¼-inch-deep) diagonal cuts in top of each loaf. Place bread in oven; immediately reduce oven temperature to 400°F. Bake 20 to 25 minutes or until lightly browned and bottoms of loaves sound hollow when gently tapped. Remove from pan; cool completely on wire rack.

2 (20-slice) loaves

PER SLICE: 60 calories, 1.5 g total fat (1 g saturated fat), 2 g protein, 9.5 g carbohydrate, 5 mg cholesterol, 135 mg sodium, 1 g fiber

Roasted Potatoes and Sage

A simple side dish can showcase vegetables and herbs from your garden or farmers market.

1½ lb. baby Yukon gold potatoes
1½ tablespoons olive oil
¾ cup fresh sage leaves

¾ teaspoon coarse salt
¼ teaspoon coarsely ground pepper
¼ teaspoon crushed red pepper, if desired

1 In large bowl, toss potatoes with olive oil. Sprinkle with sage leaves, salt, pepper and crushed red pepper.

2 Place on greased rimmed baking sheet; bake at 400°F. for 50 to 60 minutes or until tender.

8 (½-cup) servings

PER SERVING: 90 calories, 2.5 g fat (0.5 g saturated fat), 1.5 g protein, 15 g carbohydrate, 0 mg cholesterol, 155 mg sodium, 2 g fiber

Crispy Onion-Topped Mashed Potatoes

Two types of potatoes are used: Yukon gold for its buttery flavor and golden color, and russet for its fluffiness.

ONIONS

⅓ cup butter
3 tablespoons olive oil
¾ cup chopped onions
¾ cup sliced shallots

POTATOES

1 lb. russet potatoes, peeled, cut into 2-inch pieces
1 lb. Yukon gold potatoes, peeled, cut into 2-inch pieces
1½ teaspoons salt, divided
⅓ to ½ cup whole milk
¼ teaspoon freshly ground pepper

1 Heat butter and oil in medium skillet over medium heat until butter is melted. Stir in onions and shallots; cover and cook 5 minutes or until softened. Remove cover; cook an additional 18 to 20 minutes or until onion mixture is golden brown, stirring occasionally.

2 Strain onion mixture through fine strainer, reserving butter mixture and pressing on onions to extract all liquid. Place on paper towels. Place 1 tablespoon of the onion mixture in small dry nonstick skillet; cook and stir over medium heat 1 to 2 minutes or until very crispy, taking care not to overbrown.

3 Meanwhile, place potatoes in large saucepan; add enough water to cover by 1 inch. Add 1 teaspoon of the salt; bring to a boil over medium heat. Boil gently 20 to 25 minutes or until tender when pierced with fork. Drain well.

4 Bring ⅓ cup of the milk and reserved butter mixture to a simmer in small saucepan over medium heat. Keep warm.

5 Return potatoes to large saucepan; cook over medium to medium-low heat 1 to 2 minutes or until excess moisture has evaporated, shaking pan (potatoes will look dull, not moist).

6 Press potatoes through potato ricer or food mill, or mash using potato masher until no lumps remain. Slowly stir in milk mixture, adding additional warm

milk for creamier texture if desired. Add onion mixture and remaining ½ teaspoon salt and pepper; stir vigorously to fluff. Top with crispy onions.

6 (¾-cup) servings

PER SERVING: 290 calories, 17.5 g total fat (7.5 g saturated fat), 3.5 g protein, 31.5 g carbohydrate, 30 mg cholesterol, 615 mg sodium, 3.5 g fiber

Crispy Onion-Topped Mashed Potatoes

Cranberry-Wild Rice Pilaf

This recipe marries white and wild rice in a classic pilaf-style side dish. It's accented with sweet-tart dried cranberries and zesty lemon. Using basmati rice instead of white rice provides an even nuttier aroma and flavor.

½ cup wild rice
3 tablespoons butter
½ cup thinly sliced green onions
1 cup basmati or long-grain white rice
½ cup dried cranberries
2½ cups reduced-sodium chicken broth
¼ teaspoon salt
¼ teaspoon freshly ground pepper
¼ cup chopped fresh parsley
2 teaspoons grated lemon peel

1 In medium saucepan, bring 2 cups lightly salted water to a boil. Add wild rice; cook, covered, over medium-low heat 30 minutes. Drain; rinse under cold water.

2 Melt butter in large saucepan over medium heat. Add green onions; cook 2 to 3 minutes or until softened. Stir in basmati rice and dried cranberries; cook 3 minutes, stirring occasionally. Stir in wild rice. (Recipe can be made to this point up to 4 hours ahead. Cover and refrigerate.)

3 Add broth, salt and pepper; bring to a boil over high heat. Reduce heat to low; cover and simmer 15 minutes or until rice is tender. Remove from heat; let stand, covered, 5 minutes. Stir in parsley and lemon peel.

8 (½-cup) servings

PER SERVING: 200 calories, 5 g total fat (3 g saturated fat), 5 g protein, 35.5 g carbohydrate, 10 mg cholesterol, 280 mg sodium, 1.5 g fiber

Black Pepper Biscuits

Baking powder biscuits are as Southern as you can get. Flaky and tender, they're at their best served warm or shortly after emerging from a hot oven. This version is spiced up with the addition of lots of cracked pepper.

3 cups all-purpose flour
4 teaspoons sugar
4 teaspoons baking powder
2 teaspoons cracked black pepper*
1 teaspoon salt
½ cup plus 2 tablespoons unsalted butter, chilled, cut up, divided
1 cup cold whole milk

1 Heat oven to 425°F. Line two baking sheets with parchment paper. In large bowl, whisk together flour, sugar, baking powder, pepper and salt. With pastry blender or 2 knives, cut in ½ cup of the butter until mixture resembles coarse crumbs with some pea-sized pieces. Stir in milk just until soft dough forms.

2 On lightly floured surface, pat or gently roll out dough to ¾-inch thickness. With floured biscuit cutter, cut into 2-inch rounds, pushing straight down and pulling up without twisting cutter. Place on baking sheets. Press scraps together to use all the dough.

3 Melt remaining 2 tablespoons butter; brush over tops of biscuits. Bake 10 to 12 minutes or until light golden brown on tops and golden brown on bottoms. Cool briefly on wire rack.

TIP

* Cracked black pepper can be purchased in the spice aisle of the grocery store. To crack your own, place whole peppercorns in heavy resealable plastic bag; seal bag. Pound with flat side of meat mallet until coarsely chopped.

18 biscuits

PER BISCUIT: 155 calories, 7.5 g total fat (4.5 g saturated fat), 3 g protein, 18.5 g carbohydrate, 20 mg cholesterol, 250 mg sodium, .5 g fiber

Old-Fashioned Buttermilk Dinner Rolls

These tender, buttery rolls are the perfect accompaniment to family holiday celebrations. They hold a hint of sweetness and a slight tang of buttermilk. The dough can be made and shaped the day before. For the best flavor, however, bake them right before serving.

        ¾   cup warm water (110°F. to 115°F.), divided
        1   (¼-oz.) pkg. active dry yeast (2¼ teaspoons)
        ½   cup warm buttermilk (110°F. to 115°F.)
        1   egg, room temperature, beaten
        2   tablespoons unsalted butter, melted
        2   tablespoons sugar
        1½ teaspoons salt
3½ to 3¾   cups bread flour

1 Place ¼ cup of the warm water in small bowl; stir in yeast. Let stand 10 minutes or until yeast is dissolved and foamy.

2 Meanwhile, in large bowl, whisk together remaining ½ cup water, buttermilk, egg, butter, sugar and salt. Whisk in yeast mixture to combine. Slowly stir in 3½ cups of the flour, using hands if necessary, until soft dough forms, slowly adding additional ¼ cup flour as necessary to form soft dough that pulls away from sides of bowl.

3 On lightly floured surface, knead dough 7 to 10 minutes or until smooth and elastic. Place dough in lightly buttered large bowl; turn to coat all sides with butter. Cover with plastic wrap and towel; let rise in warm place until doubled in size, about 1 hour.

4 Line baking sheet with parchment paper. Gently punch dough down; turn out onto lightly floured surface. Divide dough in half; cut each half into 8 pieces. Roll each piece into desired shape; place on baking sheet. Spray plastic wrap with nonstick cooking spray; cover rolls. Let rise in warm place 30 to 40 minutes or until doubled in size. (To make ahead, shape rolls, place on baking sheet and cover with greased plastic wrap. Refrigerate 4 hours or overnight. When ready to bake, let stand at room temperature 30 minutes before baking.)

5 Meanwhile, heat oven to 375°F. Bake 17 to 20 minutes or until light golden brown.

16 rolls

PER ROLL: 135 calories, 2 g total fat (1 g saturated fat), 4 g protein, 25 g carbohydrate, 15 mg cholesterol, 235 mg sodium, 1 g fiber

Mashed Potatoes and Apples with Thyme

This contemporary version of mashed potatoes is at once buttery-rich and slightly tangy. Apple is the secret ingredient, adding an elusive nuance to the potatoes. With these full flavors, you don't need gravy.

        2   lb. red potatoes, unpeeled, cut into
            1½-inch pieces (about 6 cups)
        2   medium tart apples, peeled, cut into
            1½-inch pieces
        ½   cup regular or low-fat sour cream, room
            temperature
        3   tablespoons unsalted butter, softened
        1   tablespoon chopped fresh thyme
        ½   teaspoon salt
        ¼   teaspoon freshly ground pepper

1 Cook potatoes in large pot of boiling salted water over medium heat 5 minutes. Add apples; cook 8 to 10 minutes or until potatoes and apples are fork-tender. Drain well. Return to pot; cook and stir over medium heat 30 seconds to slightly dry potatoes and apples.

2 With potato masher or back of large spoon, coarsely mash potatoes and apples. Add sour cream, butter, thyme, salt and pepper; mash until well-blended with a few remaining lumps. (Potatoes can be made up to 1 hour ahead. Keep warm by placing pan over another pan of gently simmering water or reheat in microwave.)

8 (⅔-cup) servings

PER SERVING: 170 calories, 7.5 g total fat (4.5 g saturated fat), 2.5 g protein, 25.5 g carbohydrate, 20 mg cholesterol, 160 mg sodium, 3.5 g fiber

Old-Fashioned Buttermilk Dinner Rolls

Cornmeal Muffins with Pan-Roasted Jalapeños

Deliciously rich and buttery, these muffins are well-suited for serving with savory chili because they're not overly sweet. For an even better texture and more corn flavor, make them with stone-ground cornmeal.

- 1 teaspoon vegetable oil
- 2 jalapeño chiles, seeded, deveined
- 1¼ cups yellow cornmeal
- ¾ cup all-purpose flour
- 2 tablespoons sugar
- 1½ teaspoons baking powder
- ½ teaspoon baking soda
- ½ teaspoon salt
- 2 eggs, beaten
- 1 cup buttermilk
- ½ cup sour cream
- ¼ cup unsalted butter, melted

1 Heat oil in small skillet over medium heat until hot. Add chiles; cook and stir 2 minutes or until softened and beginning to brown. Remove chiles; cool. Finely chop.

2 Heat oven to 400°F. Grease bottoms of 12 muffin cups or line with paper liners. Whisk cornmeal, flour, sugar, baking powder, baking soda and salt in medium bowl until well-blended. Combine all remaining ingredients in large bowl. Stir cornmeal mixture into buttermilk mixture just until dry ingredients are moistened. Gently stir in chiles.

3 Spoon batter into muffin cups. Bake 15 to 18 minutes or until toothpick inserted in center comes out clean. Cool on wire rack 10 minutes; remove from pan. Serve warm or at room temperature.

12 muffins

PER MUFFIN: 165 calories, 7.5 g total fat (4 g saturated fat), 4 g protein, 21 g carbohydrate, 55 mg cholesterol, 250 mg sodium, 1 g fiber

Rainbow Italian Zucchini

Rainbow Italian Zucchini

Here's a great way to use up end-of-summer vegetables.

- 1 medium onion, coarsely chopped
- 2 tablespoons olive oil
- 1 large orange bell pepper, chopped (¾ inch)
- 2 garlic cloves, minced
- 4 medium tomatoes, coarsely chopped
- 1½ lb. zucchini, sliced (¾ inch)
- 2 teaspoons coarse salt
- ¼ teaspoon pepper
- ¼ cup chopped fresh Italian parsley
- 2 tablespoons chopped fresh basil
- 1 tablespoon chopped fresh thyme
- 1 tablespoon chopped fresh oregano

Cook onion in oil in large skillet or wok over medium-high heat 4 to 5 minutes or until softened, stirring frequently. Add bell pepper and garlic; cook 3 to 5 minutes or until pepper is softened. (Do not brown garlic because it can become bitter.) Stir in tomatoes, zucchini, salt and pepper; cover and simmer 6 to 8 minutes or until zucchini is crisp-tender. Stir in all remaining ingredients.

12 (½-cup) servings

PER SERVING: 45 calories, 2.5 g total fat (.5 g saturated fat), 1 g protein, 5.5 g carbohydrate, 0 mg cholesterol, 265 mg sodium, 1.5 g fiber

Giant Golden Popovers

Popovers are deceptively easy to make, so you can serve them any time you're looking for a quick, light bread for breakfast, lunch or dinner.

1 cup whole milk	2 egg whites
¼ teaspoon salt	1 tablespoon butter, melted
1 egg	1 cup all-purpose flour

1 In large bowl, combine milk, salt, egg and egg whites; mix with wire whisk until combined. Whisk in melted butter. Add flour; whisk just until smooth. Do not over-beat. Let batter rest 30 minutes.

2 Meanwhile, place oven rack in lower third of oven; heat to 325°F. Spray 5 cups in popover pan with nonstick cooking spray. Pour batter into sprayed cups.

3 Place on rack in lower third of oven; immediately increase oven temperature to 425°F. Bake 20 minutes.

4 Reduce oven temperature to 325°F.; bake an additional 20 minutes or until golden brown and firm. Make 1-inch slit in side of each popover with sharp knife; bake an additional 5 minutes. Serve warm.

5 popovers

PER POPOVER: 155 calories, 4 g total fat (2.5 g saturated fat), 50 mg cholesterol, 190 mg sodium, 1 g fiber

Sausage-Mushroom-Sage Dressing

This slightly spicy dressing is the perfect complement to the rest of the Thanksgiving menu. If you'd like to tone down the heat a bit, use a milder sausage.

1	cup finely diced bacon (about 5 oz.)
3	cups finely chopped onions
8	oz. button mushrooms, coarsely chopped
8	oz. spicy bulk Italian sausage
3½	cups lightly packed cubed day-old white bread (¾ inch)
1¼	cups reduced-sodium chicken broth, warm
2	eggs, beaten
½	cup chopped fresh parsley
1	tablespoon dried sage
¼	teaspoon salt
¼	teaspoon freshly ground pepper

Sausage-Mushroom-Sage Dressing

1 Heat oven to 350°F. Spray 11×7-inch glass baking dish with nonstick cooking spray. Cook bacon in large skillet over medium heat 5 to 8 minutes or until lightly browned. Add onions; cook 4 to 6 minutes or until soft. Add mushrooms; cook 3 to 4 minutes or until tender. Cool.

2 Heat medium skillet over medium-high heat until hot. Add sausage; cook 5 to 8 minutes or until lightly browned. Cool on paper towel-lined plate.

3 In large bowl, stir together bread, broth and eggs. Add bacon mixture, sausage, parsley, sage, salt and pepper; stir to combine. Spoon into pan; cover with foil. (Dressing can be made to this point up to 1 day ahead. Cover and refrigerate.)

4 Bake 30 to 45 minutes or until heated through. Remove foil during last 10 minutes of baking. (If dressing has been refrigerated, increase baking time by 5 to 10 minutes.)

10 (about ½-cup) servings

PER SERVING: 150 calories, 7.5 g total fat (2.5 g saturated fat), 8.5 g protein, 12.5 g carbohydrate, 60 mg cholesterol, 470 mg sodium, 1.5 g fiber

Roasted Italian Potatoes

Roasted potatoes, with their crispy exterior, are always a welcome side dish. Here, potatoes are accompanied by wedges of fresh fennel, which caramelize and sweeten in the oven. Roasted red peppers complete the dish. Purchased roasted peppers from the pantry are perfect for this dish.

1½	lb. fingerling or small new potatoes, unpeeled
2	medium fennel bulbs, cut into ½-inch wedges*
3	tablespoons extra-virgin olive oil
1	tablespoon chopped fresh thyme
2	teaspoons fennel seeds
2	teaspoons grated lemon peel
1½	teaspoons kosher (coarse) salt
¾	cup roasted red bell peppers, cut into 1-inch pieces

Roasted Italian Potatoes

1 Heat oven to 425°F. Cut potatoes in half lengthwise, or in quarters if large. Place in large bowl, along with fennel and oil; toss to combine.

2 Place thyme, fennel seeds, lemon peel and salt in spice grinder or mortar; grind until finely ground. Add to potato mixture; stir to coat evenly. Spread vegetables in single layer on rimmed baking sheet.

3 Bake 15 minutes; stir with large spatula. Bake an additional 10 minutes or until fennel is soft and potatoes are tender and lightly browned. (Recipe can be prepared to this point up to 2 hours ahead. Keep on baking sheet at room temperature. Baking time may need to be increased by 5 to 10 minutes.) Add peppers to baking sheet; bake 10 minutes or until potatoes are very hot.

TIP

* Fennel is a vegetable with a bulbous base and long, feathery fronds that look similar to dill. It has a sweet, delicate, anise-like flavor. To use fennel, remove the fronds and save for garnish or discard. The bulb can be sliced or chopped.

6 (¾-cup) servings

PER SERVING: 175 calories, 7 g total fat (1 g saturated fat), 3 g protein, 27.5 g carbohydrate, 0 mg cholesterol, 490 mg sodium, 5.5 g fiber

Pepper-Herb Egg Noodles

This side dish is ideal for entertaining because the noodles can be cooked in advance and then quickly reheated and tossed with the fresh herb mixture right before serving.

8	oz. egg noodles	2	tablespoons butter, melted
½	cup chopped fresh parsley	½	teaspoon pepper
½	cup chopped fresh chives	¼	teaspoon salt

1 Cook noodles according to package directions, removing from heat 1 minute before recommended cooking time. Drain and rinse. Place in bowl; cover. When ready to serve, bring saucepan of water to a boil; cook noodles 1 minute to warm. Drain.

2 Toss noodles with all remaining ingredients.

4 (1-cup) servings

PER SERVING: 260 calories, 8 g fat (4.5 g saturated fat), 7 g protein, 38 g carbohydrate, 60 mg cholesterol, 435 mg sodium, 2 g fiber

Summer Tomatoes with Warm Fresh Mozzarella

Zucchini-Olive Bread

Zucchini bread doesn't have to be sweet. This rendition teams the squash with olives and Parmesan cheese. Serve it the same day it's made, as a savory appetizer, a quick bread for brunch or an accompaniment to the main course.

- 2¼ cups all-purpose flour
- ½ cup (2 oz.) freshly shredded Parmesan cheese
- 1 tablespoon baking powder
- 1 tablespoon sugar
- ½ teaspoon salt
- ¼ teaspoon freshly ground pepper
- 3 eggs
- ⅓ cup olive oil
- ¼ cup milk
- 2 cups shredded zucchini (about 2 medium)
- ½ cup coarsely chopped pitted Kalamata olives
- 2 tablespoons minced onion

1 Heat oven to 350°F. Spray 8½x4½-inch loaf pan with nonstick cooking spray. In medium bowl, stir together flour, cheese, baking powder, sugar, salt and pepper until well-combined.

2 In large bowl, whisk together eggs, oil and milk until blended. Stir in zucchini, olives and onion. Stir flour mixture into zucchini mixture just until flour mixture is incorporated (batter will be very stiff). Spoon into pan; pat smooth with fingertips moistened with water.

3 Bake 55 to 60 minutes or until toothpick inserted in center comes out clean. Cool in pan on wire rack 10 minutes; remove from pan. Cool completely on wire rack, about 2 hours.

1 (12-slice) loaf

PER SLICE: 195 calories, 9.5 g total fat (2 g saturated fat), 6 g protein, 21 g carbohydrate, 55 mg cholesterol, 365 mg sodium, 1 g fiber

Summer Tomatoes with Warm Fresh Mozzarella

Enjoy a quintessential summer salad utilizing jewels from your very own garden.

- 3 large tomatoes, thickly sliced
- 1 tablespoon balsamic vinegar
- ¼ cup halved pitted Kalamata olives
- 3 tablespoons chopped fresh basil
- 1 tablespoon chopped fresh marjoram or oregano
- ¼ teaspoon salt
- 4 oz. sliced fresh mozzarella cheese
- 1 teaspoon extra virgin olive oil

1 Heat broiler. Place tomatoes in wide shallow baking dish. Drizzle with vinegar; sprinkle with olives, basil, marjoram and salt. Nestle cheese in between tomato slices; drizzle with oil.

2 Broil 3 to 4 minutes or until cheese is hot and just slightly melted.

6 servings

PER SERVING: 85 calories, 6 g total fat (3 g saturated fat), 4 g protein, 4.5 g carbohydrate, 15 mg cholesterol, 250 mg sodium, 1.5 g fiber

Roasted Cauliflower with Red Pepper Butter

Roasting intensifies and sweetens cauliflower's natural flavor in this appealing dish. A butter flavored with roasted red bell pepper lends richness, while bread crumbs provide a delicious toasted taste and texture.

- ¼ cup unsalted butter, melted
- 2 tablespoons finely chopped purchased roasted red bell pepper (pat dry before chopping)
- ¾ teaspoon paprika
- ¼ teaspoon salt
- ⅛ teaspoon freshly ground pepper
- 1 (1¾-lb.) head cauliflower, cut into florets (about 6 cups)
- ¼ cup unseasoned dry bread crumbs

1 In small bowl, stir together butter and bell pepper. Stir in paprika, salt and pepper until well-blended. (Mixture can be prepared up to 3 days ahead. Cover and refrigerate. Melt butter before using.)

2 Cook cauliflower in large pot of boiling salted water 1 to 3 minutes or until almost crisp-tender. Rinse under cold running water; drain well. In large bowl, toss cauliflower with red pepper butter. Add bread crumbs; toss to coat. (Cauliflower can be prepared to this point up to 2 hours ahead. Cover and refrigerate.)

3 Heat oven to 425°F. Place cauliflower on small rimmed baking sheet; bake 15 minutes or until hot and tender. Stir before serving.

8 (¾-cup) servings

PER SERVING: 85 calories, 6 g total fat (3.5 g saturated fat), 2 g protein, 6.5 g carbohydrate, 15 mg cholesterol, 120 mg sodium, 2 g fiber

Spiced Potato Wedges

A combination of smoked Spanish paprika and ancho chile powder lends sweet smokiness to the potatoes. You also can use the spice mixture as a dry rub for grilled pork, beef or chicken. If you have extra space on the grill, you can use it to cook the potatoes.

- 8 medium russet potatoes, unpeeled, cut into 1-inch wedges
- ⅓ cup vegetable oil
- 1 tablespoon smoked mild Spanish paprika*
- 1 tablespoon ancho chile powder**
- 1 tablespoon kosher (coarse) salt
- 2 teaspoons sugar
- ½ teaspoon ground coriander
- ½ teaspoon ground cumin
- ½ teaspoon ground cinnamon
- ½ teaspoon freshly ground black pepper
- ¼ teaspoon cayenne pepper

Heat oven to 400°F. Place potatoes in large bowl; toss with oil. In small bowl, stir together all remaining ingredients. Sprinkle over potatoes; toss to coat. Place potatoes on 2 rimmed baking sheets. Bake 40 to 45 minutes or until potatoes are tender.

TIPS

* Smoked paprika comes in mild and hot versions and adds a pleasant smoky taste to foods. It can be found in markets carrying foods from Spain or online at www.tienda.com. If you can't find it, substitute regular paprika.

** Regular chili powder may be substituted for ancho chile powder.

8 servings

PER SERVING: 285 calories, 9.5 g total fat (1.5 g saturated fat), 4.5 g protein, 47.5 g carbohydrate, 0 mg cholesterol, 620 mg sodium, 7 g fiber

Roasted Cauliflower with Red Pepper Butter

Rosemary-Sage Biscuits

Don't worry if your biscuits look misshapen before baking. These hearty biscuits with a touch of whole wheat are supposed to look homemade and even a little rough. The sage leaves on top darken during baking but perfume the biscuits and your entire kitchen while they bake. Serve these biscuits with grilled meat or a hearty soup.

  1 cup cake flour
  ¾ cup all-purpose flour
  ¼ cup whole wheat flour
  1 tablespoon baking powder
  2 teaspoons chopped fresh rosemary
  ¼ teaspoon salt
  6 tablespoons unsalted butter, chilled, cut up
  1 egg, beaten
  ⅔ cup whole milk
  6 fresh sage leaves

1 Heat oven to 425°F. Lightly grease baking sheet or line with parchment paper. In large bowl, combine cake flour, all-purpose flour, whole wheat flour, baking powder, rosemary and salt. With pastry blender, cut in butter until butter is size of blueberries.

2 In small bowl, whisk together egg and milk. Add to flour mixture, mixing just until soft dough forms. (Dough will be very moist and sticky.)

3 On floured surface with well-floured hands, knead dough 2 to 3 times to combine. Pat dough to form ¾-inch-thick round. Cut into 6 wedges. Press sage leaf onto top of each wedge. Place on baking sheet.

4 Bake 15 minutes or until light golden brown. Serve warm.

6 servings

PER SERVING: 290 calories, 14 g total fat (8 g saturated fat), 6 g protein, 35.5 g carbohydrate, 70 mg cholesterol, 370 mg sodium, 1.5 g fiber

Roasted Asparagus with Lemon-Tarragon Vinaigrette

Roasted Asparagus with Lemon-Tarragon Vinaigrette

Roasting, a tasty alternative to steaming, brings out the natural sweetness of asparagus.

  20 asparagus spears
  2 tablespoons fresh lemon juice
  2 tablespoons extra-virgin olive oil
  ¼ teaspoon salt
  ¼ teaspoon freshly ground pepper
  2 tablespoons chopped fresh tarragon

1 Heat oven to 450°F. Place asparagus spears in shallow baking dish. Pour lemon juice and oil over asparagus; sprinkle with salt and pepper. Turn asparagus several times to coat.

2 Bake, uncovered, 12 to 18 minutes or until crisp-tender and color has darkened slightly, turning asparagus several times during baking.

3 Sprinkle with tarragon. Serve warm or at room temperature.

4 servings

PER SERVING: 85 calories, 7 g total fat (1 g saturated fat), 2.5 g protein, 4.5 g carbohydrate, 0 mg cholesterol, 150 mg sodium, 1.5 g fiber

Wild Rice Stuffing with Dried Cranberries and Hazelnuts

Brown rice makes a great partner for wild rice because their cooking times are similar. This stuffing is an excellent side dish for roast turkey or roast pork.

2 teaspoons olive oil

2 cups chopped onions

¾ cup chopped celery

1 garlic clove, minced

4 teaspoons chopped fresh thyme or 1 teaspoon dried

¾ cup wild rice, rinsed

¾ cup short-grain brown rice

3 cups reduced-sodium chicken or vegetable broth

1 bay leaf

⅔ cup dried cranberries

¼ cup apple juice or water

½ cup (2 oz.) chopped toasted hazelnuts*

⅓ cup chopped fresh Italian parsley

½ teaspoon salt

¼ teaspoon freshly ground pepper

1 In Dutch oven or large pot, heat oil over medium heat until hot. Add onions and celery; cook 3 to 4 minutes or until softened, stirring frequently. Add garlic and thyme; cook and stir 30 seconds. Add wild rice and brown rice; stir a few seconds. Add broth and bay leaf; bring to a simmer. Reduce heat to low. Cover and simmer 50 minutes or until rice is tender and most of the liquid has been absorbed.

2 Meanwhile, in small microwave-safe bowl, combine cranberries and apple juice. Cover with plastic wrap; poke several holes in plastic wrap to vent. Microwave on high 1 to 2 minutes or until boiling. Let stand until rice is finished cooking.

3 When rice is tender, discard bay leaf. Stir in hazelnuts, parsley, salt, pepper and cranberries with juice; fluff with fork.

TIP

* To toast hazelnuts, spread on baking sheet; bake in 375°F. oven for 4 to 6 minutes or until slightly darker in color and skins begin to crack. Cool.

8 (about ¾-cup) servings

PER SERVING: 250 calories, 7 g total fat (1 g saturated fat), 7.5 g protein, 41 g carbohydrate, 0 mg cholesterol, 345 mg sodium, 4 g fiber

Wild Rice Stuffing with Dried Cranberries and Hazelnuts

Chard, Mushroom and Dill Bread Pudding

This is an ideal side dish for entertaining because it can be baked in advance and then simply reheated before serving. Select a good, chewy artisan loaf of bread (fresh or slightly stale), not one with a fluffy crumb.

6 oz. bacon, diced
1 lb. button mushrooms, sliced
2 large onions, chopped
2 teaspoons kosher (coarse) salt, divided
2 bunches Swiss chard (about 1½ lb.), chopped (½ inch)
6 eggs
2½ cups whole milk
½ cup lightly packed coarsely chopped fresh dill
½ teaspoon freshly ground pepper
1 (1½-lb.) loaf rustic Italian-style bread, cubed (1 inch)

1 Heat oven to 375°F. Spray 13 × 9-inch baking dish with nonstick cooking spray.

2 Cook bacon in large pot over medium heat 6 minutes or until partially cooked but not crisp, stirring frequently. Pour off half of the drippings. Add mushrooms, onions and ½ teaspoon of the salt. Increase heat to medium-high; cook 5 minutes or until mushrooms soften and liquid evaporates, stirring frequently.

3 Stir in chard; cover and cook 2 minutes or until wilted. Drain well, pressing down on vegetable mixture to squeeze out excess liquid.

4 In large bowl, whisk together eggs, milk, dill, pepper and remaining 1½ teaspoons salt until blended. Stir in vegetable mixture; gently fold in bread.

5 Pour mixture into baking dish (don't press down). Bake 50 to 60 minutes or until well-browned and center is firm to the touch. Cool 10 to 15 minutes.

12 (1-cup) servings

PER SERVING: 300 calories, 11 g total fat (4 g saturated fat), 13.5 g protein, 37 g carbohydrate, 120 mg cholesterol, 860 mg sodium, 3.5 g fiber

Yukon Gold Potato Latkes

Matzo meal is the traditional binder for latkes, but you can use all-purpose flour if it isn't available. Serve the latkes with a dollop of applesauce or sour cream. If you make them ahead, store them in a plastic container with paper towels between the layers.

2 lb. Yukon gold potatoes, peeled, quartered
½ medium onion, coarsely chopped
4 green onions, sliced
1 egg, beaten
2 tablespoons matzo meal
1 teaspoon salt
½ teaspoon pepper
Vegetable oil for frying

1 Grate potatoes using food processor; place in large bowl. Add onion and green onions to processor; process until finely chopped. If potatoes have exuded a lot of moisture, place in towel and squeeze out excess moisture. Return potatoes to processor; process until chopped. (Potatoes can be grated and chopped by hand.) Place in large bowl; stir in egg, matzo meal, salt and pepper.

2 Heat ¼ inch oil in large nonstick skillet over medium-high heat until hot. Working in batches of 5 or 6 latkes at a time, place about 2 tablespoons potato mixture per latke in skillet; spread to 3 inches. Cook 4 to 5 minutes or until golden brown, turning once and maintaining heat so oil bubbles around latkes.

3 Drain on paper towel-lined baking sheet. Continue with remaining potato mixture, adding additional oil as needed. Stir in any excess liquid that comes from mixture as it sits. (Latkes can be made 1 day ahead. Cover and refrigerate or freeze. Reheat on baking sheet at 375°F. for 10 minutes, turning once.)

18 (about 3-inch) latkes

PER LATKE: 70 calories, 2.5 g total fat (.5 g saturated fat), 1.5 g protein, 10.5 g carbohydrate, 10 mg cholesterol, 135 mg sodium, 1 g fiber

Desserts

Alpine Chocolate-Cherry Layer Cake

This dark chocolate cake is capped with a mound of snowy white chocolate frosting and layered with a triple-cherry filling made from dried cherries, cherry liqueur and chunky cherry preserves. It's finished with a garnish of chocolate-covered cherries.

CAKE

- 2 cups all-purpose flour
- ¾ cup unsweetened cocoa
- 1¼ teaspoons baking soda
- ¾ teaspoon salt
- ¼ teaspoon baking powder
- ¾ cup unsalted butter, softened
- 1¾ cups sugar
- 3 eggs
- 2 tablespoons kirsch or cherry juice
- 1½ teaspoons vanilla extract
- 1¼ cups hot water

FILLING

- ⅔ cup dried cherries
- 3 to 4 tablespoons kirsch or cherry juice
- 1 cup cherry preserves or jam, preferably Morello or sour cherry

FROSTING

- 4 oz. high-quality white chocolate, chopped
- 1 (8-oz.) pkg. cream cheese, softened
- 1 tablespoon kirsch, if desired
- ¾ to 1 cup powdered sugar, sifted

CHOCOLATE-COVERED CHERRIES

- 12 large maraschino cherries with stems
- 2 oz. bittersweet chocolate (preferably 60% cacao), chopped

1 Heat oven to 350°F. Grease 3 (9-inch) round pans; dust with cocoa, tapping out excess. Whisk flour, cocoa, baking soda, salt and baking powder in medium bowl. Beat butter and sugar in large bowl at medium-high speed 3 to 4 minutes or until light and fluffy. Beat in eggs one at a time until well-blended and fluffy, about 2 minutes. Beat in 2 tablespoons kirsch and vanilla. At low speed, beat in flour mixture alternately with 1¼ cups hot water just until blended, beginning and ending with flour mixture.

2 Divide batter between pans. Bake 20 to 25 minutes or until toothpick inserted in center comes out clean. Cool on wire rack 10 minutes. Invert cakes onto wire rack; cool completely. (Cakes can be made 1 day ahead. Cover and store at room temperature.)

3 Meanwhile, heat dried cherries and 3 tablespoons kirsch in small saucepan over low heat until very warm. Stir in preserves; cook and stir until preserves are melted. Cool completely. If mixture is too thick to spread, stir in additional kirsch 1 teaspoon at a time. (Filling can be made 1 day ahead. Cover and refrigerate. Bring to room temperature before using.)

4 Microwave white chocolate in small microwave-safe bowl on medium 30 to 60 seconds or until almost melted; stir until smooth. Beat cream cheese in large bowl at medium-high speed until smooth and fluffy. At low speed, beat in melted chocolate and 1 tablespoon kirsch. Beat in ¾ cup of the powdered sugar until soft and fluffy, adding additional powdered sugar to reach desired consistency.

5 Drain maraschino cherries; pat dry with paper towels. Microwave bittersweet chocolate in small microwave-safe bowl on medium 30 to 60 seconds or until almost melted; stir until smooth. Holding cherries by the stems, dip halfway into chocolate; place on wire rack. Refrigerate a few minutes to set chocolate.

6 Place 1 cake layer on serving plate or platter; spread with half of the filling. Repeat with second layer and remaining filling. Top with third layer; spread top with frosting. Right before serving, gently press chocolate-covered cherries, stem-side up, around top edge of cake. (Cake can be assembled 4 hours ahead. Cover and refrigerate. Remove from refrigerator 1 hour before serving.)

12 servings

PER SERVING: 620 calories, 25.5 g total fat (15.5 g saturated fat), 7.5 g protein, 92.5 g carbohydrate, 105 mg cholesterol, 380 mg sodium, 4 g fiber

Alpine Chocolate-Cherry Layer Cake

Lemon-Pistachio Baklava

Pistachios are the preferred nuts for baklava in Turkey. Their bright green color makes beautiful baklava, while fresh lemon peel adds a tart balance to the pastry's sweetness.

SYRUP
- 1 cup sugar
- ½ cup water
- 3 tablespoons honey
- 1½ teaspoons grated lemon peel
- 1 tablespoon lemon juice
- ½ teaspoon vanilla extract

FILLING
- 2 cups raw pistachios
- ¼ cup sugar
- 2 teaspoons finely grated lemon peel

PHYLLO
- 1 cup unsalted butter, cut up
- 24 sheets frozen phyllo dough, thawed

1 Combine all syrup ingredients in medium saucepan. Bring to a boil over medium-high heat. Reduce heat to medium or medium-low; gently boil 5 minutes or until slightly thickened. Cool. (Syrup will thicken as it cools.)

2 Place half of the pistachios in food processor; process until finely chopped. Repeat with remaining pistachios. In medium bowl, combine all filling ingredients.

3 Heat butter in microwave-safe measuring cup in microwave on high 40 to 60 seconds or until melted; skim and discard foam off top. Pour clear butter into small cup; discard remaining milky substance at bottom.

4 Heat oven to 350°F. Butter 13 × 9-inch baking pan. Unroll phyllo onto cutting board; cut to 13 × 9 inches. Discard excess phyllo, or reserve for another use. Cover phyllo with large dry towel. Lay 1 phyllo sheet in bottom of pan; brush with butter. Repeat, using 12 phyllo sheets. Evenly sprinkle filling over phyllo. Top with remaining 12 phyllo sheets, brushing each layer with butter.

5 Cut baklava crosswise into 1½-inch strips, cutting all the way to bottom. Cut diagonally to create diamond shapes, or cut into squares. Bake 25 to 30 minutes or until slightly puffed and light golden brown. Place on wire rack; immediately pour cooled syrup over baklava. Cool completely.

About 4 dozen

PER PIECE: 100 calories, 6 g total fat (2.5 g saturated fat), 1.5 g protein, 10.5 g carbohydrate, 10 mg cholesterol, 15 mg sodium, .5 g fiber

White Chocolate-Raspberry Tart

White Chocolate-Raspberry Tart

Member Marilyn Slates made this tart using a modified ganache of white chocolate and mascarpone cheese. She poured the mixture into a crust filled with fresh raspberries, and this simple, decadent dessert was born.

- Purchased dough for 1 (9-inch) single pie crust
- 1 lb. white chocolate, chopped
- ½ cup whipping cream
- ½ cup mascarpone cheese, softened
- 4 cups raspberries, divided

1 Line 9-inch tart pan with removable bottom with dough; trim edges. Bake crust according to package directions for baking unfilled pie crust. Cool completely.

2 Place chocolate in medium bowl. In small saucepan, bring cream just to a boil; pour over chocolate. Stir until melted. Stir in mascarpone cheese.

3 Place 2 cups of the raspberries in crust in single layer. Pour chocolate mixture over berries. Top with remaining 2 cups raspberries. Refrigerate at least 3 hours. Store in refrigerator.

12 servings

PER SERVING: 345 calories, 22.5 g total fat (12.5 g saturated fat), 4 g protein, 33 g carbohydrate, 25 mg cholesterol, 120 mg sodium, 3 g fiber

Tiramisù Walnut Cookies

These crisp coffee-flavored treats are like miniature biscotti with a mocha-walnut filling. Serve them with hot chocolate or rich dark-roasted coffee for dipping. Parchment paper helps in shaping these cookies.

FILLING

½ cup toasted chopped walnuts*
⅓ cup semisweet chocolate chips
¼ cup sugar
1½ teaspoons instant coffee granules
3 tablespoons coffee liqueur or cold strong coffee

COOKIES

¾ cup unsalted butter, melted
1 cup sugar
2 eggs
1 teaspoon vanilla extract
3 cups all-purpose flour
2 teaspoons baking powder
¼ teaspoon salt

GLAZE

6 oz. semisweet chocolate, chopped**

Tiramisù Walnut Cookies

1 Heat oven to 350°F. Line 2 baking sheets with parchment paper. Place walnuts, chocolate chips, ¼ cup sugar and coffee granules in food processor.*** Pulse 20 seconds or until walnuts are finely chopped and chocolate is coarsely chopped. Add liqueur; pulse to combine.

2 In large bowl, beat butter and 1 cup sugar 1½ minutes or until well-blended. Add eggs and vanilla; beat 30 seconds or until combined. In large bowl, whisk together flour, baking powder and salt. Slowly add flour mixture to butter mixture, beating at low speed until soft dough forms.

3 Divide dough into 8 equal pieces. Roll or pat out 1 piece of dough on parchment paper into 12×2-inch strip. Invert onto baking sheet; remove parchment paper. Repeat with 3 pieces of the dough, placing 2 strips on each baking sheet. Evenly spread scant 3 tablespoons filling on each strip to within ½ inch of edge. On parchment paper, pat out remaining 4 pieces dough into 12×2-inch strips. Invert over filling to create 4 logs. Remove parchment paper; press edges together. Bake, one sheet at a time, 17 to 20 minutes or until light golden brown. Place logs on wire rack; cool completely.

4 Meanwhile, place 6 oz. chocolate in large microwave-safe bowl. Microwave on medium 1 to 2 minutes or until melted. Spread chocolate over each log; refrigerate 20 minutes or until set. Cut into ½-inch slices with serrated knife using sawing motion (dip knife in hot water and wipe clean after each slice to keep edges clean).

TIPS

* To toast walnuts, spread on baking sheet; bake at 350°F. for 6 to 8 minutes or until lightly browned. Cool.

** Do not use chocolate chips for the glaze. Chips do not melt well or spread easily.

*** Walnuts and chocolate chips can be chopped by hand and combined with remaining filling ingredients in small bowl.

About 6 dozen cookies

PER COOKIE: 75 calories, 3.5 g total fat (2 g saturated fat), 1 g protein, 10 g carbohydrate, 10 mg cholesterol, 25 mg sodium, .5 g fiber

Chocolate Crunch Mousse Cake

If this cake's smooth, creamy chocolate mousse doesn't win you over, the crunchy crust and garnish will. Chopped walnuts and crisped rice cereal are coated with melted bittersweet chocolate. Part of the mixture becomes the crust, while the remainder is thinly spread on a baking sheet and allowed to chill until hardened. It's then broken into chunks for garnishing the cake.

CRUST & GARNISH

- 5 oz. bittersweet or semisweet chocolate, chopped
- 1 cup crisped rice cereal
- ⅓ cup finely chopped walnuts (size of rice cereal)

MOUSSE

- 9 oz. bittersweet or semisweet chocolate (not more than 62% cacao content), chopped
- ½ cup unsalted butter, cut up
- 4 eggs
- ¼ cup sugar

TOPPING

- ½ cup whipping cream
- 2 teaspoons sugar

1 Line bottom of 8-inch springform pan with parchment paper. Melt 5 oz. chocolate in medium heatproof bowl set over saucepan filled with 1 inch almost simmering water (bowl should not touch water). Stir frequently until almost melted. Remove from heat; stir until melted. Stir in cereal and nuts until completely coated.

2 Drop about 14 tablespoons of the mixture over bottom of pan; carefully spread into thin layer. Spread remaining mixture over parchment-lined baking sheet into thin layer. Refrigerate until hardened.

3 Meanwhile, melt 9 oz. chocolate and butter in large heatproof bowl set over saucepan filled with 1 inch almost simmering water (bowl should not touch water). Stir frequently until almost melted. Remove from heat; stir until melted.

4 Whisk eggs and ¼ cup sugar in large heatproof bowl until well-blended. Whisk in ¼ cup water. Place bowl in skillet of barely simmering water; whisk constantly until mixture reaches 160°F., 2 to 4 minutes. Remove bowl.

5 Beat egg mixture at high speed 3 to 4 minutes or until it resembles softly whipped cream. Fold one-fourth of the mixture into chocolate. Fold in half of the remaining mixture until nearly blended. Fold in remaining mixture just until blended. Spread over crust. Refrigerate overnight or until firm.

6 Beat cream and 2 teaspoons sugar in medium bowl at medium-high speed until firm but not stiff peaks form; spread over mousse. Run thin knife or spatula around side of pan to loosen cake; remove pan sides. Break refrigerated chocolate mixture into large pieces and garnish cake. Store in refrigerator.

8 servings

PER SERVING: 490 calories, 39.5 g total fat (22 g saturated fat), 7.5 g protein, 37.5 g carbohydrate, 155 mg cholesterol, 45 mg sodium, 4.5 g fiber

Chocolate Crunch Mousse Cake

Strawberry-Chocolate Meringues

This is an easy dessert because the meringues can be made ahead. The weight of the chocolate causes the meringues to fall slightly after baking, making them dense and delicious.

MERINGUES

- 1¼ **cups sugar**
- ¼ **cup Dutch-process cocoa**
- 3 **egg whites, room temperature**
- ½ **teaspoon cream of tartar**
- ¼ **teaspoon salt**

1 Place 2 baking racks in center of oven. Heat oven to 250°F. Line 2 baking sheets with parchment paper. For ease in piping meringues, draw 12 (3-inch) circles on parchment paper. Turn over and place on baking sheet. In medium bowl, whisk sugar and ¼ cup cocoa until blended. In large bowl, beat egg whites at medium-low speed until foamy. Add cream of tartar and salt. Increase speed to medium-high; beat 2½ minutes or until stiff but moist peaks form. Continue beating while adding cocoa mixture in steady stream; beat until incorporated. (Meringue may be slightly deflated but should still be stiff.)

2 Spoon meringue into pastry bag with large star tip. Pipe onto baking sheets to form 12 (3-inch) rounds. Bake 60 minutes or until firm, rotating baking sheets halfway through baking. Turn oven off; let meringues stand in oven until completely cool, at least 2 hours or overnight. (Meringues can be made up to 1 week ahead. Store in airtight container in dry place.)

STRAWBERRIES

- 4 **cups sliced strawberries**
- ¼ **cup plus 2 tablespoons sugar, divided**
- 1 **teaspoon lemon juice**
- 1¼ **cups whipping cream**
  Dutch-process cocoa for dusting

3 In medium bowl, stir together strawberries, ¼ cup of the sugar and lemon juice. Let stand 1 hour or until sugar has dissolved and strawberries are juicy. In large bowl, beat whipping cream and remaining 2 tablespoons sugar at medium-high speed until soft peaks form. Store in refrigerator.

4 To serve, place 1 meringue round on dessert plate. Top with one-sixth of the strawberry mixture and one-sixth of the whipped cream. Top with second meringue round; sprinkle with unsweetened cocoa. Repeat to make 5 additional meringues. Refrigerate any leftover assembled meringues.

6 servings

PER SERVING: 405 calories, 16.5 g total fat (10 g saturated fat), 4.5 g protein, 66 g carbohydrate, 55 mg cholesterol, 145 mg sodium, 4 g fiber

Strawberry-Chocolate Meringues

Three-Berry Cobbler

Three-Berry Cobbler

A craving for berries spurred life member Carolyn Diesen to develop this recipe. "I'm a fiend for raspberries and was trying to come up with some kind of dessert," she says. "All the berries at the store looked good so I picked up three kinds." Serve the cobbler with vanilla ice cream.

2	cups fresh blueberries
3	cups fresh raspberries
3	cups fresh blackberries
¾	cup sugar, divided
1	tablespoon lemon juice
1	teaspoon grated lemon peel
2	cups all-purpose flour
2	teaspoons baking powder
¼	teaspoon salt
½	cup butter, chilled, cut up
1	egg, lightly beaten
½	cup milk

1 Heat oven to 425°F. Spray 13 × 9-inch glass baking dish with cooking spray. Combine berries, ½ cup of the sugar, lemon juice and lemon peel in large bowl; pour into baking dish.
2 Whisk flour, remaining ¼ cup sugar, baking powder and salt in medium bowl. With pastry blender or two knives, cut in butter until mixture resembles coarse crumbs with some pea-sized pieces. Combine egg and milk; stir into flour mixture until just moistened. Spoon over berries in small mounds.
3 Bake 35 to 40 minutes or until golden brown and juices bubble in center. (If browning too quickly, cover with foil during last 5 to 10 minutes.) Serve warm.

12 servings

PER SERVING: 250 calories, 9 g total fat (5 g saturated fat), 4 g protein, 40 g carbohydrate, 40 mg cholesterol, 195 mg sodium, 5 g fiber

Chocolate Truffle Tart

This dessert takes all the elements of chocolate truffles and transforms them into a rich tart with a chocolate pastry crust. If you prefer a less sweet chocolate, use bittersweet in place of the semisweet, or use a combination of the two. Serve slices lightly dusted with cocoa powder and topped with softly whipped cream.

CRUST

¾	cup all-purpose flour
½	cup powdered sugar
¼	cup Dutch-processed cocoa
⅛	teaspoon salt
6	tablespoons unsalted butter, chilled, cut up
1	egg white
½	teaspoon vanilla extract

FILLING

12	oz. semisweet or bittersweet chocolate, coarsely chopped
1¼	cups whipping cream
2	tablespoons orange-flavored liqueur, if desired

1 In medium bowl, whisk together flour, powdered sugar, cocoa and salt. With pastry blender or 2 knives, cut in butter until mixture resembles coarse crumbs with some pea-sized pieces. In small bowl, beat egg white and vanilla until blended. Add to flour mixture; stir until dough begins to form. (Dough may be sticky.) Shape into flat round. Cover and refrigerate at least 30 minutes or up to 1 day.
2 Press dough evenly into 9-inch tart pan with removable bottom; poke bottom with fork every 2 inches. Freeze 20 minutes or until ready to bake.
3 Meanwhile, heat oven to 375°F. Bake crust 15 to 20 minutes or until dry to the touch and slightly springy when touched. If pastry begins to puff, poke lightly with fork. Cool completely on wire rack.
4 Place chocolate in medium bowl. In small saucepan, bring cream to a boil over medium heat; immediately pour over chocolate. Let stand 3 minutes to soften; stir until smooth. Stir in liqueur. Pour into crust. Refrigerate at least 4 hours or overnight. Store in refrigerator.

12 servings

PER SERVING: 320 calories, 22.5 g total fat (13.5 g saturated fat), 3.5 g protein, 31.5 g carbohydrate, 45 mg cholesterol, 40 mg sodium, 2.5 g fiber

Sour Cream-Chocolate Chip Cake

This moist yellow cake packs a triple helping of chocolate chips. Bittersweet chocolate chips have a higher cocoa content and less sugar than semisweet chips, resulting in an extra-chocolaty glaze; look for the Ghirardelli brand.

CAKE

3	cups cake flour
1	teaspoon baking powder
½	teaspoon baking soda
½	teaspoon salt
3	eggs
2	cups sugar
1	cup canola oil
2	teaspoons vanilla extract
1	cup sour cream
1½	cups semisweet chocolate chips

GLAZE

⅓	cup heavy whipping cream
¼	cup unsalted butter, cut up
2	tablespoons corn syrup
1	cup bittersweet chocolate chips

GARNISH

2	cups semisweet chocolate chips

1 Heat oven to 350°F. Spray 9½- or 10-inch tube pan with fixed bottom and 3¾-inch-high sides with nonstick cooking spray. Line bottom with parchment paper; spray paper.

2 In medium bowl, whisk together flour, baking powder, baking soda and salt until blended.

3 In large bowl, beat eggs and sugar at medium speed 2 minutes or until thick, fluffy and lightened in color. Beat in oil and vanilla at low speed until blended. Beat in flour mixture just until blended. Beat in sour cream until blended. Stir in 1½ cups semisweet chocolate chips. Spoon batter into pan.

4 Bake 55 to 60 minutes or until wooden skewer inserted in center comes out clean or with just a few crumbs attached. (If toothpick penetrates chocolate chip, test another spot.)

5 Cool in pan on wire rack 15 minutes. Invert cake onto wire rack; remove parchment. Leave bottom-side up for glazing; cool completely.

6 Meanwhile, heat cream, butter and corn syrup in medium saucepan over medium heat 2 to 3 minutes or until butter melts and mixture is hot. Remove from heat; add bittersweet chocolate chips. Let stand 1 minute. Stir until chocolate melts and glaze is smooth. Let stand at room temperature until slightly thickened.

7 With small spatula, spread glaze over top and sides of cake. Let stand 30 minutes or until glaze is set. Press 2 cups semisweet chocolate chips onto sides of cake. (Cake can be made up to 1 day ahead. Cover and store at room temperature.)

16 servings

PER SERVING: 630 calories, 36.5 g total fat (14.5 g saturated fat), 6 g protein, 78 g carbohydrate, 65 mg cholesterol, 170 mg sodium, 3 g fiber

Sour Cream-Chocolate Chip Cake

Strawberry-Orange Whipped Cream Cake

This four-layer cake, dressed with orange-accented whipped cream and whole strawberries, makes an impressive dessert for any occasion. To ensure that the cake layers rise as high as possible, take care when folding in the beaten egg whites. Overfolding can cause the whites to deflate, leading to thinner layers.

Strawberry-Orange Whipped Cream Cake

CAKE

2¾	cups cake flour
2	teaspoons baking powder
½	teaspoon salt
¾	cup unsalted butter, softened
2	cups sugar
2	teaspoons grated orange peel
1	teaspoon vanilla extract
1½	cups whole milk
6	egg whites

FILLING AND TOPPING

1½	pints (3 cups) strawberries, sliced (about 2 cups)
⅓	cup plus 1 tablespoon sugar, divided
3½	cups heavy whipping cream
1	tablespoon orange-flavored liqueur or orange juice
2	teaspoons grated orange peel
1	teaspoon vanilla extract
12	whole strawberries

1 Heat oven to 350°F. Spray bottom and sides of 2 (9 × 2-inch) round pans with nonstick cooking spray. Line bottoms of pans with parchment paper. Spray parchment; sprinkle with flour.

2 In medium bowl, stir together cake flour, baking powder and salt. In large bowl, beat butter, 2 cups sugar and 2 teaspoons orange peel at medium speed 5 minutes or until light, creamy and fluffy. Beat in 1 teaspoon vanilla until combined. At low speed, beat in flour mixture in 3 parts alternately with milk, beginning and ending with flour mixture.

3 In another large bowl, beat egg whites at medium speed 1 to 3 minutes or until soft peaks form. Stir one-fourth of the beaten egg whites into batter. Carefully fold in remaining egg whites.

4 Divide batter evenly between pans. Bake 30 to 35 minutes or until golden brown and toothpick inserted in center comes out clean. Cool on wire rack 10 minutes. Invert cakes onto wire rack; remove parchment. Cool completely.

5 In small bowl, stir together strawberries and 1 tablespoon of the sugar; let stand 30 minutes. Drain any accumulated juices from strawberries.

6 In another large bowl, beat cream, remaining ⅓ cup sugar, orange liqueur, 2 teaspoons orange peel and 1 teaspoon vanilla at medium-high speed until firm but not stiff peaks form. Reserve 3 cups of the whipped cream to frost cake. Gently fold sliced strawberries into remaining whipped cream.

7 Cut cake layers in half horizontally. Place 1 cake layer, bottom side down, on platter. Spread with about 1½ cups of the whipped cream with strawberries. Repeat with second and third cake layers. Top with fourth layer, top side up. Spread reserved whipped cream over top and sides of cake. (Cake can be made to this point up to 1 day ahead.) Arrange whole strawberries over top before serving. Cover and store in refrigerator.

12 servings

PER SERVING: 655 calories, 38.5 g total fat (24 g saturated fat), 7 g protein, 72 g carbohydrate, 130 mg cholesterol, 250 mg sodium, 1.5 g fiber

Banana Bread Pudding with Maple Sauce

Rich, creamy and decadent, this bread pudding is reminiscent of French toast. It can be served as a dessert or as a main dish for brunch. Be careful not to overbake the pudding; if it puffs up too much, the custard will begin to separate and become watery.

BREAD PUDDING

- 3½ cups whole milk
- ½ cup mashed ripe banana (1 medium brown-speckled banana)
- ¾ cup plus 1½ tablespoons sugar, divided
- 5 eggs
- 2 teaspoons vanilla extract
- 1 (12-oz.) loaf challah, brioche or other rich egg bread, cut into ¾-inch cubes (about 12 cups)
- 2 cups sliced ripe but firm bananas (3 to 4 yellow bananas without brown spots)

SAUCE

- ½ cup pure maple syrup
- ¼ cup unsalted butter
- ¼ cup packed brown sugar

1 Butter 13×9-inch glass or ceramic baking dish. In large bowl, whisk milk, mashed banana, ¾ cup of the sugar, eggs and vanilla until well-blended. Arrange half of the bread in bottom of baking dish; top with sliced bananas. Pour half of the milk mixture over bananas. Top with remaining bread; pour remaining milk mixture over bread. Let stand 30 minutes to moisten bread.

2 Meanwhile, heat oven to 325°F. Bake bread pudding 25 minutes. Sprinkle remaining 1½ tablespoons sugar evenly over pudding. Bake an additional 20 to 25 minutes or until edges have started to puff and are golden brown. Center should move slightly when baking dish is shaken but should not ripple as if liquid. Let stand 20 to 30 minutes to cool slightly.

3 Meanwhile, place all sauce ingredients in small saucepan. Simmer over medium-low heat 4 to 5 minutes or until sugar has dissolved and sauce has thickened, whisking occasionally. Serve hot sauce over warm pudding.

12 servings

PER SERVING: 335 calories, 10 g total fat (5 g saturated fat), 8 g protein, 54 g carbohydrate, 120 mg cholesterol, 115 mg sodium, 1 g fiber

Banana Bread Pudding with Maple Sauce

Chocolate-Raspberry Cake

As if a fudgy, chocolate-intense dessert weren't enough, this cake goes one better by incorporating a puree of fresh raspberries. The resulting flavor will intoxicate your taste buds.

CAKE

2	cups fresh raspberries
1⅔	cups sugar, divided
10	oz. semisweet chocolate, chopped
¾	cup unsalted butter, cut up
5	eggs
1	cup all-purpose flour
½	teaspoon salt

CAKE

½	cup whipping cream
1	teaspoon powdered sugar
1	teaspoon raspberry flavoring syrup

GARNISH

Powdered sugar

2 cups fresh raspberries

Chocolate-Raspberry Cake

1 Heat oven to 350°F. Spray bottom of 9-inch springform pan with cooking spray; line with parchment paper. Spray paper.

2 Puree 2 cups raspberries in blender or food processor. Strain through fine strainer (you should have about 1 cup puree). Combine puree and ⅔ cup of the sugar in small saucepan; bring to a boil over medium heat. Reduce heat to low; simmer 20 to 30 minutes or until thickened and reduced to ⅔ cup, stirring frequently.

3 Melt chocolate and butter in large heatproof bowl set over saucepan of barely simmering water (bowl should not touch water); stir until smooth. Remove from heat; stir in raspberry puree.

4 Whisk remaining 1 cup sugar into chocolate mixture. Whisk in eggs one at a time. Whisk flour and salt in small bowl; fold into chocolate mixture in two additions until well-blended. Pour into pan.

5 Bake 45 to 55 minutes or until toothpick inserted in center comes out clean. Cool on wire rack 20 minutes; remove sides of pan. Cool completely. (Cake may sink slightly during baking.)

6 Meanwhile, beat all whipped cream ingredients in large bowl at medium-high speed until soft peaks form. Sprinkle cake with powdered sugar. Serve with whipped cream; garnish with 2 cups raspberries.

12 servings

PER SERVING: 445 calories, 24.5 g total fat (14 g saturated fat), 5.5 g protein, 57 g carbohydrate, 130 mg cholesterol, 210 mg sodium, 4 g fiber

Outrageous Carrot Cake

This lavish cake boasts three layers loaded with carrots, pineapple, coconut and walnuts. It's filled and crowned with a cream cheese frosting. While cake layers are often created by slicing a single layer horizontally, the fruit and nuts in this cake make that difficult, so the batter is baked in three pans.

Outrageous Carrot Cake

CAKE

- 3 cups all-purpose flour
- 2 teaspoons baking soda
- 1 teaspoon salt
- 1 tablespoon plus 1 teaspoon ground cinnamon
- 6 eggs
- 2½ cups sugar
- 1½ cups canola oil
- 2½ cups finely grated carrots (about 6 carrots)
- 2 (8-oz.) cans crushed pineapple in juice, well-drained*
- 1 cup shredded sweetened coconut
- 1 cup finely chopped walnuts

FROSTING

- 12 oz. cream cheese, softened
- 1 cup unsalted butter, softened
- 2 teaspoons vanilla extract
- 6 cups powdered sugar
- 1½ cups finely chopped walnuts, if desired

1 Evenly space 2 baking racks in oven. Heat oven to 350°F. Spray bottom and sides of 3 (9×2-inch) round cake pans with nonstick cooking spray. Line bottoms with parchment paper; spray parchment with nonstick cooking spray.

2 Sift flour, baking soda, salt and cinnamon into medium bowl.

3 In large bowl, beat eggs and sugar at medium speed 1 to 3 minutes or until thickened and slightly lighter in color. Beat in oil at low speed. Stir in flour mixture until blended. Stir in carrots, pineapple, coconut and 1 cup walnuts until blended. Divide batter evenly among pans. Bake 25 minutes; turn and reverse cake pans. Bake an additional 10 minutes or until toothpick inserted in center comes out clean and cake pulls slightly away from sides of pan. Cool in pans on wire rack 15 minutes. Invert onto wire rack; remove parchment. Cool completely.

4 To make frosting, beat cream cheese and butter in large bowl at medium speed 3 minutes or until blended and smooth. Beat in vanilla. Add powdered sugar; beat at low speed 1 minute or until blended and smooth.

5 Place 1 cake layer on serving platter or cardboard round; spread with 1 cup frosting. Repeat. Top with remaining cake layer; spread top and sides with thin layer of frosting. Coat sides with another smooth layer of frosting; spread remaining frosting on top. Press 1½ cups walnuts onto sides of cake. (Cake can be made up to 2 days ahead and refrigerated, or 3 weeks ahead and frozen. To freeze, place cake in freezer until frosting is firm; wrap in plastic wrap, then heavy-duty foil. To defrost, place in refrigerator overnight; remove wrapping. Serve at room temperature.) Refrigerate leftovers.

TIP

* If pineapple has any large pieces, finely chop.

20 servings

PER SERVING: 755 calories, 45 g total fat (13.5 g saturated fat), 8 g protein, 84.5 g carbohydrate, 105 mg cholesterol, 330 mg sodium, 2.5 g fiber

Best-Ever Pecan Pie

Caramel-like and rich without being overly sweet, this is one dessert that really lives up to its name. Because the filling is a type of custard, it's important not to overbake it or else it will develop a curdled texture. Serve it with vanilla ice cream or softly whipped cream.

CRUST

- 1½ cups all-purpose flour
- ¾ cup unsalted butter, chilled, cut up
- 1 tablespoon sugar
- ⅛ teaspoon salt
- 2 to 3 tablespoons ice water

FILLING

- 3 eggs
- 1 cup dark corn syrup
- ¾ cup packed light brown sugar
- ¼ cup unsalted butter, melted, cooled
- 2 tablespoons whipping cream
- 1½ teaspoons vanilla extract
- 2 cups toasted pecan halves*

1 In large bowl, beat flour, ¾ cup butter, sugar and salt at low speed until mixture resembles coarse crumbs with some pea-sized pieces. Add 2 tablespoons of the water; stir until dough begins to form, adding additional water 1 teaspoon at a time if necessary. Shape into 6-inch flat round; cover and refrigerate 30 to 40 minutes.

2 On lightly floured surface, roll dough into 12-inch round. Place in 9-inch pie pan; trim dough, leaving ¼-inch overhang. Fold overhang under, even with edge of pan; crimp edge. Freeze 15 minutes.

3 Meanwhile, heat oven to 350°F. In medium bowl, whisk together eggs and corn syrup. Whisk in brown sugar, melted butter, cream and vanilla until blended.

4 Place pecans in crust; pour filling over pecans. Bake 45 to 55 minutes or until filling just begins to puff and is light golden brown. (If top begins to brown too quickly toward end of baking, cover loosely with foil.)

TIP

* To toast pecans, place on baking sheet; bake at 350°F. for 6 to 8 minutes or until slightly darker in color. Cool.

8 servings

PER SERVING: 705 calories, 44 g total fat (17.5 g saturated fat), 7.5 g protein, 76 g carbohydrate, 145 mg cholesterol, 120 mg sodium, 3 g fiber

Best-Ever Pecan Pie

Pumpkin-Praline Cheesecake

A crunchy praline-like topping is the perfect foil for this soft, creamy cheesecake. The rich pumpkin filling is scented with all the right spices, just like your favorite pumpkin pie.

CRUST

- 1 cup graham cracker crumbs
- ¼ cup unsalted butter, melted
- 1 tablespoon packed brown sugar
- ½ cup finely chopped toasted pecans*

CHEESECAKE

- 3 (8-oz.) pkg. cream cheese, softened
- 1 cup canned pure pumpkin
- 1 cup packed brown sugar
- 1½ teaspoons ground cinnamon
- ¾ teaspoon ground ginger
- ½ teaspoon ground cloves
- 4 eggs
- 1 tablespoon dark rum, if desired

TOPPING

- ½ cup packed brown sugar
- ½ cup whipping cream
- ¾ cup coarsely chopped toasted pecans*

1 Wrap bottom and sides of 9-inch springform pan with heavy-duty foil. In medium bowl, stir together all crust ingredients except pecans; press into bottom of pan. Sprinkle ½ cup pecans over crust. Refrigerate while preparing filling.

2 Heat oven to 300°F. Place cream cheese in food processor; process until smooth and creamy. Add pumpkin, 1 cup brown sugar, cinnamon, ginger and cloves; pulse to combine. Add eggs two at a time; pulse until well-blended. Add rum; pulse to combine. (Cheesecake also can be made with electric mixer.) Pour into pan.

3 Place springform pan in large shallow roasting or broiler pan. Fill pan with enough hot water to come halfway up sides of springform pan. Bake 65 to 75 minutes or until edges are puffed and top is dry to the touch. Center should move slightly when pan is tapped but should not ripple as if liquid. Remove cake from water bath; remove foil. Cool on wire rack 1 hour. Refrigerate at least 8 hours or overnight.

4 Place ½ cup brown sugar and cream in small saucepan; heat over medium heat until sugar dissolves, stirring frequently. Reduce heat to medium-low; simmer 5 minutes or until thickened (you should be able to see bottom of pan when stirring). (Topping will thicken more as it cools.)

5 Remove from heat; stir in ¾ cup pecans. Let stand until cool, 10 to 15 minutes. Pour over cheesecake, spreading with spatula. Refrigerate at least 30 minutes or until set. Store in refrigerator.

TIP

* To toast pecans, place on baking sheet; bake at 350°F. for 6 to 8 minutes or until slightly darker in color. Cool.

12 servings

PER SERVING: 510 calories, 37.5 g total fat (18.5 g saturated fat), 8 g protein, 39 g carbohydrate, 155 mg cholesterol, 245 mg sodium, 2 g fiber

Pumpkin-Praline Cheesecake

Orange Grove Butter Cookies with Toasted Macadamia Nuts

These divine, buttery cookies deserve a place on your cookie plate! Cut from thickly rolled dough, the resulting cookies look like little cakes. Their intense flavor comes from toasting the macadamia nuts and using orange oil (look for it in the spice aisle).

COOKIES

1	cup sugar
1	cup unsalted butter, softened, cut up
½	cup macadamia nuts, toasted, finely chopped*
1	tablespoon grated orange peel
1	egg
3	tablespoons half-and-half or orange juice
1	teaspoon vanilla extract
1	teaspoon orange oil or orange extract
3	cups all-purpose flour
1½	teaspoons baking powder
¼	teaspoon salt

GLAZE AND GARNISH

2	cups powdered sugar
4 to 5	tablespoons fresh orange juice**
¼	teaspoon orange oil or orange extract***
1	teaspoon grated orange peel
24	macadamia nuts, halved

Orange Grove Butter Cookies with Toasted Macadamia Nuts

1 Line 2 baking sheets with parchment paper. Place sugar, butter, ½ cup nuts and 1 tablespoon orange peel in food processor. (Dough also can be made using mixer.) Pulse until combined; process 20 to 30 seconds or until mixture is blended. Add egg, half-and-half, vanilla and 1 teaspoon orange oil; pulse briefly to blend. Add flour, baking powder and salt; pulse until dough starts to form.

2 Turn out onto lightly floured surface; divide dough in half. Knead each half until smooth; pat into flat rounds. Cover and refrigerate 2 hours.

3 When ready to bake, heat oven to 350°F. On lightly floured surface, roll half of the dough into 6-inch round ¾ inch thick. Cut cookies with 1- to 1¼-inch round scalloped cookie cutter; place 1 inch apart on baking sheet. Repeat with remaining dough. Combine scraps and trimmings; roll out and cut with cookie cutter. Bake, one sheet at a time, 12 to 15 minutes or until just golden brown around edges.

4 Meanwhile, in small bowl, whisk together powdered sugar, 4 tablespoons of the orange juice, ¼ teaspoon orange oil and 1 teaspoon orange peel. Add remaining 1 tablespoon orange juice, if necessary.

5 Place cookies on wire rack; cool completely. Spread each cookie with glaze; top each with macadamia nut half.

TIPS

* To toast macadamia nuts, spread on baking sheet; bake at 350°F. for 5 to 7 minutes or until nuts are golden brown. Cool.

** Substitute 1 to 2 tablespoons orange-flavored liqueur for part of the orange juice, if desired.

*** Citrus oils replicate the intense flavor of citrus rind. To locate citrus oil, go to www.cooking club.com and click on Featured Links.

About 4 dozen cookies

PER COOKIE: 120 calories, 6 g total fat (3 g saturated fat), 1 g protein, 16 g carbohydrate, 15 mg cholesterol, 30 mg sodium, .5 g fiber

Chocolate-Vanilla Swirl Cheesecake

This luscious dessert is the ultimate homage to cream cheese. Chocolate and vanilla batters are swirled together for a delicious contrast of flavor and texture. You'll want to make it at least 1 day ahead to let the flavors develop.

CRUST

- 1½ cups chocolate cookie crumbs*
- 5 tablespoons unsalted butter, melted
- 3 tablespoons sugar
- 1½ teaspoons instant espresso coffee powder

CAKE

- 6 oz. 70% bittersweet chocolate, chopped
- 3 (8-oz.) pkg. cream cheese, softened
- ⅔ cup sugar
- ¼ teaspoon salt
- 2 eggs, room temperature
- ½ teaspoon vanilla extract

1 Heat oven to 350°F. Combine all crust ingredients in medium bowl. Press into bottom and 1¼ inches up sides of 8-inch springform pan. Bake 10 minutes. Cool completely on wire rack.

2 Reduce oven temperature to 325°F. Heat chocolate and 6 tablespoons water in medium heatproof bowl set over saucepan filled with 1 inch almost simmering water (bowl should not touch water). Stir frequently until almost melted. Remove from heat; stir until melted.

3 Beat cream cheese in large bowl at medium speed 30 seconds or just until smooth. Beat in ⅔ cup sugar and salt until smooth and creamy. Beat in eggs one at a time just until blended. Measure 2 cups of the batter; stir into melted chocolate. Stir vanilla into remaining plain batter.

4 Place springform pan on baking sheet. Pour 1¼ cups of the chocolate batter into crust. Pour 1¼ cups of the vanilla batter over chocolate batter. Reserve ¼ cup of the chocolate batter; spread remaining batter over vanilla layer. Spoon remaining vanilla batter in small dollops

over chocolate batter. Spoon reserved chocolate batter into center of each dollop. Marble batters with small knife (do not overblend).

5 Bake cake on baking sheet at 325°F. for 40 to 50 minutes or until edges are puffed and top is dry to the touch. Center should move slightly when pan is tapped but should not ripple as if liquid. Cool completely on wire rack. Refrigerate overnight. (Cake can be made 2 days ahead.) Store in refrigerator.

TIP

* Crush chocolate wafer cookies or chocolate sandwich cookies in food processor or in plastic bag with rolling pin.

12 servings

PER SERVING: 440 calories, 32.5 g total fat (19.5 g saturated fat), 7 g protein, 34 g carbohydrate, 110 mg cholesterol, 310 mg sodium, 1.5 g fiber

Chocolate-Vanilla Swirl Cheesecake

Coconut-Key Lime-Meringue Tarts

From the coconut crust to the lime filling, these individual tarts sparkle with tastes of the tropics. If you can't find the small, distinctly perfumed Key limes for which the dessert is named, regular limes (called Persian) can be substituted. The tarts are best served the same day they're assembled.

CRUST

1¾	cups graham cracker crumbs
¾	cup sweetened flaked coconut
¼	cup sugar
½	teaspoon grated fresh ginger
½	cup unsalted butter, melted

FILLING

4	egg yolks
2	eggs
1¼	cups sugar
½	cup fresh Key or regular lime juice
1	tablespoon grated lime peel
⅛	teaspoon salt
¼	cup unsalted butter, cut up

MERINGUE

4	egg whites
¼	teaspoon cream of tartar
½	cup sugar
¼	teaspoon almond extract
¼	cup sweetened flaked coconut

Coconut-Key Lime-Meringue Tarts

1 Heat oven to 375°F. In medium bowl, stir together graham cracker crumbs, ¾ cup coconut, ¼ cup sugar and ginger. Stir in melted butter until all crumbs are moistened. Press packed ¼ cup crumb mixture into bottom and up sides of 8 (4-inch) mini tart pans with removable bottoms. (Pat firmly to make even crusts.) Place tart pans on large baking sheet. Bake 8 to 10 minutes or until crusts are fragrant and a shade darker. Cool completely on wire rack. (Crusts will puff during baking but will deflate while cooling.) (Crusts can be made up to 1 day ahead. Cover and store at room temperature.)

2 In medium nonreactive saucepan, whisk egg yolks and eggs until blended. Whisk in 1¼ cups sugar, lime juice, lime peel and salt. Add ¼ cup butter. Cook over medium heat, stirring constantly, 8 to 10 minutes or until mixture coats back of a spoon and just begins to come to a boil (do not let it come to a full boil). (Filling can be made up to 1 day ahead. Cover and refrigerate. Heat until hot before using.)

3 Heat oven to 400°F. In large bowl, beat egg whites at medium speed until frothy. Beat in cream of tartar until soft peaks form. Beat in ½ cup sugar, 1 tablespoon at a time, until stiff shiny peaks form. Beat in almond extract.

4 Working quickly, assemble tarts one at a time. (Tarts need to be assembled one at a time to ensure meringue is spread over hot filling.) Spoon ¼ cup of the hot lime curd into crust; top with one-eighth of the meringue mixture by mounding in center and then spreading to edges to touch crust. Repeat with remaining crusts. Sprinkle each tart with one-eighth of the coconut. Bake 5 to 7 minutes or until meringue is light golden brown and coconut is toasted. Cool completely 1 to 2 hours. Remove from tart pans before serving. (Tarts can be made up to 4 hours ahead. Cover and refrigerate.)

8 tarts

PER TART: 525 calories, 26 g total fat (15.5 g saturated fat), 6 g protein, 70 g carbohydrate, 205 mg cholesterol, 215 mg sodium, .5 g fiber

Fresh Fruit Crisp

This basic recipe works using a variety of fruits, such as peaches, nectarines, plums, apples, pears or blueberries. You can mix and match the fruits, but remember to taste them before baking. Depending on the season and time of year, they may require a little more or a little less sugar.

> 4 cups fruit
> ⅓ cup sugar
> 1 tablespoon cornstarch
>   Cornmeal-Almond Topping

1 Heat oven to 375°F. Spray 5- to 7-cup ceramic or glass baking dish, oval gratin or 8-inch square baking pan with nonstick cooking spray. In large bowl, gently stir together fruit, sugar and cornstarch. Spoon fruit mixture into baking dish; sprinkle with topping, squeezing some of it together with your hands to create some larger clumps.

2 Bake 30 to 40 minutes or until top is golden brown and fruit juices bubble heavily at the edges and begin to bubble towards the center. Serve warm or at room temperature.

6 servings

PER SERVING: 90 calories, .5 g total fat (0 g saturated fat), 1 g protein, 22.5 g carbohydrate, 0 mg cholesterol, 0 mg sodium, 3.5 g fiber (Figures based on an average of several fruits. Add topping nutrition for complete nutrition.)

CORNMEAL-ALMOND TOPPING

Add a bright, light finish to fresh fruit with this cornmeal-accented topping. The cornmeal, along with the almonds, provides a slight crunchiness. The topping is particularly good over fresh berries and/or peaches.

> ¾ cup all-purpose flour
> ⅓ cup sugar
> ¼ cup cornmeal
> 2 teaspoons grated orange peel
> ¼ teaspoon ground nutmeg
> ¼ teaspoon salt
> ½ cup unsalted butter, chilled, cut up
> ¼ cup sliced almonds

In large bowl, stir together all ingredients except butter and almonds. With pastry blender or 2 knives, cut in butter until mixture is crumbly with some pieces the size of blueberries. Sprinkle almonds over topping before baking.

6 servings

PER SERVING: 280 calories, 17.5 g total fat (10 g saturated fat), 3 g protein, 28.5 g carbohydrate, 40 mg cholesterol, 100 mg sodium, 1 g fiber

Fresh Fruit Crisp

Hazelnut-Cherry Reine de Saba

This classic French cake is typically made with ground almonds. Here we've substituted toasted hazelnuts and added dried cherries. Made with just a little flour, it's deliciously moist and dense in the center.

CAKE

- ½ cup hazelnuts
- ⅔ cup all-purpose flour
- Dash salt
- ½ cup dried cherries
- 2 tablespoons Kirsch or orange juice
- 4 oz. semisweet chocolate, chopped
- ½ cup unsalted butter, cut up
- 3 eggs separated
- ¾ cup sugar
- ⅛ teaspoon almond extract
- Powdered sugar

GANACHE

- 6 oz. semisweet chocolate, chopped
- ½ cup whipping cream
- 1 tablespoon Kirsch or additional whipping cream

Hazelnut-Cherry Reine de Saba

1 Heat oven to 350°F. Grease 9×1½-inch round cake pan; line bottom with parchment paper. Grease parchment; flour bottom and sides of pan.

2 Place hazelnuts in small baking pan; bake 7 to 9 minutes or until skins begin to loosen and nuts begin to brown. Wrap nuts in paper towels; let stand 5 minutes. Rub with paper towels to remove as much of the outer skins as possible; cool. Place cooled nuts, flour and salt in food processor; process until finely ground.

3 Meanwhile, in small bowl, combine cherries and 2 tablespoons Kirsch; let stand 30 minutes. In medium heatproof bowl, microwave 4 oz. chocolate and butter on medium 1 to 2 minutes or until butter is melted and chocolate is soft. Stir until smooth; cool to room temperature.

4 In large bowl, beat egg yolks and all but 2 tablespoons of the sugar at medium speed 4 minutes or until thick and pale yellow. Reduce speed to low; beat in chocolate mixture until blended. Stir in cherries with soaking liquid and almond extract. Stir in flour mixture.

5 In another large bowl, beat egg whites at medium-high speed 1 minute or until soft peaks form. Add remaining 2 tablespoons sugar; beat until slightly stiff peaks form (do not overbeat). Stir one-fourth of the egg white mixture into chocolate mixture to lighten batter; fold in remaining whites. (Mixture will still be fairly stiff.) Spread in pan.

6 Bake 25 to 30 minutes or until toothpick inserted 2 inches from side of pan comes out almost clean with a few crumbs attached. Cool in pan on wire rack. To remove cake, invert onto plate; remove parchment. Invert onto serving platter. Dust lightly with powdered sugar before serving.

7 Meanwhile, in medium heatproof bowl, microwave 6 oz. chocolate and ½ cup whipping cream* on medium 2 minutes or until cream is hot and chocolate is softened. Stir until smooth. Stir in 1 tablespoon Kirsch. (Ganache can be made up to 3 days ahead. Cover and refrigerate. Reheat gently over low heat or in microwave on medium just until warm.) To serve, cut cake into 8 pieces; place on dessert plates. Spoon ganache over cake.

TIP

* If using additional 1 tablespoon whipping cream instead of Kirsch, add at this time.

8 servings

PER SERVING: 555 calories, 34 g total fat (17 g saturated fat), 7 g protein, 61 g carbohydrate, 125 mg cholesterol, 70 mg sodium, 3 g fiber

Very Lemon Cake with Lush Lemon Frosting

This cake bursts with lemony flavor, thanks to a triple dose from peel, curd and juice. The soft frosting is a creamy contrast to the coarse texture of the cake, and there's enough of it to generously cover every inch.

CAKE

- 2 cups all-purpose flour
- 2 teaspoons baking powder
- ½ teaspoon baking soda
- ½ teaspoon salt
- ¾ cup unsalted butter, softened
- 1½ cups sugar
- 1 tablespoon grated lemon peel
- 3 eggs
- ⅔ cup whole milk
- 2 tablespoons lemon juice
- 1 teaspoon vanilla extract

FROSTING

- 1 (8-oz.) pkg. cream cheese, softened
- ½ cup unsalted butter, softened
- ½ cup purchased lemon curd
- 2 tablespoons grated lemon peel
- 4 cups powdered sugar

1 Heat oven to 350°F. Spray 13×9-inch baking pan with cooking spray. Whisk flour, baking powder, baking soda and salt in medium bowl.

2 Beat ¾ cup butter and sugar in large bowl at medium speed 4 minutes or until light and fluffy. Beat in 1 tablespoon lemon peel. Add eggs one at a time, beating well after each addition. Combine milk, lemon juice and vanilla in small bowl. At low speed, beat in flour mixture in 3 parts alternately with milk mixture just until blended, beginning and ending with flour mixture.

3 Spread batter in pan. Bake 35 to 40 minutes or until deep golden brown and toothpick inserted in center comes out clean. Cool completely on wire rack.

4 Beat cream cheese, ½ cup butter, lemon curd and 2 tablespoons lemon peel at medium speed 2 minutes or until smooth. Slowly add powdered sugar; beat 2 minutes or until light and fluffy. Spread frosting over cake. Cover and refrigerate. Serve at room temperature. Store in refrigerator.

24 servings

PER SERVING: 315 calories, 14 g total fat (8.5 g saturated fat), 3 g protein, 45 g carbohydrate, 70 mg cholesterol, 160 mg sodium, .5 g fiber

Very Lemon Cake with Lush Lemon Frosting

Tropical Coconut Crème Brûlée

For variety, this mild, coconut-flavored crème brûlée is baked in small gratin dishes, which allows for more of the crisp caramelized topping.

4	cups whipping cream	1	lemon
1	cup grated unsweetened coconut	8	egg yolks
½	cup sugar	¾	cup packed light brown sugar
½	vanilla bean or 2 teaspoons vanilla extract		

1 In large saucepan, combine cream, coconut and sugar. If using vanilla bean, cut in half lengthwise; scrape out vanilla seeds. Add scraped pod and seeds to cream mixture. (If using vanilla extract, add in step 3.) With vegetable peeler, peel 6- to 8-inch strip of peel from lemon; add to cream mixture. Heat mixture until small bubbles form around edge of pan. Remove saucepan from heat; cover and steep 20 minutes.

2 Heat oven to 300°F. Place 8 (½- to ¾-cup) shallow round or oval gratin dishes or ramekins in shallow roasting pan.

3 In large bowl, beat egg yolks. Strain cream mixture through fine strainer into egg yolks, whisking to combine. If using vanilla extract, stir into custard. Pour into baking dishes. Add enough boiling water to roasting pan to reach halfway up sides of baking dishes. Cover pan securely with foil.

4 Bake 30 to 40 minutes or until custards are set but still quivery like gelatin.

5 With tongs, remove baking dishes from hot water; cool on wire rack 30 to 40 minutes or until room temperature. Cover with plastic wrap; refrigerate at least 1 hour or up to 24 hours.

6 Place oven rack 8 inches from broiler; heat broiler. Push brown sugar through strainer over each custard, allowing about 1½ tablespoons per custard. Using fingers, gently spread brown sugar to distribute evenly. Place ramekins in shallow roasting pan; surround ramekins with ice cubes.

7 Broil 8 inches from heat 3 to 6 minutes or until brown sugar melts and caramelizes, watching carefully to prevent burning. Cool to room temperature. Store in refrigerator. (If made more than 4 hours ahead, topping will begin to soften and will no longer be crisp.)

8 servings

PER SERVING: 540 calories, 42 g total fat (24.5 g saturated fat), 345 mg cholesterol, 55 mg sodium, 0 g fiber

Italian Chocolate-Amaretto Mousse

This Italian version of chocolate mousse is flavored with Amaretto and coffee, with delicious results! It's rich and creamy and fairly fuss-free, using chocolate chips instead of chopped chocolate.

8	egg yolks	12	oz. semisweet chocolate chips
¼	cup sugar	½	cup strong coffee, hot
¼	cup Amaretto liqueur or ½ teaspoon almond extract	2½	cups heavy whipping cream

1 In medium bowl, whisk egg yolks and sugar until lemon-colored and fluffy. Whisk in liqueur.

2 Place chocolate chips and coffee in medium heatproof bowl; place over saucepan of barely simmering water (bowl should not touch water). Whisk until melted and smooth. Slowly whisk egg yolk mixture into chocolate mixture. Cook and whisk until mixture reaches 160°F., about 4 minutes. Remove bowl from saucepan; pour into large bowl. Cool 30 minutes or until lukewarm.

3 Meanwhile, beat cream in large bowl at medium-high speed until firm but not stiff peaks form. Stir one-third of the whipped cream into cooled chocolate mixture until completely blended; gently fold in remaining whipped cream until well-mixed. Divide mixture among 8 stemmed glasses or serving dishes; refrigerate at least 2 hours.

8 (1-cup) servings

PER SERVING: 560 calories, 44.5 g total fat (26.5 g saturated fat), 6 g protein, 38 g carbohydrate, 305 mg cholesterol, 40 mg sodium, 2.5 g fiber

Chocolate Angel Food Cake with Triple-Chocolate Glaze

This cake is tall and airy, but don't be fooled by its lightness. The cake is moist, with a cocoa-rich flavor, and its triple-chocolate glaze is enough to entice any chocolate lover.

CAKE

- ¼ cup Dutch-processed cocoa
- ¼ cup hot water
- ¾ cup all-purpose flour
- ½ cup powdered sugar
- ¼ teaspoon salt
- 1½ cups egg whites (10 to 12 large), cool room temperature*
- 1½ teaspoons cream of tartar
- 1 teaspoon vanilla extract
- 1¼ cups superfine sugar

SEMISWEET CHOCOLATE GLAZE

- 4 oz. semisweet chocolate, chopped
- 4 tablespoons unsalted butter, softened, cut up
- 1 tablespoon light corn syrup

MILK CHOCOLATE GLAZE

- 2 oz. milk chocolate, chopped
- 2 tablespoons unsalted butter, softened, cut up
- 1½ teaspoons corn syrup

WHITE CHOCOLATE GLAZE

- 2 oz. white chocolate, chopped
- 2 tablespoons unsalted butter, softened, cut up
- 2 teaspoons whipping cream
- 1½ teaspoons corn syrup

1 Heat oven to 350°F. In small bowl, stir together cocoa and hot water until cocoa is dissolved.

2 Place flour, powdered sugar and salt in medium bowl. Sift 3 times to evenly distribute ingredients.

3 Place egg whites in large bowl; beat at medium-low speed until loose and foamy. Add cream of tartar and vanilla; beat at medium-high speed until soft peaks just begin to form. With mixer running, slowly add superfine sugar in steady stream, beating just until egg whites are glossy and hold peaks that slightly bend at the tip. (Do not overbeat; peaks should not be dry and stiff.) Place about 1 cup of the egg white mixture in small bowl. Add cocoa mixture; stir until thoroughly combined.

4 Place chocolate mixture over remaining egg white mixture. Immediately sift one-third of the flour mixture over chocolate mixture; gently fold to incorporate. Repeat with remaining flour mixture, making sure no lumps of flour remain but being careful egg whites do not deflate. Gently spoon mixture into ungreased 10-inch tube pan with removable bottom. Run long narrow spatula through cake to eliminate any large air bubbles; gently smooth top.

5 Bake 35 to 40 minutes or until cake springs back when gently touched and skewer inserted in center comes out clean. (Top may crack as it bakes.) Invert cake onto neck of bottle or funnel, or let stand upside-down on feet attached to tube pan. Cool completely in pan 2 to 3 hours.

6 To remove cake from pan, slide thin narrow knife or spatula around edges of pan and tube. Lift tube out of pan; invert cake onto serving platter.

7 Place all semisweet chocolate glaze ingredients in small saucepan. Heat over low heat, stirring constantly, until chocolate is melted and smooth. Remove from heat; let stand until slightly thickened. Drizzle over cake.

8 Place all milk chocolate glaze ingredients in small saucepan. Heat over low heat, stirring constantly, until chocolate is melted and smooth. Remove from heat; let stand until slightly thickened. Drizzle over cake.

9 Place all white chocolate glaze ingredients in small saucepan. Heat over low heat, stirring constantly, until chocolate is partially melted. Remove from heat; continue stirring until chocolate is melted and smooth. Let stand until slightly thickened; drizzle over cake.

TIP

*To bring egg whites to cool room temperature, separate eggs and place whites in large bowl. (Discard yolks or save for another use.) Place bowl in sink or pan filled with 2 to 3 inches of hot tap water. Let stand 1 to 3 minutes or until whites are at cool room temperature, stirring occasionally.

12 servings

PER SERVING: 325 calories, 14 g total fat (8.5 g saturated fat), 5.5 g protein, 47.5 g carbohydrate, 25 mg cholesterol, 115 mg sodium, 1.5 g fiber

Nutty Drumstick Squares

These ice cream squares are reminiscent of the classic frozen cone. Because they're made in a large pan, they're perfect for a crowd. Cut the dessert before a party, arrange on a platter, cover and return to the freezer until you're ready to serve it.

CRUST

1	(4-oz.) pkg. sugar cones (12 cones)
½	cup chopped lightly salted peanuts

SAUCE

1	cup half-and-half
3	tablespoons unsalted butter, cut up
3¼	cups semisweet chocolate chips
1½	teaspoons vanilla extract

FILLING

2	quarts French vanilla ice cream*
1	cup chopped lightly salted peanuts

Nutty Drumstick Squares

1 Line 13 × 9-inch baking pan with heavy-duty aluminum foil, leaving extra foil extending over edges. Place 6 of the sugar cones in resealable plastic bag; seal bag. Crush cones with rolling pin into ½- to 1-inch pieces. Repeat with remaining 6 cones. (You should have about 2 cups crushed cones.) In medium bowl, stir together 1½ cups of the crushed cones and ½ cup peanuts. Spread evenly over bottom of pan.

2 Place half-and-half and butter in heavy medium saucepan; heat over medium heat until butter melts, tiny bubbles appear around edge of saucepan and mixture reaches about 160°F. Remove from heat; add chocolate chips. Let stand 1 minute; stir. If necessary, return saucepan to low heat just until chocolate is completely melted, stirring constantly. Remove from heat; stir in vanilla. Drizzle half of the sauce over crust, spreading carefully to completely cover. Freeze at least 20 minutes or until firm.

3 Spread ice cream evenly over sauce; spoon remaining sauce over ice cream. Sprinkle with 1 cup peanuts and remaining ½ cup crushed cones. Freeze until firm, 4 hours or overnight. (Dessert can be made up to 3 days ahead. Cover and freeze.) To serve, lift foil and dessert from pan; cut into 16 pieces. Freeze leftovers

TIP

*Soften ice cream in refrigerator until spreadable but not melting, 10 to 20 minutes.

16 servings

PER SERVING: 445 calories, 28.5 g total fat (14 g saturated fat), 8.5 g protein, 46 g carbohydrate, 40 mg cholesterol, 120 mg sodium, 3 g fiber

Chocolate Angel Food Cake with Triple-Chocolate Glaze

Hanukkah Honey Puffs

Variations on this recipe are prepared for Hanukkah celebrations in Egypt, Morocco, India and Greece. Orange-flavored liqueur makes them unforgettable.

HONEY PUFFS

- 1 (¼-oz.) pkg. active dry yeast
- 3 tablespoons sugar
- 1½ cups warm water (110°F. to 115°F.)
- ½ teaspoon salt
- ½ teaspoon cinnamon
- 1½ teaspoons grated lemon peel
- 1 tablespoon orange-flavored liqueur or orange juice
- 1 egg, beaten
- 2 cups all-purpose flour
  Oil for deep frying

SYRUP

- ¾ cup sugar
- 2 tablespoons honey
- ½ cup water
- 2 tablespoons orange-flavored liqueur or orange juice

1 In large bowl, combine yeast, 3 tablespoons sugar and ½ cup of the warm water; mix well. Let stand 10 minutes or until mixture looks foamy.

2 Whisk in remaining 1 cup warm water, salt, cinnamon, lemon peel, 1 tablespoon liqueur and egg until well mixed. Add flour; whisk until smooth. Dough will be consistency of thick cake batter. Cover bowl with kitchen towel; set aside in warm place 1 to 1½ hours or until almost doubled in size.

3 Meanwhile, in medium saucepan, combine ¾ cup sugar, honey and ½ cup water; mix well. Bring to a boil, stirring occasionally. Boil gently without stirring 10 minutes. Remove saucepan from heat; stir in 2 tablespoons liqueur. Cool. (Syrup can be made up to 24 hours ahead. Cover and refrigerate. Bring to room temperature before using.)

Hanukkah Honey Puffs

4 Line baking sheet with paper towels. Beat dough briefly to remove air bubbles. To cook honey puffs, pour 1 inch oil into large saucepan. Heat to 375°F. To test oil, drop 1 teaspoon batter into oil; count to 30. If dough does not rise to surface, continue to heat oil.

5 When oil is ready, drop dough by teaspoonfuls into hot oil. Do not crowd. Fry honey puffs about 3 minutes or until golden brown on bottom. Turn; fry 2 to 3 minutes or until golden brown all over. Remove with slotted spoon; drain on lined baking sheet. (Honey puffs can be made up to 3 hours ahead. Reheat by placing on baking sheet; bake at 350°F. for 3 to 5 minutes or until warm and slightly crisp.) To serve, spoon syrup over honey puffs. Serve warm.

4 dozen honey puffs

PER HONEY PUFF: 60 calories, 2.5 g total fat (.5 g saturated fat), .5 g protein, 9 g carbohydrate, 5 mg cholesterol, 25 mg sodium, 0 g fiber

Mixed Berry Tart with Raspberry Glaze

Frozen raspberries in sugar syrup make an excellent fruit glaze; they cook down quickly and thicken to a perfect consistency. Serve the tart with a bowl of sweetened, freshly whipped cream. Don't overbeat the cream; it should fall gently off the spoon and flow between the berries.

CRUST

5	tablespoons sliced almonds, toasted*
1	cup all-purpose flour
¼	cup sugar
⅛	teaspoon salt
6	tablespoons unsalted butter, chilled, cut up
1	egg
¼	teaspoon almond extract

GLAZE

1	(10-oz.) pkg. frozen raspberries in syrup, thawed
3	tablespoons sugar

FILLING

2	cups strawberries, quartered
1	cup blueberries
1	cup raspberries

1 Reserve 2 tablespoons of the toasted almonds for garnish. Pulse remaining 3 tablespoons toasted almonds in food processor until ground. Add flour, ¼ cup sugar and salt; pulse to mix. Add butter; pulse until butter is size of small peas. In small bowl, whisk together egg and almond extract; add to flour mixture. Pulse until dough is moist and crumbly. (Dough also can be made in bowl using pastry blender or two knives.) Shape dough into flat round. With lightly floured hands, press dough evenly into bottom and up sides of 9-inch tart pan with removable bottom. Pierce dough all over with fork. Refrigerate 30 minutes or until cold.

2 Meanwhile, heat oven to 400°F. Line dough with foil sprayed with nonstick cooking spray; bake 15 minutes. Remove foil; if crust is puffed, prick several times with fork. Bake an additional 10 to 15 minutes or until golden brown; cool completely on wire rack. (Crust can be made up to 1 day ahead. Cover and store at room temperature.)

3 Meanwhile, place thawed raspberries with syrup in blender; blend until smooth. Strain to remove seeds. Place strained raspberry juice and 3 tablespoons sugar in large skillet. Bring to a boil over high heat; boil 4 minutes or until slightly thickened and reduced to ½ cup. Cool to room temperature. (Glaze can be made up to 1 day ahead. Cover and refrigerate.)

4 To assemble tart, brush bottom of crust with glaze. Arrange strawberries over glaze. Place blueberries over strawberries; top with raspberries. Brush remaining glaze over fruit. Garnish with sliced almonds. (Tart can be assembled up to 2 hours ahead.) Store in refrigerator.

TIP

* To toast almonds, place on baking sheet; bake at 400°F. for 3 to 5 minutes or until golden brown. Cool.

8 servings

PER SERVING: 275 calories, 11.5 g total fat (6 g saturated fat), 4 g protein, 40 g carbohydrate, 50 mg cholesterol, 45 mg sodium, 4 g fiber

Mixed Berry Tart with Raspberry Glaze

Raspberry-Nectarine Pie

There's no need to peel the nectarines, and you don't have to worry about making a picture-perfect lattice topping; the colorful filling softens the edges of even the most rough-hewn crisscross as it bubbles up. Tapioca is the thickener of choice because it cooks up clear and glossy, allowing the bright colors of the fruit to shine. Serve the pie with whipped cream.

CRUST

- 1 recipe Old-Fashioned Flaky Pie Crust (see page 141)
- 1 tablespoon milk
- 2 teaspoons sugar

FILLING

- 1 cup sugar
- 3 tablespoons quick-cooking tapioca
- ½ teaspoon ground nutmeg
- ¼ teaspoon ground cardamom
- 5 large firm but ripe nectarines, sliced (½ inch) (7 cups)
- 1 pint (2 cups) raspberries
- 1 tablespoon lemon juice

1 Place oven rack on lowest level; place baking sheet on rack. Heat oven to 425°F. Divide pie dough in half; refrigerate 1 piece. On lightly floured surface, roll remaining piece into 12-inch round. (Edge can be rough and you can pinch together any tears.) Roll dough over rolling pin; unroll into 9-inch pie pan. Let dough hang over edge of pan.

2 In large bowl, stir together 1 cup sugar, tapioca, nutmeg and cardamom. Add nectarines, raspberries and lemon juice; stir gently to combine. Spoon filling into pie crust. Refrigerate while rolling out lattice.

3 On lightly floured surface, roll remaining dough into 12-inch round. Cut into 5 (1¼-inch) strips. Place 3 strips lengthwise over pie; trim edges to inside of pie pan. Place remaining 2 strips crosswise over pie; trim edges. Fold edge of bottom crust over edges of strips. Brush dough with milk; sprinkle with 2 teaspoons sugar.

4 Place pie on baking sheet; bake at 425°F. for 30 minutes. Reduce oven temperature to 400°F. (If crust is brown, cover with foil, leaving center open for steam.) Bake at 400°F. for 15 minutes. Reduce oven temperature to 375°F.; bake an additional 15 to 25 minutes or until juices are bubbly and crust is rich golden brown. Cool on wire rack.

8 servings

PER SERVING: 530 calories, 22.5 g total fat (10 g saturated fat), 6 g protein, 80.5 g carbohydrate, 30 mg cholesterol, 300 mg sodium, 6.5 g fiber

Raspberry-Nectarine Pie

Chocolate-Kahlúa Soufflés

These individual soufflés are impressive to serve but actually quite easy to make. Kahlúa helps boost their deep chocolate flavor. The recipe can be doubled to serve four.

- 4 oz. semisweet chocolate, chopped
- 2 tablespoons Kahlúa (coffee-flavored liqueur) or cold strong coffee
- 2 egg yolks
- 2 tablespoons sugar, divided
- 3 egg whites
  Powdered sugar

1 Grease 2 (10-oz.) ramekins with butter; sprinkle with sugar. Wipe top ¼ inch of ramekins to provide surface for soufflés to cling to.

2 Place 13 × 9-inch baking pan half-filled with water on bottom oven rack. Heat oven to 400°F.

3 Place chocolate and Kahlúa in heatproof medium bowl. Bring 1 inch water to a boil in medium saucepan. Remove from heat. Place bowl with chocolate mixture over water (bowl should not touch water). Let stand until chocolate is melted, stirring occasionally.

4 In medium bowl, whisk egg yolks and 1 tablespoon of the sugar until mixture thickens and turns light yellow. In large bowl, beat egg whites and remaining 1 tablespoon sugar at medium-high speed until stiff, but not dry, peaks form.

Chocolate-Kahlúa Soufflés

5 Slowly stir chocolate mixture into egg yolk mixture. Stir in one-third of the egg white mixture. Gently fold in remaining egg white mixture. Spoon mixture into ramekins; place on baking sheet. (Soufflés can be made to this point up to 3 hours ahead. Cover and refrigerate.)

6 Bake 13 to 16 minutes or until soufflés have risen and sides feel slightly firm. Sprinkle with powdered sugar.

2 servings

PER SERVING: 450 calories, 22 g total fat (11.5 g saturated fat), 10.5 g protein, 57.5 g carbohydrate, 215 mg cholesterol, 95 mg sodium, 3.5 g fiber

Old-Fashioned Flaky Pie Crust

Two different fats contribute to this crust's flaky texture. Vegetable shortening melts slower than butter, creating extra flakiness, and butter adds richness and superb flavor. But the secret ingredient is cider vinegar, which breaks down the gluten in the flour for a tender, more delicate crust.

- 2½ cups all-purpose flour
- 1 teaspoon salt
- 8 tablespoons unsalted butter, chilled, cut up
- 6 tablespoons shortening, chilled, cut up
- 5 to 7 tablespoons ice water
- 1½ teaspoons cider vinegar

In large bowl, stir together flour and salt. With pastry blender or 2 knives, cut in butter and shortening until mixture resembles coarse crumbs with some pea-sized pieces. Slowly add 5 tablespoons of the water and vinegar, stirring until dough just begins to come together. (If dough is too dry, sprinkle with additional water.) (Dough also can be made in food processor.) Form into flat round. Cover and refrigerate at least 1 hour or up to 2 days.

1 (9-inch) double-crust pie crust

PER 1/8 OF RECIPE: 330 calories, 21.5 g total fat (10 g saturated fat), 4 g protein, 30 g carbohydrate, 30 mg cholesterol, 295 mg sodium, 1 g fiber

Coffee Ice Cream

Coffee Ice Cream

Member Heather Gardner tinkered with a vanilla ice cream recipe to create an indulgence she says reminds her of Häagen-Dazs ice cream. Garnish with a crushed coffee bean, if desired.

2	pasteurized eggs*
1¼	cups sugar
2½	cups whole milk
1	cup whipping cream
¾	cup evaporated milk
¼	cup half-and-half
¼	cup instant coffee granules
2½	teaspoons vanilla extract
¼	teaspoon salt

1 In large bowl, beat eggs and sugar at medium speed 4 minutes or until light-colored and thick. Add all remaining ingredients one at a time, beating well after each addition. Beat until well-blended.
2 Freeze in ice cream machine according to manufacturer's instructions.

TIP

* It is important to use pasteurized eggs in this recipe because the eggs are not cooked. Pasteurized whole eggs are now sold in most grocery stores. If you cannot find them, use ½ cup egg substitute in place of the eggs.

10 (¾-cup) servings

PER SERVING: 325 calories, 15.5 g total fat (9.5 g saturated fat), 6.5 g protein, 39.5 g carbohydrate, 105 mg cholesterol, 165 mg sodium, 0 g fiber

Orchard-Fresh Apple Pie

This is apple pie as it should be: strong on the apple flavor with a touch of cinnamon, nutmeg and cloves. Cooking down a mixture of apple juice, sugar, flour and spices results in a syrup that helps give the pie its intense taste. The best apples to use are Jonagold, Fuji or Braeburn.

	Dough for 1 (9-inch) deep-dish double-crust pie
¾	cup unfiltered or fresh apple juice
½	cup plus ½ tablespoon sugar, divided
¾	teaspoon ground cinnamon
½	teaspoon ground nutmeg
⅛	teaspoon ground cloves
¼	cup all-purpose flour
3	lb. apples, peeled, sliced (⅛ to ¼ inch) (about 10 cups)

1 Heat oven to 400°F. Line 9-inch deep-dish pie pan with 1 circle of dough. Combine apple juice, ½ cup of the sugar, cinnamon, nutmeg and cloves in small saucepan; bring to a boil over medium heat. Simmer 10 minutes or until syrup has reduced to ½ cup. Whisk in flour until combined. (Syrup will be very thick.)
2 Toss apples with syrup in large bowl. Pour into pie crust, pressing to mound apples. Top with remaining circle of dough; gently press around edges. Trim dough to ½-inch overhang; fold under edge of bottom crust. Press down gently to seal; flute or crimp edge. Make 4 or 5 slits in top crust to allow steam to escape during baking; sprinkle with remaining ½ tablespoon sugar.
3 Bake 50 to 60 minutes or until crust is golden brown and apples are tender, covering edge with foil during last 15 minutes of baking if browning too quickly. (Test apples by poking small knife into slit in pie.) Cool on wire rack to room temperature.

8 servings

PER SERVING: 335 calories, 12 g total fat (3 g saturated fat), 3.5 g protein, 55.5 g carbohydrate, 0 mg cholesterol, 235 mg sodium, 3 g fiber

Nutmeg-Eggnog Cake with Rum Glaze

Nutmeg permeates this moist, delicate-textured cake that's made with eggnog and topped with a sweet rum-flavored glaze. It's ideal for a dessert buffet. Freeze the leftover eggnog to make the cake another time.

CAKE

- 1¼ cups unsalted butter, softened
- 1½ cups sugar
- 6 egg yolks
- 1 tablespoon rum, or ¼ teaspoon rum extract mixed with 1 tablespoon water
- 1½ teaspoons vanilla extract
- 3 cups sifted cake flour
- 2½ teaspoons baking powder
- 2 teaspoons ground nutmeg
- 1 teaspoon ground cinnamon
- ½ teaspoon salt
- 1 cup purchased eggnog

GLAZE

- 1 cup powdered sugar
- 1 to 2 tablespoons milk
- 1½ teaspoons rum or ⅛ teaspoon rum extract
- ½ teaspoon vanilla extract
- ¼ cup sliced almonds

1 Heat oven to 350°F. Generously grease 8- to 10-cup Bundt pan with shortening. Sprinkle with flour; tap pan to remove excess flour.

2 In large bowl, beat butter at medium speed 1 minute or until blended. Add sugar; beat 5 minutes or until light and fluffy. Add egg yolks two at a time, beating well after each addition. Beat in 1 tablespoon rum and 1½ teaspoons vanilla until incorporated.

3 In another large bowl, whisk together cake flour, baking powder, nutmeg, cinnamon and salt. At low speed, beat flour mixture into batter in 3 parts alternately with eggnog just until blended, beginning and ending with flour mixture. Do not overbeat.

4 Spoon batter into pan. Level with spatula; tap pan firmly on counter several times to settle batter. Bake 45 to 60 minutes or until wooden skewer inserted in center comes out clean and edges of cake start to pull away from sides of pan.

5 Cool on wire rack 10 to 15 minutes. Invert cake onto wire rack; cool completely.

6 Meanwhile, in small bowl, whisk together all glaze ingredients except almonds, adding milk until of desired consistency. Drizzle glaze over top of cake; sprinkle with almonds. Let stand until glaze is set. (Cake can be made up to 1 day ahead.)

12 servings

PER SERVING: 505 calories, 24.5 g total fat (14 g saturated fat), 5.5 g protein, 66 g carbohydrate, 165 mg cholesterol, 220 mg sodium, 1 g fiber

Nutmeg-Eggnog Cake with Rum Glaze

Dried Cherry, Chocolate and Almond Pound Cake

This moist, dense cake is even more flavorful the day after baking, making it a perfect do-ahead party dessert.

CAKE

- 1 cup chopped dried cherries
- ¼ cup Kirsch or cherry-flavored juice*
- 3 cups all-purpose flour
- ¼ cup unsweetened cocoa
- 1 teaspoon ground cinnamon
- 1¼ teaspoons baking powder
- ½ teaspoon baking soda
- ½ teaspoon salt
- 1 cup plus 2 tablespoons toasted sliced almonds, divided**
- 1 cup unsalted butter, softened
- 2 cups sugar
- 1 teaspoon vanilla extract
- ½ teaspoon almond extract
- 1 (7-oz.) pkg. almond paste
- 5 eggs
- 1 cup regular or low-fat sour cream
- 1 cup mini semisweet chocolate chips

GLAZE

- 6 oz. semisweet chocolate, chopped
- 3 tablespoons light corn syrup
- ¼ cup whipping cream
- 2 tablespoons unsalted butter

1 Heat oven to 325°F. Grease 10-inch tube pan with removable bottom or 12-cup Bundt pan with shortening; sprinkle with flour. Place cherries and Kirsch in small bowl; let stand at least 30 minutes or up to 2 hours. In large bowl, whisk together flour, cocoa, cinnamon, baking powder, baking soda and salt.

2 Reserve 2 tablespoons of the sliced almonds for garnish; chop remaining almonds. In another large bowl, beat 1 cup butter and sugar at medium speed 5 minutes or until light and fluffy. Beat in vanilla and almond extract. Shred almond paste with cheese grater; beat into butter mixture until smooth. Beat in eggs one at a time, beating well after each addition. Reduce speed to low; beat in flour mixture in 3 parts alternately with sour cream, beginning and ending with flour mixture. Do not overbeat. Stir in cherries with liquid, chocolate chips and chopped almonds.

3 Spoon batter into pan. Bake 1 hour 30 minutes to 1 hour 40 minutes or until rich golden brown and skewer inserted in center comes out clean. Cool in pan on wire rack 1 hour. To remove cake from pan, slide thin narrow knife or spatula around edges of pan and tube. Lift tube out of pan; invert cake onto wire rack. Remove pan bottom. Cool completely.

4 Meanwhile, place all glaze ingredients in medium saucepan; heat over low heat until chocolate is melted and smooth, stirring frequently. Cool glaze until slightly thickened. Pour glaze over cooled cake; garnish with reserved sliced almonds. Let stand until set.

TIPS

* Kirsch is German for cherries and refers to cherry brandy.

** To toast sliced almonds, place on baking sheet; bake at 325°F. for 8 to 10 minutes or until light golden brown. Cool.

12 servings

PER SERVING: 815 calories, 43 g total fat (21 g saturated fat), 12.5 g protein, 102.5 g carbohydrate, 155 mg cholesterol, 250 mg sodium, 6.5 g fiber

Caramel-Pear Pie

The richness of caramel and the bright flavor of pear meet up in this Americanized version of a classic French dessert, tarte Tatin. If you're new to making caramel, reduce the heat to low as the sugar starts to caramelize to minimize the chances of it getting too dark. Serve the pie with a scoop of vanilla ice cream or a drizzle of crème fraîche.

Dough for 1 (9-inch) double-crust pie

- 3 **tablespoons all-purpose flour, divided**
- 1 **tablespoon ground almonds**
- 3 **lb. Bartlett pears (about 6), peeled, quartered**
- 1 **tablespoon pear or apple cognac, if desired**
- 2 **tablespoons unsalted butter**
- ½ **cup sugar**

1 Heat oven to 400°F. Line 9-inch pie pan with 1 circle of dough. Sprinkle 1 tablespoon of the flour and ground almonds over bottom of crust; refrigerate while preparing filling.

2 Toss pears with cognac in large bowl. Melt butter in large skillet over medium heat. Add sugar; cook and stir 7 to 8 minutes or until golden brown. (At first, caramel will appear crystallized, followed by a separating of the butter and sugar. It will smooth out as it begins to brown.) Whisk in remaining 2 tablespoons flour until combined. Add pears; reduce heat to low. (Some of the caramel will harden.) Cook and stir 3 to 5 minutes or until caramel melts and coats pears. Place pears in pie crust; pour remaining caramel over pears.

3 Cut remaining circle of dough into 10 (¾-inch-wide) strips. Weave strips into lattice over pie filling, letting strips overhang pie pan. Trim strips to ½-inch overhang; fold under edge of bottom crust. Press down gently to seal; flute or crimp edge.

4 Bake 45 to 55 minutes or until crust is golden brown and filling is bubbly, covering edge with foil after 20 minutes if browning too quickly. Cool on wire rack to room temperature.

8 servings

PER SERVING: 350 calories, 14 g total fat (4.5 g saturated fat), 3 g protein, 55.5 g carbohydrate, 10 mg cholesterol, 205 mg sodium, 5.5 g fiber

Rhubarb-Strawberry Streusel Tart

Rhubarb-Strawberry Streusel Tart

Rhubarb and strawberries are a perfect spring marriage. In this tart, they're topped with a brown sugar streusel that uses chopped pecans to provide an appealing crunch.

Dough for 1 (9- to 10-inch) pie crust

- 3 **cups sliced rhubarb (¾ inch)**
- 3 **cups strawberries, halved if large**
- 1½ **cups sugar**
- ¼ **cup cornstarch**
- ¼ **cup all-purpose flour**
- ¼ **cup packed brown sugar**
- 2 **tablespoons butter, softened**
- ¼ **cup finely chopped pecans**

1 Heat oven to 375°F. Line 10-inch tart pan with removable bottom or ceramic pan with dough; trim edges. Place on rimmed baking sheet.

2 In large bowl, stir together rhubarb, strawberries, sugar and cornstarch; place in crust.

3 In medium bowl, stir together flour and brown sugar. With pastry blender or 2 knives, cut in butter until mixture resembles coarse crumbs with some pea-sized pieces. Stir in pecans. Sprinkle over tart. Place tart with baking sheet in oven; bake 55 to 65 minutes or until edges and center are bubbly and streusel is golden brown.

8 servings

PER SERVING: 355 calories, 11 g total fat (3.5 g saturated fat), 2.5 g protein, 64.5 g carbohydrate, 10 mg cholesterol, 125 mg sodium, 2.5 g fiber

Maple-Pecan Layer Cake

This two-layer cake is loaded with pecans and topped with a buttery, creamy frosting. While the nuts can be ground in a food processor, using a nut grater will produce a darker, nuttier taste because the more finely ground nuts are better dispersed throughout the cake. If possible, use grade B maple syrup; it's darker in color and has a stronger maple flavor.

CAKE

- ⅔ cup unsalted butter, softened
- 1⅓ cups sugar
- 4 eggs
- 1½ teaspoons vanilla extract
- 1 cup all-purpose flour
- ½ teaspoon salt
- ½ teaspoon baking soda
- ¼ teaspoon baking powder
- 1 cup finely grated or ground toasted pecans*
- ⅔ cup sour cream

FROSTING

- 3 cups powdered sugar, sifted
- ½ cup unsalted butter, softened
- ½ cup maple syrup
- ¼ cup finely chopped toasted pecans**

1 Heat oven to 350°F. Grease 2 (9 × 2-inch) round pans. Line bottoms with parchment paper; grease paper.

2 In large bowl, beat ⅔ cup butter and sugar at medium speed 4 to 5 minutes or until light and creamy. In small bowl, whisk together eggs and vanilla; beat into butter mixture in two parts.

3 In medium bowl, whisk together flour, salt, baking soda and baking powder. Whisk in 1 cup pecans. At low speed, beat into butter mixture in 3 parts alternately with sour cream, beginning and ending with flour mixture. Divide batter evenly between pans.

4 Bake 30 minutes or until golden brown and toothpick inserted in center comes out clean. Cool on wire rack 10 minutes. Invert cakes onto wire rack; remove parchment. Cool completely.

5 Meanwhile, in medium bowl, beat powdered sugar and ½ cup butter at medium-low speed until blended. Slowly beat in maple syrup until smooth and creamy.

6 Spread half of the frosting over one cake layer; top with second cake layer. Frost top of cake with remaining frosting; sprinkle with ¼ cup pecans.

TIPS

* If using nut grater, grate approximately 1 cup toasted pecan halves and measure 1 cup. If using food processor, pulse scant 1 cup toasted pecan halves with 1 tablespoon of the flour until finely ground; measure 1 cup.

** To toast pecans, place on baking sheet; bake at 350°F. for 6 to 8 minutes or until slightly darker in color. Cool.

12 servings

PER SERVING: 555 calories, 29.5 g total fat (14 g saturated fat), 4.5 g protein, 71 g carbohydrate, 125 mg cholesterol, 190 mg sodium, 1.5 g fiber

Maple-Pecan Layer Cake

Peanut Butter-Chocolate Mousse Cake

This impressive dessert is a peanut butter lover's delight. A chocolate cookie crust with crunchy roasted peanuts and a hint of cinnamon holds a dreamy filling of peanut butter mousse. Make sure you give it plenty of time to chill before serving.

CRUST

- 1¼ cups chocolate cookie crumbs*
- ¼ cup finely chopped unsalted roasted peanuts
- 3 tablespoons sugar
- ½ teaspoon ground cinnamon
- ¼ cup unsalted butter, melted

MOUSSE

- 1¼ cups creamy peanut butter
- 1 (8-oz.) pkg. cream cheese, softened
- 1¼ cups powdered sugar
- 1 tablespoon vanilla extract
- 1⅓ cups whipping cream

TOPPING

- ⅓ cup whipping cream
- 3 tablespoons sugar
- 2 teaspoons instant espresso coffee powder
- 4 oz. semisweet chocolate, chopped
- ½ teaspoon vanilla extract

Peanut Butter-Chocolate Mousse Cake

1 Heat oven to 325°F. In medium bowl, stir together cookie crumbs, peanuts, 3 tablespoons sugar and cinnamon. Add melted butter; stir until evenly moistened. Press evenly into bottom and 1 inch up sides of 9-inch springform pan. Bake 10 minutes or until crust is firm. Cool.

2 In large bowl, beat peanut butter and cream cheese at low speed until blended. Add powdered sugar and 1 tablespoon vanilla; beat until smooth.

3 In another large bowl, beat 1⅓ cups cream at medium-high to high speed until soft peaks form. Fold into peanut butter mixture in three parts; pour into crust. Place in refrigerator while preparing topping.

4 Place ⅓ cup cream, 3 tablespoons sugar and espresso coffee powder in small saucepan; heat over medium heat until sugar dissolves, tiny bubbles appear around edge of saucepan and mixture reaches about 160°F., stirring occasionally. Remove from heat; add chocolate. Let stand 1 minute; stir until smooth. If necessary, return saucepan to low heat just until chocolate is completely melted, stirring constantly. Remove from heat; stir in ½ teaspoon vanilla. Cool 5 minutes. Spread topping evenly over mousse filling. Cover and refrigerate until well-chilled, at least 4 hours. Store in refrigerator.

TIP

* Look for 100-percent chocolate cookie crumbs, such as the Oreo brand, which are located in the supermarket baking section near graham cracker crumbs or in the ice cream topping section. Do not use Oreo Crunchies, which are broken Oreo cookies that also contain the creme filling. If you can't find chocolate cookies in crumb form, purchase chocolate wafer cookies (such as the Famous brand) and crush them into fine crumbs.

12 servings

PER SERVING: 625 calories, 44.5 g total fat (19 g saturated fat), 11.5 g protein, 49.5 g carbohydrate, 70 mg cholesterol, 290 mg sodium, 3 g fiber

Raspberry-Almond-Cream Cheese Cookies

These delicate-shaped cookies look like miniature Danish pastries. The cream cheese filling, topped with glistening raspberry jam, is neatly enveloped in a tender sugar cookie. To make it easier to work with, the dough should stay slightly cool during the shaping process. If it becomes too warm, stop and place it in the refrigerator for 5 to 10 minutes before continuing.

FILLING

- 1 (8-oz.) pkg. cream cheese, softened
- 1 egg yolk
- 2 tablespoons sugar
- 2 tablespoons all-purpose flour
- ¼ teaspoon almond extract
- ½ cup raspberry preserves
- ½ cup sliced almonds

DOUGH

- 1 cup unsalted butter, softened
- 1⅓ cups sugar
- 2 eggs
- 2 teaspoons vanilla extract
- 3¼ to 3½ cups all-purpose flour
- 2 teaspoons baking powder
- ¼ teaspoon salt
- Powdered sugar

1 Place all filling ingredients except preserves and almonds in food processor. (Filling and dough also can be made using mixer.) Process 10 to 20 seconds or until combined. Place in small bowl; cover and refrigerate while preparing dough.

2 Place butter and 1⅓ cups sugar in food processor. Pulse 10 times or until combined; process 10 to 20 seconds or until soft and creamy. Add eggs and vanilla; process until combined. In medium bowl, stir together 3¼ cups of the flour, baking powder and salt. Add half of the flour mixture to food processor; pulse briefly to combine. Add remaining flour mixture; pulse just until incorporated. Turn dough out onto lightly floured surface; knead briefly until smooth, adding up to an additional ¼ cup flour if dough is too soft.

3 Divide dough in half; press into flat rounds ½ inch thick. Wrap in plastic wrap; refrigerate 30 to 60 minutes or until firm.

4 When ready to bake, heat oven to 350°F. Line 2 baking sheets with parchment paper.

5 On lightly floured surface, roll out 1 dough round to ⅛ inch thickness. With 2½-inch round cookie cutter, cut dough into 24 circles; place on baking sheet. Spread each circle with about ¾ teaspoon filling; place scant ½ teaspoon preserves in center. Sprinkle with a few almond slices. Pinch 2 sides together in middle (cookies will look like Danish pastry with cream cheese and raspberry filling peeking out). Repeat with remaining dough, rerolling excess dough. If dough becomes soft, place baking sheet in refrigerator until dough is firm before baking.

6 Bake, one sheet at a time, 10 to 12 minutes or until light brown. Place cookies on wire rack; cool completely. Sprinkle with powdered sugar.

About 5 dozen cookies

PER COOKIE: 100 calories, 5 g total fat (3 g saturated fat), 1.5 g protein, 12.5 g carbohydrate, 25 mg cholesterol, 40 mg sodium, .5 g fiber

Menu Ideas

Lemon-Garlic Grilled Chicken with Basil Aioli, page 29

Spring

MARDI GRAS GATHERING

Short Ribs Jambalaya
page 78

Bayou Cakes with Remoulade Sauce
page 10

Black Pepper Biscuits
page 105

Southern Greens with Hot Bacon Vinaigrette
page 91

Banana Bread Pudding with Maple Sauce
page 124

CASUAL SALMON FOR 4

Rosemary Roasted Salmon
page 28

Steamed asparagus with lemon pepper

Warm New Potato and Spring Pea Salad
page 89

Strawberry-Chocolate Meringues
page 120

BRIDAL SHOWER BRUNCH

Strawberry-Walnut Salad with Warm Goat Cheese
page 92

Greek Chicken Pot Pie
page 34

Roasted Asparagus with Lemon-Tarragon Vinaigrette
page 112

White Chocolate-Raspberry Tart
page 117

LAMB FOR EASTER

Roast Rack of Lamb with Blackberry Crust
page 49

Mixed Greens with Hazelnuts and Goat Cheese
page 86

Steamed sugar snap peas and baby carrots

Roasted new potatoes

Giant Golden Popovers
page 108

Strawberry-Orange Whipped Cream Cake
page 123

SPRING HERBAL DINNER

Mint Pesto-Stuffed Chicken Breasts
page 60

Chard, Mushroom and Dill Bread Pudding
page 114

Spring Herb Salad with Champagne Vinaigrette
page 84

Rhubarb-Strawberry Streusel Tart
page 145

Italicized items are menu suggestions; recipes not included.

Summer

BACKYARD MEXICAN BUFFET

Traditional Guacamole
page 17

Mexican Black Bean-Orange Dip
page 17

**Garlic-Lime Chicken Drumettes
with Chipotle Mayonnaise**
page 12

Tequila-Chile-Marinated Pork Chops
page 69

Grilled Corn and Black Bean Salad
page 94

Cornmeal Muffins with Pan-Roasted Jalapenos
page 107

Coffee Ice Cream
page 142

FOURTH OF JULY PICNIC

Creamy Summer Vegetable Dip
page 23

Lemon-Garlic Grilled Chicken with Basil Aioli
page 29

Red Potato Salad with Feta and Olives
page 88

**Green and Yellow Bean Salad
with Tomato-Basil Topping**
page 84

Watermelon slices

Mixed Berry Tart with Raspberry Glaze
page 139

SOUTHERN STEAK DINNER

**Grilled T-Bone Steaks
with Bourbon-Peppercorn Mop Sauce**
page 44

Grilled Corn and Black Bean Salad
page 94

Spiced Potato Wedges
page 111

**Summer Salad
with Buttermilk-Dill Dressing**
page 92

Raspberry-Nectarine Pie
page 140

A TASTE OF THAI

**Marinated Thai
Chicken Breasts**
page 55

*Rice noodles tossed
with sesame oil*

Asian Shredded Slaw
page 83

Steamed snow peas

**Coconut-Key Lime-
Meringue Tarts**
page 131

MEDITERRANEAN EVENING
WITH FRIENDS

Pistachio-Coated Shrimp
page 15

Grilled Pork Tenderloin Spiedini
page 63

Mediterranean Rice and Fennel Salad
page 82

Tomato-Zucchini Gratin
page 99

Very Lemon Cake with Lush Lemon Frosting
page 134

Italicized items are menu suggestions; recipes not included.

Fall

SUNDAY NIGHT PIZZA

Tomato-Olive Pizza with Fresh Mushrooms
page 49

Rustic Pizza Crust
page 48

Tomato-Basil Pizza Sauce
page 48

Tossed Greens with Balsamic Vinaigrette and Romano Cheese
page 89

Coffee Ice Cream
page 142

Tiramisu Walnut Cookies
page 118

RUSTIC ITALIAN-STYLE MEAL

Spicy Herbed Olive Melange
page 14

Fennel-Roasted Pork Rib Roast
page 53

Tossed Greens with Balsamic Vinaigrette and Romano Cheese
page 89

Roasted Italian Potatoes
page 109

Italian Chocolate-Amaretto Mousse
page 135

AN APPLE AFFAIR

Crown Roast of Pork with Porcini, Fennel and Apple Stuffing
page 30

Porcini, Fennel and Apple Stuffing
page 96

Apple, Walnut and Blue Cheese Salad
page 82

Orchard-Fresh Apple Pie
page 142

*Italicized items are menu suggestions;
recipes not included.*

Winter

HANUKKAH

Roasted Red Pepper Hummus
page 26

Braised Chicken with Orange and Ginger
page 76

Yukon Gold Potato Latkes
page 114

Green beans

Walnut-Endive Salad
page 85

Hanukkah Honey Puffs
page 138

CELEBRATION BEEF DINNER

Figs Stuffed with Gorgonzola and Walnuts
page 9

**Marinated Beef Tenderloin with
Roasted Shallots and Port Reduction**
page 61

Baby Baked Potato Fans
page 97

Broccoli Florets with Lemon Crumbs
page 96

Walnut-Pear Salad with Cranberry Vinaigrette
page 86

Chocolate Truffle Tart
page 121

SPARKLING NEW YEAR

Warm Cheese with Nuts
page 9

Wild Mushroom Turnovers
page 20

**Sea Scallops with
Champagne Buerre Blanc**
page 35

Steamed julienned carrots, leeks and celery

**Spring Herb Salad with
Champagne Vinaigrette**
page 84

Chocolate-Vanilla Swirl Cheesecake
page 130

*Italicized items are menu suggestions;
recipes not included.*

Index